PRAISE FOR
APOPHATIC PATHS FROM EUROPE TO CHINA

"Up to now François Jullien's conception of Chinese thought has not had a full representation in English. This book responds to that gap and opens a dialogue with other traditions of apophasis."

— Haun Saussy, author of *Great Walls of Discourse and Other Adventures in Cultural China*

"By highlighting Western phenomena that are comparable to the Chinese, mainly in the apophatic tradition, Franke succeeds in exposing the biases and blind spots in Jullien's as well as in Hall's and Ames's respective treatment of Chinese 'philosophy.' This book will stand as an important resource for the future of scholarly debates in these areas."

— Karl-Heinz Pohl, editor of *Chinese Thought in a Global Context: A Dialogue Between Chinese and Western Philosophical Approaches*

APOPHATIC PATHS
from Europe to China

SUNY series in Chinese Philosophy and Culture

Roger T. Ames, editor

APOPHATIC PATHS
from Europe to China

REGIONS WITHOUT BORDERS

William Franke

Published by State University of New York Press, Albany

© 2018 State University of New York

All rights reserved

No part of this book may be used or reproduced in any manner whatsoever without written permission. No part of this book may be stored in a retrieval system or transmitted in any form or by any means including electronic, electrostatic, magnetic tape, mechanical, photocopying, recording, or otherwise without the prior permission in writing of the publisher.

For information, contact State University of New York Press, Albany, NY
www.sunypress.edu

Production, Jenn Bennett
Marketing, Kate R. Seburyamo

Library of Congress Cataloging-in-Publication Data

Names: Franke, William, author
Title: Apophatic paths from Europe to China : regions without borders
Description: Albany : State University of New York Press, [2018] | Series:
  SUNY series in Chinese philosophy and culture | Includes bibliographical references and index.
Identifiers: ISBN 9781438468570 (hardcover   ) | ISBN 9781438468587 (pbk.   ) | ISBN 9781438468594 (ebook)
Further information is available at the Library of Congress.

10 9 8 7 6 5 4 3 2 1

To Li Jiu Ping 李菊萍 *(Lemon)*
and Wang Hai Juan 王海涓 *(Daisy)*

Leap into the boundless and make it your own.

—Zhuangzi

Ultimate speech is to be rid of speech; ultimate action is to be rid of action.

—Zhuangzi

CONTENTS

List of Illustrations — xi

Preface and Argument — xiii

Chapter 1 All or Nothing?: Nature in Chinese Thought and the Apophatic Occident — 1

Chapter 2 Nothing and the Poetic "Making" of Sense — 37

Chapter 3 Immanence: The Last Word? — 85

Chapter 4 Universalism, or the Nothing That Is All — 141

Chapter 5 An Extra Word on Originality — 199

Epilogue Intercultural Dia-logue and Its Apophatic Interstices — 213

Appendix Analytic Table of Contents — 235

Index — 237

ILLUSTRATIONS

Figure 1.1. Peter Paul Rubens, *Abundantia*, 1630. Oil on panel. 2

Figure 1.2. Ni Zan, *Woods and Valleys of Mount Yü*, China, Yuan Dynasty, 1372. Hanging scroll; ink on paper. 17

Figure 1.3. Ni Zan, *Twin Trees by the South Bank*, China, Yuan Dynasty, 1353. Hanging scroll; ink on paper. 18

PREFACE AND ARGUMENT

This book is part of a larger project of rethinking philosophy and culture across historical ages and geographical continents through "apophatic" lenses or, in other words, through the perspective of negation, of what does not appear, of what is not and cannot be said. The apophatic thinking pursued here undertakes this task through bringing about its own metamorphosis into a programmatically intercultural philosophy. This entails attempting to think ideas not just within the bounds of a given cultural frame, with its inevitable background assumptions, but rather in unbounded ways in relation to other cultures and their different conceptual frameworks. Such thinking aims to negate, if not to neutralize, first one's own and finally any cultural framework. The possibility of relativizing culture per se by playing one culture off against the other—of stepping back and gaining critical perspective with respect to any and all cultural preconditioning, and then perchance of facing something absolute that is fleetingly glimpsed in the interstices between cultures—is the momentous breakthrough of intercultural philosophy. By negating all that is culturally relative, such philosophy opens into a dimension of the absolute that can perhaps be best interpreted as theological, or at least as religious, in nature. This "dimension" has been the source of representations of divinity throughout the history of religions and in mythologies the world over.

This uncircumscribable, unfathomable dimension intrinsic to experience as such is the real bugbear, making culture such a volatile, conflictual, aporetic, and unmasterable challenge for philosophical thinking, as well as for the multicultural—modern or modernizing—societies that in our time are seen to be mushrooming all across the planet. Reflecting on culture philosophically is not just a matter of comparing different forms and variants of manifest phenomena. More fundamentally, it entails sounding out the ungraspable ground of all cultural expressions, whether this abyss is imagined as residing in human nature and its inalienable freedom exceeding the confines of any possible definition of identity; or in language, with its differential structure opening to infinity; or in a divine endowment and destiny that transcend human knowing.

We are creatures of culture even before we are self-consciously aware as subjects or agents. And centrally at stake in the philosophy of culture, most conspicuously since the Enlightenment, is the question of universality. The title in hand will eventually be subsumed under a broader rubric: *The Universality of What Is Not: The Apophatic Turn in Critical Thinking*. The present volume is issued as a first installment, complete and coherent in itself, of that more comprehensive project. The broader project works from the insights of negative theology as it emerges in Western civilization from antiquity, especially in Neoplatonism, and develops in medieval and baroque mysticisms, continuing all the way to modern and postmodern expressions in philosophy, religion, literature, and the arts. The work being presented now carries the self-critical vocation of such negative (or, literally, "apophatic") thought into unconfined regions beyond what is recognized as "the West" through encounter with Eastern, particularly Chinese, traditions and their characteristic modes of thought.

Crucial to this book's agenda, accordingly, is the endeavor to discern and renew the claim of universality as rethought and reconfigured within the predicament of philosophy today considered specifically as a cultural or, more exactly, an *inter*cultural predicament. Nothing could be more classically philosophical than the quest for universal knowledge and for a universal or common ethical and political practice. But how are we to think of universality in our times, after the concussions of postmodern thought and culture and in the midst of our current historical crisis, with its pervasive fragmentation and sectarianism? A conviction concerning the preeminent, perhaps paradoxical value of theology—specifically in its infinitely self-critical form as negative theology—as a guide to this rethinking animates my previous works in this vein, particularly my books *On What Cannot Be Said* (2007) and *A Philosophy of the Unsayable* (2014). The special focus of the present volume is on the intercultural aspects and underpinnings of such an apophatic philosophy. In order to illuminate this focus from below and by a more particularized light than that of purportedly pure, universal reason, it will be useful and appropriate to begin in an autobiographical mode with a retrospective reflection placing the author's personal path from Europe to China in its geographical and historical context.

PREFACE AND ARGUMENT   xv

HISTORICAL-AUTOBIOGRAPHICAL INTRODUCTION

I write from within China, or more exactly from Macao, a Special Administrative Region (SAR) of the People's Republic of China. This special status is legislated to last for a limited time only—until 2049—for exactly fifty years starting from the 1999 handover of Macao to China by the Portuguese colonial government. This scenario is roughly synchronized with the similar handover of Hong Kong to China by Great Britain in 1997. But particularly Macao today has become the theatre of a great experiment being conducted by the People's Republic of China in an attempt to test the viability of opening its territory to Western-style intellectual freedom and unrestricted cultural exchange, while still maintaining an authoritarian form of government centered in Beijing. If this kind of controlled freedom can be fostered in Macao without creating a climate of revolt against the central Chinese government, maybe the model can be extended to other areas in the interior of the mainland. Something like this, we may surmise, might lie behind the reasoning of the regime in Beijing. There is much at stake for the future of China and, consequently, of the world in seeking to find ways of forging a viable form of compatibility between such overtly divergent types of civilization. The university, too, has an important role to play in this refashioning.

Within the first decade of the new millennium, the University of Macao began announcing its goal of hiring leading Western academics as part of its all-out bid to become a world-class research institution with a mandate from Beijing. In effect, whether intentionally or not, the aim was to revive Macao's historical role as gateway to the West. Historically, especially in the early modern period, Macao had been the key point of entry into China for the Christian missionaries who first infiltrated and initiated consequential contacts with this ancient empire. It has remained a primary port of entry for Westerners and their wares—including, not least, their ideas—ever since.

When in 2011 I accepted an appointment as Professor of Philosophy and Religions at the University of Macao, I imagined myself to be following in the wake of Matteo Ricci, the Italian Jesuit who arrived in the Portuguese mission and trading post of Macau (anglicized as "Macao") in 1582. He opened the door for genuine acquaintance and far-reaching exchange with the cultures of China, settling into and setting out from precisely this southeast Chinese peninsular seaport, which became, reciprocally, a door to the West for the Chinese. In fact, Macao's Chinese name *Aò Mén*

(澳門) is built on the Mandarin character 門 (*Mén*) for "door." The pictogram for this word lends itself to being construed as representing the two facing leaves of a swinging double door such as is familiar, ironically, from the decor of saloon sets in Hollywood westerns!

Working from this rather eccentric outpost on the rim of Greater China, Matteo Ricci (re)opened Western inroads into the "Central Kingdom," *Zhōng Guó* (中国)—China, in the literal sense of its name. Ricci's phenomenal linguistic and scientific talents enabled him to master the Chinese language and begin translating its classics. He produced the earliest Western translations of the canonical Four Books (*Sì shū* 四書) of Confucianism: the *Great Learning* (*Dà Xué* 大學), the *Analects* (*Lúnyǔ* 論語), the *Mencius* (*Mèngzǐ* 孟子), and the *Doctrine of the Mean* (*Zhōngyōng* 中庸). He counts as the outstanding intellectual figure among the first modern Europeans to penetrate the mysteries of the Chinese Orient.

My taking up a post in Macao was an adventurous turn in my more than two-decade-old career as a professor of comparative literature in the United States at Vanderbilt University. I had pursued this career also in Europe and Asia, thanks to several sabbatical years and to visiting appointments in Germany, Austria, France, Italy, and Hong Kong. My research had come to concentrate more and more on the apophatic—that is, on the unsayable, as it is manifest in philosophical, religious, literary, and artistic productions. I had cultivated and researched this topic as it flourishes in Western traditions and in the European languages that I passionately read and speak. But at a certain point I was compelled to pursue my interest in this type of thinking also eastward in relation to Asian cultures. The wisdom of the unsayable is even more pronounced and widespread in the most influential of Asian traditions ranging from the ancient Chinese, especially Daoism, to the Indian, particularly the Advaita Vedanta, which itself derives from the Vedas and Upanishads and issues in various forms of Buddhism.

I had written extensively on Western traditions from Plato to postmodernism, yet as a scholar of comparative literature and philosophy and religion, I could not help but discern on the horizon the ineluctable challenge of going global. I had taught comparative literature at the University of Hong Kong in 2005, and I was appointed there in 2011 as Professor of European Studies with tenure and an initial year's leave. However, before actually moving into that position, I swapped it for another role as head of the nascent Philosophy and Religious Studies Program at the nearby University of Macao. This seemed to open even more novel and adventurous prospects of building something truly unique and answering to the call of this particular world-historical moment. My wife, the French poet Béatrice

Machet, was also hired by the University of Macao to teach creative writing, and she too was able to contribute richly to the intercultural experiment that we undertook together.

This French connection, however, is also crucial and even more directly pertinent to the book in yet another respect. My discovery and exploration of classical Chinese culture had been guided all along by François Jullien, the eminent French philosopher and sinologist, professor at the Paris Diderot University and titular Chair on Alterity at the College of World Studies (Chaire sur l'altérité, le Collège d'études mondiales). Thanks to Jullien's many books, but also to the opportunity to interact with him directly at colloquia in Cerisy-la-Salle in France and at the Academia Sinica in Taipei, Taiwan, I have been able to develop my ideas concerning the apophatic aspects of Chinese thought in dialogue with his magisterial presentation of classical Chinese texts and culture. His philosophical approach to sinology first enabled me to enter into this apparently most foreign of worlds and engage with its thinking.

So much, then, for my own circuitous route to this subject. Some explanation was called for in order to account for how a philosopher of Western humanities and a Dante scholar should have embarked on this foray into Far Eastern, particularly Chinese philosophy and literature. Such ventures are, in fact, sometimes necessary in the name of what more specialized scholarship, for all the precision of its analyses, cannot completely grasp or fathom. Of all topics, especially this one, that of the unsayable, inevitably spans intellectual disciplines and geographical divides—even as it straddles cultural and spiritual universes—and erases their ostensible, yet illusory, boundaries.

INTRODUCTION TO AN
INTERCULTURAL PHILOSOPHY OF UNIVERSALISM

This book turns on two main axes. One is disciplinary, reaching from theology and philosophy to literature and culture generally. The other is geographical, stretching from Europe to China, or more broadly from the West to "the rest." These are the dimensions along which the universality of apophatic vision pivots between the covers of this book—and also beyond it, in the open expanse of the emerging world that we inhabit today, even as it turns toward and into tomorrow. The hope here is to put us in touch with a kind of connecting tissue that will facilitate our passage, more or less gracefully, across borders and through the transitions before us towards what lies beyond words, towards what has constantly been expressed in traditional religious practices and doctrines concerning other worlds and afterlives, those ultimate symbols of otherness.

The question of why look to China when we have plenty of alterity already within our own vicinity in the West points us to the importance of *culture* in our approach to what words always prove inadequate to grasp. We have only our cultures—with their symbols and concepts and rites and everyday practices—to work from in our attempt to articulate and communicate our experience of the real. The *comparison* of cultures brings out the effects of their mediation of anything and everything that can be considered as real or absolute—that is, as reaching beyond historical and cultural contingencies. Such comparison enables us to discern each culture's specific possibilities, its characteristic decisions, and its symptomatic exclusions. The intercultural becomes itself a kind of revelation once we recognize the cultural relativity of all our conceptualities. At a minimum, it is a revelation of unrevealability. All cultural grammars and vocabularies are seeking to mediate—or are in any case referred to, at least potentially—a common undifferentiated whole, an unlimited ambit that envelops us all already before we can define or differentiate it or even conceive of our particular questions and specific angles of vision. This holds whether the enveloping ambit is considered to be real or virtual, ultimate or proximate, everyday or sacred and sublime. What is aimed at and projected here is the perspective of globality—with the proviso that globality requires the negation of every mere perspective, including, recursively, the negator's own. This negation is thus actually a negation of negation and opens into unlimited affirmation, an open embrace of all that is positively present in any culture taken as a means of reaching out beyond oneself.

Recognizing the otherness of cultures and recognizing culture per se as introducing a factor of alterity, then, is necessary in order that we may distinguish ourselves and our representations from the absolutely real—from that which simply is—so as to perceive it as such and relate ourselves to it consciously as other than ourselves and our own reflections. We need to become conscious of culture in order to look beyond it to what is not it—to the strangeness of what asserts itself as real beyond our cultural and conceptual grasp, beyond our linguistic shaping and molding. We discover that there is nothing quite like the experience of intercultural difference to provoke this search and to induce us to seek after this widened, deepened outlook.

Of course, any distinction between the absolutely real and our own only relative grasp of it can be made only within language and therefore also from within a culture, since language is always embedded within culture. Nevertheless, such a distinction between the absolute and the relative proves to be necessary for any given language, as soon as it reflects on the unsurpassable incompleteness of all of its own actual formulations and their inability to exhaust the infinity of possible expressions. A language cannot exhaustively formulate the contextual whole to which it is beholden and which informs its every expression. It cannot completely or explicitly say all that it means, all that is conveyed by means of it. Language resorts instead to indirect forms of expression such as metaphor and analogy in order to suggestively refract, through particular images, this unencompassable whole context that bears on its meaning. Characteristic of such metaphorical modes is that they always allow and invite further formulations highlighting other, untold aspects of their subject that remain relatively unilluminated from the particular angle of vision enabled by any one image. Each particular culture is distinguished by the choice of metaphors it privileges for approaching the real, while the real as such remains in excess of its construal within any given culture's conceptual framework.

If the necessity of gaining intercultural perspective, then, answers to the question of why we might turn to a presumably faraway, foreign culture such as China as the paradigmatic Other in preference to any of our own internal others, still the question remains: Why not any other culture at all? Might not all other cultures serve for "working the gaps" ("travailler les écarts")—to use Jullien's language—between (and within) cultures? It is, indeed, the relation of all with all that is ultimately the arena within which revelation through culture takes place.

Holistic thinking, relating to the all, has long been recognized as a characteristic virtue and forte of Chinese culture. I believe that Chinese classical wisdom possesses very special—if not strictly incomparable—resources for addressing precisely this problem of the unthinkable wholeness to which we must nevertheless relate ourselves arguably as a condition of the validity of all our thinking. However, quite apart from any such ultimate, foundational considerations, Jullien has a contingent, historical justification for focusing specifically on China, and he spells it out over and over again from book to book in factual, historical terms: China is the world's other great, continuously existing civilization alongside the West but separate from it. China's cultural heritage is equally textualized and interpreted and dialecticized, having as long a history as the West—and even longer and more continuous. These are grounds for why a special sort of disclosure can be expected from this particular comparison—nevertheless not, I must insist, to the exclusion of other possible comparisons. No other culture is less valid or potentially fecund as a foil for comparison, even though all are specifically differentiated and would cast very different lights upon our own cultural predicament.

The Chinese foil certainly offers its own particular vantage points, including perhaps some unique advantages. However, my purpose is, in any case, not to sharpen our focus on China; it is ultimately to see what is working in *any and all* cultures *beyond* their borders and definitions and irrespective of their specific characters. Not to fetishize any given culture but rather to see it as a means of expression, as an enabling form of thought or as a filter of perception, is what Jullien's thought, too—sometimes inadvertently and yet consistently—recommends, quite beyond his own fixation on China as his constant Other of reference. The paradigms and intellectual structures that may be defined and differentiated as characteristic of one or another culture are not uninteresting, but they are not ultimate. They open a way towards another reality that culture does not encompass, one that it nevertheless refracts and alludes to by representing it in negative.

As Jullien wisely observes, one cannot exit from one's own frame of thinking, with its blind spots and prejudices, except by entering into another universe of thinking, and this is what he does through his strategic choice, his heuristic self-displacement to China as the ultimate "heterotopy." However, even this gesture of self-dispossession and self-critique does not go without questioning. In Jullien's own words, "One cannot effectively flush out the arbitrariness of one's thinking except in departing from it; and, thus, by entering into another. But what can this strategic elsewhere be, which will make us break the ties that we are unaware of? Where can it be found?" ("On ne peut débusquer l'arbitraire de sa pensée, en effet, qu'en la *quittant*; et, pour ce, en entrant dans une autre. Mais quel peut être cet ailleurs stratégique qui nous fera rompre des amarres que nous n'envisageons pas? Où le trouver?")[1]

Precisely this question leads to the rationale that I find for entering into theology as a way to exit from the reductiveness of any human way of thinking. For theology is a *way* (much like the *Dao* as guiding principle of Chinese thought) that relativizes all our human rationalizing and places us into another world of thought, one where our measures or criteria or standards are no longer definitive or authoritative. The radical displacement entailed by theology is one type of response that Jullien seems not to have envisaged to his own question of how to answer to the challenge of thinking out of and from alterity. Theology, at its core, consists in nothing but

---

1. *Entrer dans une pensée ou Des possibles de l'esprit* (Paris: Gallimard, 2012), 12.

its reference to an Other whom we cannot so much as define—one who rather defines *us* and disposes of us together with all that is.

The present monograph treats the question of culture in the gap between European and Chinese thought as a space that invites particularly to *negative* theological interpretation. This project of interpretation will be fully developed only with the subsequent portions of the larger project mentioned at the outset of this Preface. The work now put forward in these pages concentrates, instead, on opening the *space* of intercultural philosophy as a region without borders. This region is rather a plurality of regions, such as "China" and "the West," which can be apprehended only through their mutual relations with one another and only as negated. The work is thus made to open upon the indescribably and unfathomably Other, the Other that inspires philosophical wonder, as well as unbounded religious awe and—at least for some—even worship.

ACKNOWLEDGMENTS

The book is dedicated gratefully to two former graduate students who worked patiently day by day to initiate me into speaking and reading their language.

I thank the Government of Macao for a generous multi-year research grant and the University of Macao and its staff, especially Maggie Wong and Isa Chan of the Program in Philosophy and Religious Studies, for supporting this project in myriad ways. Also indispensable were Molly Lei and the staff working for the interlibrary loan service. I owe symmetrical thanks in the other direction to Jim Webb and the Vanderbilt Interlibrary Loan service.

An earlier version of some sections of the first chapter appeared as "All or Nothing?—Nature in Chinese Thought and the Apophatic Occident" in *Comparative Philosophy* 5/2 (2014): 4–24, Special Issue edited by Mario Wenning. This reflection was initiated in response to an invitation from Professor Wenning to contribute to a colloquium sponsored by the Alexander von Humboldt-Stiftung on "Nature–Time–Responsibility" at the University of Macao in April, 2013.

Some parts of chapter 2 were delivered at the International Summit Dialogue and Forum "What Is World Literature? Tension between the Local and the Universal" at Beijing Normal University, October 17, 2015, and appear as "Nothingness and the Aspiration to Universality in the Poetic 'Making' of Sense: An Essay in Comparative East-West Poetics" in *Asian Philosophy: An International Journal of the Philosophical Traditions of the*

East 26/3 (2016): 241–64, copyright Taylor & Francis, available online at http://www.tandfonline.com. doi:10.1080/09552367.2016.1206687. Other sections were delivered as a keynote address, "Apophatic Paths from Europe to China: Method and Mysticism in Intercultural Philosophy," at the annual conference of the Mystical Theology Network, University of Glasgow, Scotland, December 15, 2016.

Selected sections of chapter 3 form part of an essay "Classical Chinese Thought and the Sense of Transcendence" in *Transcendence, Immanence, and Intercultural Philosophy*, eds. Nahum Brown and William Franke (London: Palgrave Macmillan, 2016).

The beginning of chapter 4 was the basis of a talk at the 23rd World Congress of Philosophy at the University of Athens, Greece, August 2–11, 2013. In a different redaction, it served as a keynote address for "Cognition, Religion, and Science": A Conference of the International Association for the History of Religions (IAHR), cosponsored by the Toronto Institute for the Advanced Study of Religion, January 13–14, 2015. Some early sections of chapter 4 appear as an essay in *Contemporary Debates in Negative Theology: Philosophical Soundings of the Unsayable*, eds. Nahum Brown and J. Aaron Simmons (New York: Palgrave, 2017). The last section of chapter 4 is reframed as "The Ethical Import of (Negative) Theology in Intercultural Dialogue: Eine *Auseinandersetzung* mit François Jullien," in *Ethik zwischen Vernunft und Glaube. Brennpunkte und Gegenwartsfragen im interkulturellen Diskurs* [*Transcending Boundaries. Practical Philosophy from Intercultural Perspectives*], ed. Walter Schweidler (Eichstätt/Ingoldstadt: Academia Verlag, 2015), series: West-östliche Denkwege, 75–90.

The concluding Epilogue, recapitulating the book's theses and epitomizing its fundamental gesture in a condensed rhetorical form, is based on an English translation of my lecture at the 2013 Cerisy colloquium "Des possibles de la pensée: Autour des travaux François Jullien." The French text, "Le dia-logue et son au-delà apophatique: avec François Jullien," has been published together with other papers from the colloquium in *Des possible de la pensée: Autour des travaux François Jullien*, eds. Françoise Gaillard and Philippe Ratte (Paris: Editions Hermann, 2015), 277–98. This essay was also the basis for my extemporaneous presentation to the Académie du Midi symposium on "Wisdom East and West" at Alet-les-bains in France on June 10, 2014. An English version appears as "The Philosopher or the Sage: Apophaticism in Europe and China" in *Wisdom East and West: Symposium of Académie du Midi*, eds. Hans-Georg Moeller and Andrew Whitehead (London: Bloomsbury Academic, 2016), 55–73.

Chapter 1

ALL OR NOTHING?
Nature in Chinese Thought and the Apophatic Occident

Nature, in Western literature and art, is by most accounts a figure of openhanded generosity and nurturing. Iconographically, "she" is represented most palpably and intimately by the nursing breast. Nature, however, can also be epitomized by a cornucopia teeming with delectable comestibles. Enticingly placed on display, her bounty promises to satiate all comers.[1] This latter image represents nature's more extroverted side turned toward universal outreach. She beckons to all and sundry, spilling her goods from the wide-open mouth of the "horn of plenty." Mother Nature gives to all freely of her seemingly inexhaustible stores and knows no measure of restraint. At least until recently, her ever-renewable resources have appeared in their fabulous copiousness to be practically beyond all possibility of depletion.

Abundance and productiveness are in this way built in at the foundations of the myth of nature. To this extent, nature evidently presents itself, at first flush, as an eminently positive and saturated concept. What we will find, however, is that it is only as negation and emptiness, as the negative par excellence, that nature can truly serve as a universal source and unlimited resource. Recognizing the intrinsic negativity of nature, moreover, will prove to be the antidote necessary for disabusing us of delusions that we can heedlessly manage and manipulate our environment in accordance with our own self-willed desires. Such recognition makes us realize that we must first mind this vacuum and conform ourselves to nature's silent dictates.

---

1. Both emblems figure together suggestively in Peter Paul Rubens's painting of the Roman goddess *Abundantia* (1630). See figure 1.

FIGURE 1.1. Peter Paul Rubens, *Abundantia*, 1630. Oil on panel. Image courtesy of the National Museum of Western Art, Tokyo.

In medieval allegorical poems such as the *De planctu naturae* by Alain de Lille (Alanus de Insulis, 1117–1203), *Natura* appears as a prolific producer of life and letters alike. She pullulates with numberless progeny of material, fleshly things. But she also generates their scarcely containable significances, without stint or limit. Her natural creativity is typically understood through its likeness to the inventive capabilities of language. Things and meanings alike tumble out from the lap of Nature, whose generative powers are fecundated by the creative Word, the divine *Verbum* or *Logos*. This prolific productiveness is then further reflected, or imitated and multiplied, by poets through the fantasy-filled, prodigious words of literature.

Taking up the relay from Alain de Lille, Jean de Meun (1240–1305) continues to elaborate the allegorical representation of Nature and of Nature's priest, Genius, in *Le Roman de la Rose*. Unbound by the normal constraints of convention and culture, Natura and her male counterpart Genius, writing with his "pen," his phallic *stylus*, have their own unrestrained capacities of *poiesis*. They produce both words and every species of being according to its kind, as well as freaks and solecisms. Deviations from proper expression and orthography are placed in parallel with the miscarriages of nature by these medieval poets who are employing a practically inescapable analogy.[2]

Monstrosities (literally "showings," as in "de*monstr*ations"), both material and linguistic, render conspicuous some of the intriguing excesses and ambiguities of natural generation. They do so especially when the human penchant for deviancy mixes its own mischief into the process of engendering—for example, by bastardizing pure, noble genealogical lines.[3] The linguistic mode of operation of nature in this medieval imagining may seem, at first, to provide another positive way of representing natural creativity—namely, in terms of manifest, familiar phenomena of language. However, it also brings us near to recognition of the negativity at nature's source and origin, since language is inherently negative, engendered by difference, always *not* what things are themselves in their unmediated simplicity.

Tellingly, a negation projected backward from language can be detected at the root of the very notion of simplicity. The word "simple" is itself produced by negation: it breaks down etymologically into its Latin components *sine* or *sin* (without) and *plic* (fold). The simple is that which is without

---

2. Illuminating on this score is Alexandre Leupin, *Barbarolexis: Medieval Writing and Sexuality* (Cambridge, MA: Harvard University Press, 1989).

3. R. Howard Bloch, *Etymologies and Genealogies: A Literary Anthropology of the French Middle Ages* (Chicago, IL: University of Chicago Press, 1983) ingeniously elaborates on this vertiginous topic.

folds; it is the negation of *complexity*, which means being compounded of or with (*cum* = *com*) various folds (*plexi*). In these terms, simplicity can first be conceived only in and through the (en)foldings of language.

Despite such inherent negativities, nature commonly stands for the manifest, the positively present: it is a kataphatic concept, if ever there was one. We call nature what is immediately at hand, springing up spontaneously—*sponte sua*—given, or literally birthed (*natus*) of itself. It is thus prior to the transformative activities brought to bear by human agents and their conceptualities and technologies. Is there, then, any warrant for considering what is *not,* or what withdraws from being and speech, to be in any way natural? Are such elusive *non*phenomena or negative phenomena not defined precisely by their being *un*natural, by their refusing life, and by their denial of being as it is naturally given to us in the world of ordinary experience? Exuberance and positivity, as opposed to all the ascetic, world-denying negations introduced by religion, have long been the keynote of nature in classic representations such as Lucretius's epicurean celebration of the love goddess Venus. So fecund in the production of life throughout the manifest physical universe, she serves as emblem of a rapturously natural way of living.[4]

Admittedly, representations of nature, even in the West, are not uniformly positive. There have been negative moments in Western literature expressing, for example, a sense of being punished and persecuted by nature. Giacomo Leopardi, in "La Ginestra," desperately cries out, from the depths of Romantic melancholia and despair, against "step-mother nature" ("la noverca natura"). And he is only echoing a topos that is forged already within the heart of Roman classicism by Cicero in his *De Republica,* book 3 in a passage best known from a citation by Saint Augustine in book 4 of his *Contra Pelagium.* Many have confessed themselves appalled by nature's indifferent destruction or cruelty. Wordsworth's famous "nature red in tooth and claw" betrays dismay at the ferocious but universal spectacle of natural predation among animals, and Hobbes, with his "state of nature," unflinchingly recognizes treacherous killing as all too natural for humans as well. Although in yet another key of moral consternation, Voltaire's poem on the 1755 earthquake in Lisbon ("Poème sur le désastre de Lisbonne") is similarly based on observation of the perversity of the supposed laws of nature as an "empire of destruction" ("De la destruction la nature est l'empire").

Such expressions capture obvious, undeniable facts of nature, crucial facets of its appearance in the world of phenomenal manifestation. In decadent phases of culture, nature can even become an object of loathing

---

4. Lucretius, *De rerum natura* (*On the Nature of Things*), book I, lines 1–43.

and horror. Charles Baudelaire's imagining of "the flowers of evil" (*Les fleurs du mal*, 1857–68) pushes repugnance vis-à-vis nature, at least when it is undissembled by art, to pathological extremes. This comes across overpoweringly, for example, in view of a rotting carcass in "Une Charogne." And in "Rêve Parisienne," Baudelaire banishes from his dream utopia the spectacle of "vegetable irregularity" ("végetal irrégularité") in favor of artificial geometrical constructions of marble and metal in a Paris purged of every vestige of nature. The ideal is pure art without nature rather than an equilibrium and symbiosis between the two.

However, beyond any of these richly suggestive and divergent figurations, whether positive or negative in emotional tonality and moral valence, there is another possible face of nature, or more exactly an *effacement*, in which nature is what invisibly and imperceptibly encompasses us all. And this is the relation in which a deeper and subtler sense of negativity emerges. In this case, nature is precisely what never appears as such nor ever can be exactly apprehended or defined. For perception and expression inevitably entail human mediation and cultural transmission by semiotic and hermeneutic means that distort and occult the natural.

To the end of placing this cultural mediation of whatever we can apprehend of the natural order under examination, so as to take up our distance from it, we are well advised to travel east. Certain classical cultures of Asia seem most apt to suggest an original idea of how nature might find its least inadequate image in what does *not* appear at all. They expose the deepest affinities between cultures in their approach to nature as consisting in what *cannot* be articulated.[5] Specifically, I propose to take up an observation post located in view of ancient Chinese wisdom in both its classical (Confucian) formulation and the (Daoist) dialectical antithesis of that doctrine. This is one strategic position from which we can descry a conception of nature as inherently negative, as the apophatic par excellence.

According to the Chinese conceptions, beneath or within the phenomenal appearances that gaily dance before the windows of our senses as employed in ordinary perception, there is something else, something that does not as such appear, an invisible dimension. In traditional Chinese wisdom, however, this hidden reality is not typically thought to transcend nature into a purely metaphysical, indeed an *un*natural realm. This invisible dimension is found, rather, in the inscrutability immanent in things

---

5. J. Baird Callicott and Roger T. Ames, eds., *Nature in Asian Traditions of Thought: Essays in Environmental Philosophy* (Albany: State University of New York Press, 1989) can serve as a landmark and guidepost along this itinerary.

in nature as a process of ongoing, inarrestable change. The phenomenal universe is taken to be the veil of a mystery that has no name or concept, although, taken as the immanent All, it is commonly identified with nature through a great variety of mythological forms of expression.

In dominant currents in Western philosophy, this numinous and fathomless nature has typically been suppressed for the sake of positively thinking the all, the universal, the whole. In the West, nature typically was and is taken to be a sub-realm of the whole of being, thus the object of only limited knowledge by lower faculties, particularly the physical senses of sight and hearing, smell and taste and touch. This hierarchical domination has involved suppression also of the apophatic wisdom that shadows Western metaphysics at every step along its way through history. Indeed the subordination of nature, its reduction to being merely a resource for human use and exploitation, turns out to be an indicator of a loss of sensibility for the apophatic. I intend to expose this history from an eccentric vantage point by following the lead of one of the great contemporary mediators of philosophical thinking between European and Chinese thought—François Jullien.

As I construe Jullien's project, the key to it is, precisely, apophatic awareness, and this is what places Chinese wisdom on a common ground with certain deep strata in Western thinking, marking out a fertile field for dialogue that can point indicatively to a dimension that is effectively universal. The question of the representations of nature in the West and in the East respectively serves perfectly to bring out the stakes of apophasis as a miraculous "open sesame" in this encounter between cultures. This is so because the characteristic efforts of both cultures clearly show that, taken radically, nature is beyond all possibility of representation.

To begin to pry open this perspective, we might turn first to Jullien's analysis of "silent transformation" as apprehended especially in traditional Chinese wisdom as a peculiarly ungraspable form of negation—the type of negation that I call "apophatic." Jullien explains, through reference to the process of aging, the invisible dimension of nature, which has just been invoked.[6] Although invisible as such, aging is nevertheless taking place in every moment and in every part of our bodies and of our entire lives. Aging determines every aspect of our being, working at the surface of our skin, but also in our psychological depths. It is continuous and total and,

---

6. *Les transformations silencieuses* (Paris: Grasset, 2008), trans. Krysztof Fijalkowski and Michael Richardson as *The Silent Transformations* (Chicago, IL: University of Chicago Press, 2011).

for these very reasons, paradoxically invisible. While specific phenomena tell of our age, the global fact itself is not as such perceptible and escapes our notice minute by minute, hour by hour, day by day, month by month. Aging operates silently in us and in the end destroys our earthly existence altogether (provided that we are spared other more precipitous deaths). As such, however, aging escapes our consciousness. We are unaware of its full deployment and ramifications across every aspect of our being . . . even while it is relentlessly going on in us all the time. Only in moments of comparison, for instance, with earlier photos, does the transformation become conspicuous—and then poignantly, even pathetically, so. Jullien is willing to speak here of a "revelation," albeit with a caveat to the effect that he does not mean thereby anything "mystical" in nature. I take his analysis of the phenomenon of aging, nevertheless, as exemplary of an applied form of apophatic vision. Whether one considers it to be "mystical" or not, I maintain that such vision is accessible equally to Western and to Eastern thought. Whether the apophatic must be differently inflected as transcendent or as immanent as it operates in one or the other of these diverse cultural spheres is a crucial issue that is pursued by this inquiry.

THE NATURE OF *DAO*, OR THE *DAO* OF NATURE

The idea of nature as an All that always eludes us, I contend, is thus a universal theme. Positioned between Eastern and Western paradigms, this theme raises the possibility of a relation to a universal philosophical truth. Such an idea of nature occurs in the sources of philosophical reflection in Chinese tradition with the *Dao-de-Jing* (道德经), which is traditionally attributed to Laozi (sixth to fifth century BC). Its very first composition is emblematic of the book's naturalist vision of an ineffable mystery immanent within all that lives and is:

道可道, 非常道. 名可名, 非常名. 無名天地之始; 有名萬物之母. 故常無欲, 以觀其妙; 常有欲, 以觀其徼. 此兩者, 同出而異名, 同謂之玄. 玄之又玄, 衆妙之門.

The way that can be spoken of
Is not the constant way;
The name that can be named
Is not the constant name.

The nameless was the beginning of heaven and earth;
The named was the mother of the myriad creatures.

Hence always rid yourself of desires in order to observe its secrets;
But always allow yourself to have desires in order to observe its manifestations.

These two are the same
But diverge in name as they issue forth.
Being the same they are called mysteries,
Mystery upon mystery—
The gateway of the manifold secrets. (Lau, trans.)[7]

The named and the nameless, the secret and the manifest, desire and its absence, form a unity: deeply the same, they diverge *in name* as they emerge into manifest unity as "the same." Opposites, even when they are distinguished in thought and discourse, do not definitively separate but remain beholden each to a deeper or more intrinsic nature, in which they are really one.

Accordingly, the way or *Dao*, like the moon, has at least two faces, one manifest and one hidden. Still, however, more deeply or inwardly, it remains one and the same. Nature is evoked here, but not under any graspable, definable concept such as the emergent (*ta physis*) or the perceptible or sensory (*to aistheton*), as two common Greek concepts of nature would have it. Such manifestations belong to nature (as does everything whatsoever), but they do not define it. The way remains a "mystery." Neither does the way exclude what is unchanging and withdraws from manifestation. There is no assertion here of the existence of anything other than nature, but nature itself in this depth dimension is mysteriously other to all that we perceive and know. The nature of the *Dao* is to be without nature and beyond nature in any shape or form that we can grasp or name or measure.

---

7. I compare different translations of Laozi's *Tao Te Ching*, including those by D.C. Lau (New York: Penguin Books, 1963); Arthur Waley (London: Wordsworth Editions, 1997); Paul J. Lin, *A Translation of Lao Tzu's Tao Te Ching and Wang Pi's Commentary* (Ann Arbor: University of Michigan Press, 1977); and James Legge, *The Texts of Taoism*, 2 vols. (Oxford: Clarendon Press, 1891 / London: Humphry Milford, 1891). The Chinese text is taken from the Legge edition (http://ctext.org/dao-de-jing). In the case of the citations, except in the book titles, '*tao*' is replaced by the *pinyin* transliteration '*dao*' for the original Chinese character '道'.

In this "way" (*Dao*), negation of an indeterminate or indeterminable sort is built in at the fathomless source of nature. Prima facie, nature is a full and robust idea, the epitome of plenty. The *Dao* is clearly figured as Mother of all things, and yet it remains indescribable and formless in itself: it remains apart from any such figurable relation with the universe. This is the case again, and in just these terms, in the twenty-fifth composition of the *Dao-de-Jing*:

有物混成，先天地生．寂兮寥兮，獨立不改，周行而不殆，可以為天下母．吾不知其名，字之曰道，強為之名曰大．

There was something undefined and complete, coming into existence before Heaven and Earth. How still it was and formless, standing alone, and undergoing no change, reaching everywhere and in no danger (of being exhausted)! It may be regarded as the Mother of all things.

I do not know its name, and I give it the designation of the Dao (the Way or Course). Making an effort (further) to give it a name I call it The Great. (James Legge, trans.)

Prior to heaven and earth and other binary poles producing change, there is here, just as in creation myths, something antecedent and without change, in some sense a Nothing from which everything comes. It may be figured, metaphorically, as the Mother of all. The maternal images of *Dao* as nurturing all things are elaborated further in poem 51: "Thus it is that the Dao produces (all things), nourishes them, brings them to their full growth, nurses them, completes them, matures them, maintains them, and overspreads them" (James Legge, trans.). And again, in poem 52 we read:

天下有始，以為天下母．既得[1]其母，以[2]知其子，

That which was the beginning of all things under heaven
We may speak of as the "mother" of all things.
He who apprehends the mother
Thereby knows the sons. (Waley, trans.)

The sixth chapter of the *Dao-de-Jing* also contributes to this figuring of the *Dao* as a mysterious female source, a sort of Mother Nature, immanent and inexhaustible.

谷神不死，是謂玄牝。玄牝之門，是謂天地根。綿綿若存，用之不勤。

The valley spirit never dies,
It is called the mystic female.
The door of the mystic female
Is the root of heaven and earth.
Being interminable and seeming to endure,
It can be used without toil. (Paul J. Lin, trans.)

Nature, as the ultimate source of all that exists, is at the same time equated here and in Daoist texts more generally with Nothing—certainly with nothing that can be named or known. The figures of Nothing are persistent and pervasive. Here they appear as an emptiness that is inexhaustible, despite the fact that the notion of a thinking, which is a thinking of Nothing, also has something that is most unnatural about it. The sense of Nothing here is all-pervading: it is conceptualized in Daoism as a way without content, a way which cannot be said (as we have just seen in the opening line of the *Dao-de-Jing* 1), and as an emptiness—to which a whole range especially of Buddhist schools and texts bear witness. These presumably metaphysical notions of nothingness, if they are indeed metaphysical, are not thought of as exiting from and transcending nature but rather as realizing its inherent process and dynamic. Everything that is anything is considered to be part of one All that does not exceed the bounds of the world: it is all still in the end simply natural.

In the West, too, the All has all along been equated also with the Nothing. However, generally this has been so not so much, or at least not so explicitly, in the mainstream of its metaphysical tradition as in certain of its countercurrents. This idea of Nothing as a universal emanating source is developed penetratingly by the negative theology particularly of ancient Neoplatonic philosophers from Plotinus to Damascius. It is generally to be found, thereafter, as something of a radical fringe in relation to the tradition of orthodox Christian theology that takes it over and builds on it. Such a figure of the Nothing passes from Eriugena and Eckhart through Nicolaus Cusanus and Jakob Böhme to Hegel. It is especially common in esoteric traditions and can be traced specifically to the *Corpus Hermeticum*.[8] Recent revivals and revisitings of Western apophatic tradition have suggested that

---

8. See Glenn Alexander Magee, *Hegel and the Hermetic Tradition* (Ithaca, NY: Cornell University Press, 2001).

this supposed marginalization is mistaken and that the Nothing (nothing conceptualizable or knowable) should be recognized as hidden at the core of mainstream Christian theology from Augustine to at least Aquinas in the West, as well as in Orthodox theology from its Greek origins.[9]

Clearly, China, even in some of the most widely circulated and authoritative expressions of its philosophy, has conceived of nature as the All and of Nothing as the heart of it. There are, of course, significant tensions between Daoist mystical interpretations and Confucian socially pragmatic approaches. Yet they agree in recommending that we harmonize with nature by erasure, or at least moderation, of ourselves and our own self-willed activity. Non-action, *wú wéi* (无为), is the apophatic path that they indicate as an ethical application of this "natural" apprehension of and response to the universe. The action of non-action aims to enable us to move flexibly in alignment with the ebb and flow of nature. Indeed, it is because nature is itself a disappearing act that a negative form of behavior turns out, paradoxically, to be the best way of harmonizing with it.

The negativity of thought and action that adheres to nature does not produce or posit an abstract metaphysical Nothing. Instead, it releases the ungraspable concreteness of things by removal of conceptual limits and barriers, by letting things be all that they are or can be even beyond our powers of conception. Nature is most truly defined not by anything that it is but only by what it is not. This is the kind of negativity associated, for example, with something tasteless. Insipidness is the negation of any strong flavor or distinct character. Yet the relative nothingness of the insipid is inhabited potentially by every nature or quality that could be positively perceived as a determination in a given register of sensation. This is the negative in the sense of the neuter. Such neutrality can lead us beyond determinate sensation into a more mysterious kind of negativity at the heart of nature itself. For Jullien, this is an emphatically *immanent* form of negativity, as we will see in the next section. And yet he, too, cannot help but describe it also as "the transcendent Font of reality ('Heaven')" ("Fonds transcendant de la réalité [le 'Ciel']").[10]

---

9. My own efforts in this revisionary direction of reconstructing the tradition of Western thought can be found in *On What Cannot Be Said: Apophatic Discourses in Philosophy, Religion, Literature, and the Arts*, 2 vols. (Notre Dame, IN: University of Notre Dame Press, 2007).

10. Jullien, *Dialogue sur la morale* (Paris: Grasset, 1995). This language appears persistently, for example, at 54, 73, 143, 166.

According to reigning stereotypes, following nature and harmonizing with it is the way to fulfillment in the philosophy of the East, whereas the West is typically held to take the opposite tack of striving to master and contain nature or, alternatively, to escape from it. However, these generalizations can be tested and probed and put under pressure until they metamorphose into their opposites.[11] Whenever Western tradition is seen in the light of apophasis as its deepest thinking, true mastery is always found only in the surrender to the Nothing at the core of an all-encompassing Nature that cannot be adequately named in this or in any other way. Such has been the drift of the apophatic logic that counterpoints Western thought all along its course through history, exemplarily in the *De divisione naturae* (Περί φύσεων) by John Scott Eriugena (810–77). What is meant here, however, is not exactly *Nothing* in a strongly abstract, positively metaphysical sense. Let us begin to approach Jullien by following his investigation of nothing rather in the *neutral* sense simply of *blandness* as he derives this notion, working in the gap ("écart") between Eastern and Western cultures, from Chinese sources.

IN PRAISE OF BLANDNESS: LITOTES OF THE NEUTER

In order to gain a first, global impression of the purport of Jullien's philosophical vision and its overriding message, specifically in terms of the peculiar logic or *il*logic of negativity, it is instructive to turn to his little treatise on blandness, *Éloge de la fadeur*.[12] This work synoptically encompasses many of his seminal insights in an accessible and paradoxically *poignant* manner. Its outlook and overview can serve for a preliminary probing, in an

---

11. Modern Western sciences of nature, especially the postclassical physics of quantum mechanics and relativity theory, are seen to converge with Daoist mysticism in their discovery of an enigmatic nothingness at the heart of nature by Fritjov Capra in his cult-creating book *The Tao of Physics: An Exploration of the Parallels between Modern Physics and Eastern Mysticism* (Boston, MA: Shambhala, 1975). This book was followed up by *The Hidden Connection*, *The Turning Point*, *The Web of Life*, and others.

12. *Éloge de la fadeur: À partir de la pensée et de l'esthétique de la Chine* (Arles: Éditions Philippe Picquier, 1991). The work is available in an English translation by Paula M. Varsano as *In Praise of Blandness: Proceeding from Chinese Thought and Aesthetics* (New York: Zone Books, 2004). However, citations in this subsection and throughout the book are translated directly from the French.

apophatic key, of the connections between Nature, Nothing, Immanence, Universality, and Originality (the topics to be explored in turn in the successive chapters of this book).

The bland ("le fade"), *dàn* 淡, seems, at first, to be merely negative. It lacks any distinguishing quality. Yet this apparently neutral condition can turn out to be the most potent and productive condition of all, for it is potentially all qualities: and it can be them in an indeterminate and infinite way. Spiced with a little imagination, there is nothing that the bland cannot become, for there is nothing that it excludes. With no distinctive property of its own, it is open in all directions and can be the basis for suggesting every other quality into which the neutral receptivity to any and every quality whatever might metamorphose. Blandness has no intrinsic limits. The bland transgresses the law of the excluded middle: it becomes rather an all-*inclusive* middle confounding logical oppositions and antitheses.

As Jullien presents it, in relaying ancient and perennial Chinese wisdom, in which the tastelessness of water is exemplary, the bland absorbs every other quality or savor that could possibly contrast with it. In its own amorphousness, it is open to all forms and consequently has infinite potential for expansion. The bland is *in* all savors and *is* them virtually: it is, at least potentially, their truth. It expands dynamically on a horizontal plain without requiring any vertical, metaphysical breakthrough to some other, higher order of reality. It is a dynamic infinite that is constantly in act and knows no stable, achieved state of completeness. Its completeness and perfection remain part of an infinite, ongoing process from which no abstraction need or can be made.

One suggestive vocabulary for this neutral state of blandness is that of the neuter. Blandness, in the sense that Jullien derives from many centuries of Chinese literature and landscape painting, as well as of critical commentary and theoretical reflection on art and music, compares closely with the idea of the neuter as expounded by Maurice Blanchot and Roland Barthes.[13] These authors, among others, have pursued kindred insights in the margins of Western philosophy and aesthetic reflection. My claim is

---

13. Roland Barthes, *Le neutre: Cours au Collège de France* (1977–78) (Paris: Seuil, 2002), trans. Rosalind E. Krauss as *The Neutral: Lecture Course at the Collège de France (1977–1978)* (New York: Columbia University Press, 2007). Maurice Blanchot, *Le pas au-delà* (Paris: Gallimard, 1973). On this pervasive motif in Blanchot, which is diffused throughout his mature works, see Christophe Bident, "The Movements of the Neuter," in *After Blanchot: Literature, Criticism, Philosophy*, eds. Leslie Hill, Brian Nelson, and Dimitris Vardoulakis (Newark: University of Delaware Press, 2004), 13–34.

that the natural and yet negative forms of thought that Jullien finds in the East have been gestated also in the West, particularly in its apophatic currents. These currents develop especially from the critique of idolatry, in which worship of nature, in the form of concrete objects taken as gods, is negated.[14] Bringing out this affinity can give us a perspective on Jullien's treatment and expose some of his own biases. Such a procedure is meant to further the self-critical process by means of which apophatic thinking remains continually in evolution through thinking always also against itself.

Another of Jullien's works, *La Grande image n'a pas de forme* (*The Great Image Has No Form*) is a veritable manifesto of apophatic thought in relation to the experience of painting and particularly of the invisible at the extreme limit of the visible—at its frayed ends, where visibility fades into indistinctness. Rather than separating from the visible altogether so as to constitute itself as an intelligible order, visibility in this manner turns into invisibility. This type of insight is concentrated particularly into chapter 4 on the "vague" and "indistinct."[15] The techniques of Chinese landscape painting are designed not to paint reality as a positive object but to de-paint, to disfigure, and to de-signify. More than discreet objects, such painting presents the circumambient atmosphere from which all distinct visible aspects emerge and into which they are once again reabsorbed. The special vocation of this painting is to show or to intimate the great process of reality underway in everything not as a state of being but as the continual appearing and disappearing of all into all.

Venetian painting from Giorgione to Titian and Tintoretto is similarly concerned with the enveloping atmosphere of all, as Bernard Berenson so memorably showed in his *Venetian Painters of the Renaissance* (1894). But Jullien minimizes the development of these insights in the West, briefly alluding only to Poussin and Chateaubriand as fugitive and irresolute exceptions and only in order to maintain that a clear contrast nevertheless exists. He denies that his method does anything more than enhance the readability and thus the fecundity of each tradition in its own intrinsic coherence. But he nevertheless insists on the exclusion of theology and even on its impossi-

---

14. Moshe Halbertal and Avishai Margalit, *Idolatry*, trans. (from Hebrew) Naomi Goldblum (Cambridge, MA: Harvard University Press, 1992).

15. *La Grande image n'a pas de forme: À partir des Arts de peindre de la Chine ancienne* (Paris: Seuil, 2003), 59 (cf. 35, 43). Available in English translation by Jane Marie Todd as *The Great Image Has No Form, On the Nonobject through Painting* (Chicago: University of Chicago Press, 2009). Jullien extends key aspects of this argument in *Vivre de paysage ou l'impensé de la raison* (Paris: Gallimard, 2014).

bility in Chinese thought (*Grande image*, 58, 27, etc.) in order to ground the two traditions' supposedly completely different approaches. The one works through transcendence, hence theology, and the other completely without it in order to express what in the end is a common reality or shared experience ("une commune expérience ou du moins qu'on peut partager," 72).

While there is certainly a warrant for Jullien's saying that the Chinese aesthetic of the invisible does not impose another plain of reality separate from the visible, he is perhaps not fully justified in concluding therefore that in Chinese thought all transpires on a single, continuous plane of immanence. Such a *representation,* if taken to exclude transcendence or anything not on the same plane of immanence, is as erroneous as is the representation of an other world or a higher (intelligible) order, for both types of representation are in reality but relations to something unrepresentable. However, both are also potentially—and poetically—fertile as forms of inevitable *mis*representation. What is activated or called up in either case is, in effect, the unrepresentable. To the extent that we can approach it only through inadequate representations, the field of representation that is opened is one of infinite potential planes (one is reminded of Deleuze and Guattari's *mille plateaux*) like parallel worlds. These worlds, I submit, should be recognized as including other worlds, even other worlds such as Dante has imagined in his *Divine Comedy*, without limit. Such openness to other even so-called "fictional" worlds is compatible with and even required by an ontology of the non-existence of *the* world such as Markus Gabriel develops in *Warum es die Welt nicht gibt*.[16]

Jullien should not be allowed to substitute another representation—"immanence"—as if that were the one truly adequate representation and fundamentally unlike the representations propounding transcendence, which he shows to be inadequate. The question is not one of transcendence or of immanence but of the limitations of representation per se and of its "beyond" (or its "before," "upstream" from the source). Daoist theorists of painting from medieval Tang (618–907) and Song (960–1279) times down to early modern theorists, notably Shitao (1644–1707) in the Qing dynasty, agree that painting concerns something absolute at the origin of all. They contemplate this origin without the figures of God or the Demiurge. Indeed, they envision it as undifferentiated and formless, and therefore as not representable or articulable at all, except in its evasion of expression and

---

16. Markus Gabriel, *Warum es die Welt nicht gibt* (Berlin: Ullstein, 2013), trans. Gregory S. Moss as *Why the World Does Not Exist* (Cambridge, UK: Polity Press, 2015).

comprehension. Hence the tops of mountains are lost in fog that shades into sky, and the tips of trees blend into the indefiniteness of the background.[17] This manner shows Laozi's unnameable, undifferentiated bottom (*fond*) of the invisible, as Jullien writes, citing *Laozi* profusely, in *La grande image* (see especially 44–47).

The first stroke ("trait") of a painting in its uniqueness and before all differentiation contains all existents in itself, the whole of creation in its emergence and in the full amplitude of its potency (53). Jullien expressly recognizes that Chinese theorists, particularly Shitao, envisage painting's "vocation to the absolute" and to expressing "the unsayable" (54). Such a metaphysical quest becomes explicit at many junctures in the history of European art. Modern painting in the West, with Picasso and Braque, finally exceeds the constraints of linear perspective—which had been taken since the Renaissance as canonical for representing the real—and shows things simultaneously from multiple perspectives. This is to transcend the bounds of any one determinate form in the direction of the great image that has no form, to evoke once again as leitmotif this paradoxically self-negating figure forged by the *Laozi*. In the fourth chapter of his homonymous book (*La grande image n'a pas de forme*), Jullien describes a logic of non-exclusion of the great form that remains open to all "compossibles." It is a unity that is neither synthetic nor symbolic, as would be the case in Western onto-theological conceptions, but rather "Daoesque, in the sense that one [determination] does not exclude the other, one [applies] at the same time as the other" (95). We might just as well say that this is an apophatic logic, one availing itself of non-exclusive terms that do not appropriate and circumscribe such conceptions within one culture to the exclusion of others. According to such a logic, every conception is rather a de-conception. Not even conceptions of transcendence can by rights be excluded from the *Dao*—on the condition that they be taken *as conceptions* (and therefore as a species of representation), even if always as conceptions of what transcends conception itself. As such, they are only determinate (com)possibilities among others.

The virtue of Jullien's representation of the plane of immanence is that this plane is presumably infinite and open to all, all that cannot be seen *yet* in the temporal succession of images on a plane in which each presence is always already yielding to its own absence. Jullien's image can be very persuasive inasmuch as it seems to allow for heterogeneity and for the invisible in the form of always further images or presences (presences-absences)

---

17. Paintings by Ni Zan (1301–74) offer suggestive illustrations. See figures 2 and 3.

FIGURE 1.2. Ni Zan, *Woods and Valleys of Mount Yü*, China, Yuan Dynasty, 1372. Hanging scroll; ink on paper. Image © Metropolitan Museum of Art.

FIGURE 1.3. Ni Zan, *Twin Trees by the South Bank*, China, Yuan Dynasty, 1353. Hanging scroll; ink on paper. Image © Princeton University Art Museum.

that are not yet visible and that will be different, even very different, from the present ones. Such a plane of immanence is open to the invisible and infinite. Yet there is also in Chinese wisdom a sense of the radical difference of what cannot be grasped or represented. The sacred or holy is such a heterogeneous element, and it cannot be located and confined to the plane of immanence. The world does not consist only in an unending series of images all on the same plane. Things are governed from a higher level, even though this principle, the *Dao*, like God, cannot be represented as a member of the series. Chinese wisdom does work without the representation of God, but it nevertheless knows the dimension of the unprespresentable. Jullien, in following Chinese wisdom (to the extent that he adheres to it), is explicating apophatic logic in its approach to the unrepresentable.

At the end of *Éloge de la fadeur*, Jullien characterizes 'blandness" in Chinese thought and culture as a sort of immanent transcendence active at the root and center of the whole process of reality: it does not open upon "another world," and it dispenses with "faith":

> Ni simple litote ni fadeur affectée (ou conduite à se compliquer) l'insipidité chinoise, celle que symbolise la limpidité de l'eau "à la base de toutes les saveurs," est une conversion dont l'*au-delà* est en elle-même: conduisant la conscience à la *racine* du réel, au *centre* dont découle le procès des choses, elle est la voie de l'approfondissement (vers le simple, le naturel, l'essentiel), du détachement (loin du particulier, de l'individuel, du contingent). Sa transcendance ne débouche pas sur un autre monde, elle est vécue sur le mode même de l'immanence (pris dans cette perspective, les deux termes cessent enfin de s'opposer). La fadeur est cette expérience de la "transcendance" réconciliée avec la nature—dispensée de la foi. (127)

> Neither simple litotes nor affected blandness (induced to complicate itself), Chinese insipidity, that which the limpidity of water "at the base of all savors" symbolizes, is a conversion of which the *beyond* is itself: conducting consciousness to the *root* of the real, to the *center* from which flows the process of things, it is the way of deepening (towards the simple, natural, essential), of detachment (far from the particular, the individual, the contingent). Its transcendence does not enter upon another world but is lived in the mode even of immanence (taken in this perspective, the two terms cease finally to oppose one another).

Blandness is this experience of "transcendence" reconciled with nature—dispensed from faith.

Part of my purpose in what follows is to probe the possible "partis pris," or biases, and the discernible "atavisms" lurking within these otherwise lucid judgments.[18] It is important to bring reflection to bear on what might represent imperceptible automatisms hailing from what remains unthought in the shadows of this brilliantly illuminating thinking. In particular, the concluding statement here is arguably skewed by Jullien's own anticlerical prejudices, along with those of French lay culture generally, against any type of religious faith or otherworldliness, especially those characteristic of Christianity.

Jullien embraces a form of immanent transcendence within the real rather than of transcendence to a reality beyond. He seems to find the solution to the impasses of Western metaphysical thinking in what purportedly, at least in an initial moment of representation, is the wholly other thinking of an ancient Chinese Orient. He has been criticized by certain fellow sinologists for this alleged use of Chinese cultural capital converted into his own currency of Western philosophy and inflated by the exoticism of the other.[19] To demonstrate the purportedly alien nature of Chinese thought, Jullien typically starts from examples of Western thinkers, like Hegel, who could not really appreciate a value in Chinese culture such as blandness, which is distinguished only by what it is *not*. For Hegel, Confucius's "insipid" prescriptions lacked all speculative content and did not say anything that attained to the genuinely philosophical (12).[20] Even Roland Barthes, after his Chinese voyage in 1975, lacked confidence that "blandness" (*dàn* 淡) could really be the right word for the most revered quality

---

18. The terms within scare quotes are often repeated in Jullien's own *oeuvre* and were among the signposts adopted for the 2013 Cerisy Colloquium "Des possible de la pensée: Autour des travaux de François Jullien" staking out the contemporary import of his work. The colloquium's acts have since appeared as *Des possible de la pensée: Autour des travaux François Jullien*, eds. Françoise Gaillard and Philippe Ratte (Paris: Editions Hermann, 2015).

19. See Jean-François Billeter, *Contre François Jullien* (Paris: Éditions Allia, 2006). This is discussed below in the subsection "Universality in the (Apophatic) Gap between China and the West" of chapter 4.

20. Hegel's critique of Laozi is analyzed carefully and answered judiciously by Kwok Kui Wong, "Hegel's Criticism of Laozi and its Implications," *Philosophy East & West* 61/1 (2011): 56–79, in terms of Laozi's own form of dialectic and concreteness, which are missed by Hegel.

in ancient Chinese art and literature and culture and, accordingly, proposed that the Chinese word might be better translated as "peacefulness" (10–11).

Eulogizing insipidity is, of course, a reversal of normal or at least prevalent values ("renversement generalisé des valeurs," 23). It is purposefully undertaken, according to Jullien, in order to "evoke the essential." Blandness is not exactly *a* quality, not a distinct one at any rate, but in some sense the open possibility of all qualities—the capacity for being perceived as any specific quality and as all such qualities potentially. Taken in this way, blandness turns out to be much more essential than any given taste or flavor, however intense and exalted. For it is not definable or delimited. It is infinite. Every specific quality in some sense manifests a particular transformation of this indistinct but universal *capacity* to be something definite and distinct that is the peculiar virtue of the insipid. The insipid is infinitely transformable, and there is no particular savor or quality that it excludes. Blandness is the universal medium in and from which every savor arises. It is the magma of their transformation from one into the other because it has no boundaries of its own. I have already suggested that blandness is a kind of neuter ("le neutre") in the vocabulary of Blanchot and Barthes, and Jullien does, in fact, adopt this term. Insipidness, so construed, eliminates boundaries and barriers, so that everything flows into everything else. This type of unblocking can be imagined most readily for a specific spectrum of tastes and colors, but it is not restricted to any given field of objects: it can open into a general promiscuousness of all with all in a kind of universal, mystic union.

The vocabulary of the mystical used by Western writers such as Novalis may be alien to Jullien's taste—just as it was often treated with suspicion by Blanchot and Barthes. And yet it, too, has some pertinence, at least if it is heard apophatically as opening out beyond all its own merely heuristic conceptual bounds, since nothing should, in principle, be excluded from this universal vision and limitless capability.

Jullien's purpose is not to drive all things together into union in a mystic consummation so much as to deploy the insipid and its praise in carefully, concretely delimited, pragmatic and social contexts, where insipidity can operate with surpassing efficaciousness. Not a rigorous spiritual asceticism but rather total engagement with the world is the goal. "It is not a matter of a morality of solitariness, of living withdrawn from the world, because its lesson is valid first on the political plane and concerns management of one's affairs" ("Il ne s'agit point là d'une morale de solitaires, vivant retirés du monde, car la leçon vaut d'abord sur le plan politique et concerne la gestion des affaires," 26). In the state of indifferentiation and indeed of indifference, in the sense of being without partisanship, the spirit conforms to the underlying state of things beneath all invidious distinctions and definitions.

Even in allowing for an underlying reality of things astir within or beneath the surface evidence of the manifest, there is still no overarching sense of things to be discerned beneath them (107). It is just that all things transcend themselves in the inarrestable flow of time. Instead of producing the tension of allegory, in which signifiers tend towards a final sense that must be deciphered by consciousness tensely charged and concentrated, the insipid for Jullien does just the opposite: it "discharges consciousness" ("Elle décharge la conscience," 107). In this manner, blandness undoes all transcendent meaning, exposing it as myth. Its "transcendence" is completely natural, as the final chapter of *L'Éloge* (chap. 15: "La transcendance est naturelle"), endeavors to demonstrate.

TRANSCENDENCE AND IMMANENCE OF THE *DAO*

There is a hint here (in the last quotation) that simply opting for immanence over transcendence is not completely adequate either; it is still based on a logic of exclusion. Even those writing ostensibly against theology often acknowledge this. Theodor Adorno points to this dialectic in remarking that immanence, however necessary to all expression of anything transcendent, if absolutized, is itself, in effect, divinized: "No absolute can be expressed otherwise than in topics and categories of immanence, although neither in its conditionality nor as its totality is immanence to be deified."[21] Adorno wishes to rule out this possibility, but for apophatics "divinity" is not unequivocally to be ruled out: it ambiguously haunts the limits of thought and saying. Adorno himself recognizes dialectic as embodying a kind of mystical impulse ("mystische Impuls"), as itself a sort of secularized mysticism. Dialectic envisions and even effectuates a kind of coincidence of opposites (*coincidentia oppositorum*), for example, of the eternal with the most ephemeral ("das Vergänglichste"). Most importantly, Adorno's negative dialectics enacts a critical self-reflection ("Selbst-reflexion des Denkens") in which thinking resolutely thinks *against itself*. Adorno's striving to avoid enclosure in immanence leads him to a method of critique that descries

---

21. From "Meditationen zur Metaphysik," the final chapter of *Negative Dialektik*, quoted from *On What Cannot Be Said*, vol. 2, 269. Original in *Negative Dialektik* (Frankfurt a. M.: Suhrkamp, 1966): "Kein Absolutes ist anders auszudrücken als in Stoffen und Kategorien der Immanenz, während doch weder diese in ihrer Bedingtheit noch ihr totaler Inbegriff zu vergotten ist" (397).

transcendence as springing from immanence itself.[22] Adorno discovers this dimension of transcendence in immanence precisely in the "micrology" of the cracks and crevices through which the world is revealed as estranged ("die Welt ähnlich sich versetzt, verfremdet, ihre Risse und Schründe offenbart") and through which Messianic light ("Messianischen Lichte"), the light of knowledge but also of redemption, penetrates ("Erkentniss hat kein Licht, als das von der Erlösung her auf die Welt scheint").[23] Transcendence in this sense, as an impulse prompting to critique of what already factually exists, is necessary to avoid the totalizing self-enclosure of immanence. Like the bland, the minimal is revealing of something that is not manifest except negatively, through cracks and lacks. And yet, even as such, it can become peculiarly redeeming. Indeed, there is a negative theological discourse on the minimal that can trace its pedigree back through classical apophatic sources in Western tradition such as Nicholas of Cusa's *De docta ignorantia*. Cusa employs a mathematical imagery in order to treat God as both the maximum and the minimum. In his apophatic vision, in which these terms are "understood incomprehensibly," they actually "coincide" (book I, chapter 4).

Adorno's employment of the notion of the minimal, given its connections with apophatic tradition, serves as a reminder of how contemporary philosophy of even a secular and socially-oriented nature in the tradition of the Frankfurt school may find it necessary to leave space for some notion of metaphysical transcendence. In fact, Adorno's "Meditationen zur Metaphysik" in the third part of his *Negative Dialektik* struggles with and remains suspended by this tension. In order, then, to allow the possibility of transcendence and perhaps even of divinity to remain open and in play, as in classical sources of negative or apophatic theology, we might productively counterpoint Jullien's anti-Christian perspective on Chinese tradition also with that of a contemporary Christian mystical writer. There has, after all, been a continuous stream of such interpreters of Chinese classical tradition since the sixteenth-century Jesuits. One such heir and propagator is Thomas Merton.[24]

---

22. Fabian Heubel adroitly treats Adorno's negative dialectical understanding of the interpenetration of transcendence and immanence in relation to Chinese thinking in "Immanente Transzendenz im Spannungsfeld von europäischer Sinologie, kritischer Theorie und zeitgenössischem Konfuzianismus," *Polylog: Zeitschrift für Interkulturellen Philosophie* 26 (2011): 91–114, citation 96

23. Adorno, *Minima Moralia, Reflexion aus dem beschädigten Leben* (Frankfurt a. M.: Suhrkamp, 1951), 333–34. Citations are from the book's concluding paragraph ("Zum Ende"), which I translate and paraphrase.

24. See particularly Thomas Merton, *Mystics and Zen Masters* (New York: Farrar, Straus and Giroux, 1967 [1961]).

According to this view, whether as the metaphysical *Dao* of the Daoists or in its more ethically oriented form in Confucianism, classical Chinese thought is based on a transcendent nature or principle of order and harmony. The thrust of Laozi's thought is to recover the innate goodness of nature in a state prior to society and reflection, which are inevitably corrupt. Principled humanity and moral righteousness, in this perspective, are already degenerate forms symptomatic of a state of decline from the *Dao*. Social virtues of filial piety and paternal affection appear only when natural, spontaneous relations of harmony have already been broken or are forsaken. Conscious, deliberate virtue emerges only as an antidote to vice and so is more a symptom of illness than of good health. Laozi states this most explicitly in a few lapidary verses in poem 18 of the *Dao-de-jing*.

大道廢, 有仁義; 智慧出, 有大偽; 六親不和, 有孝慈; 國家昏亂, 有忠臣.

When the great way falls into disuse
There are benevolence and rectitude;
When cleverness emerges
There is great hypocrisy;
When the six relations are at variance
There are filial children;
When the state is benighted
There are loyal ministers. (Lau, trans.)

Laozi's Daoism envisages, at least negatively (without, that is, concretely imagining it in detailed representations or narrative), something like an Edenic existence, which, from a social point of view, is anarchic. Concerned chiefly with humanity in a state of society, Confucian thinkers often consider Daoism impracticable and sometimes even deleterious, to the extent that it can tend to undermine the authority necessary for social cohesion.

The doctrine of Confucius, "Master Kong" (Kǒng Fūzǐ, 孔夫子, or "Kong Tzu," as Latinized by the Jesuits, like Lao Tzu, or Laozi, meaning "Old Master"[25]) is based rather on faith in humanity (*rén* 仁) or on the *Dao* as immanent in human nature. It is rooted in a social class, the

---

25. Both transliterations, Laozi (Jullien) and Lao Tzu (Merton), in the Pinyin and Wade-Giles systems of Romanization respectively, have wide currency and need to be recognized.

cultivated military aristocracy (*ru* 儒) and their six talents (charioteering, archery, music, history, numbers, and ceremony or ritual). It undoubtedly still has something of an aura of transcendent mystery about it: from the *Dao*, human order springs up in ways that cannot be fully comprehended in human terms. Nevertheless, these skills can (and must) be consciously cultivated. Whereas Lao Tzu's ideal is the uncut block before the sculptor begins carving it, Confucius considers how to shape the individual who can build and participate in a harmonious, well-ordered society. Everything depends on being in harmony with heaven and on "visible expression of the hidden reality of the universe" through rites, or *lǐ* 禮 (Merton, 60). Rather than the inscrutable, incomprehensible Way of the Daoists, in Confucianism and specifically in *The Great Learning* (*Dà Xué*, 大學), "the real, the ethical *Dao*, is celebrated, solemnized, and clarified by rites." Yet precisely the religious or spiritual basis of Confucian social morality is brought out through this emphasis on rites: "Thus, moral action is at the same time contemplative and liturgical. Symbolic ceremony gives morality a character of deeper realization. The Confucian ethic is not only not automatic, not the product of inert routine. It is more than merely spontaneous. It is the *fruit of spiritual awareness*" (Merton, 61; Merton's italics).

Without Merton's basis of faith, but with acute attention to a "magical dimension" of human existence that becomes manifest especially in the quality of human virtue (*rén*) whereby it becomes possible to bring about prodigies effortlessly, Herbert Fingarette similarly interprets Confucius's human community as a "holy rite." Ultimate dignity is based neither on the individual nor on society but rather on "the flowering of humanity in the ceremonial acts of men," and this involves a "participation in divinity."[26]

Curiously, despite the obvious contrast in their approaches, Merton is actually very close to Jullien in one decisive respect. Wm. Theodore de Bary, in a highly appreciative essay on Merton's sinological writings, notes Merton's "foreshortened 'timeless' view of Confucianism" in terms that would apply well also to Jullien.[27] Both authors, Merton because he is a "poet" and Jullien as primarily a philosopher, read the Confucian classics as speaking

---

26. Herbert Fingarette, *Confucius: The Secular as Sacred* (New York: Harper and Row, 1972), 78. A comparable sort of bifocalism is recommended by Henry Rosemont Jr., *Rationality and Religious Experience: The Continuing Relevance of the World's Spiritual Traditions* (La Salle, IL: Open Court, 2001).

27. Wm. Theodore de Bary, "Thomas Merton, Matteo Ricci, and Confucianism," *The Great Conversation: Education for a World Community* (New York: Columbia University Press, 2014), 366.

directly to them as individuals and as contemporary in relative abstraction from their social context and millenary history.

The diverging emphases on immanence and on transcendence, as found in Jullien and in Merton respectively, are not to be set against each other but rather to be held together in tension. Both are actually in agreement on the mutual dependence or co-implication of transcendence and immanence. What we need to probe critically, and finally to explode, are the exclusionary myths that nevertheless adhere to any particular path of thought and that limit our capacity for understanding and empathy. Such is exactly the spirit of the *Dao*, furthermore, as expounded by many who can approach it through their own native language. Among them, Longxi Zhang (张隆溪) emphasizes the *Dao*'s straddling of transcendence and immanence precisely by its ineffable or, I would say, apophatic character:

> According to Laozi the philosopher, *Dao* is both immanent and transcendent; it is the begetter of all things; therefore, it is not and cannot be named after any of these things. In other words, *Dao* is the ineffable, the "mystery of mysteries" beyond the power of language. Even the name *Dao* is not a name in itself: "I do not know its name; so I just call it *Dao*." "The *Dao* is forever nameless." Laozi makes it clear that the totality of the *Dao* is kept intact only in knowing silence; hence this famous paradox that "the one who knows does not speak; the one who speaks does not know."[28]

Similarly, Zonqi Cai advocates a "nondualistic" understanding of the traditional Chinese thinkers' approach to "ultimate reality" as "ultimate Process" that spans both the immanence and transcendence of nature and humanity: "The early Chinese worldviews . . . entail either a 'naturalization' of conscious beings in the numinous realms (ancestral spirits, the high god, Heaven, etc.), or a 'supernaturalization' of actual processes in the world of nature and man (the cosmological *li*, Confucius' Dao of human history, the all-inclusive Dao of the *Changes*)."[29] In either case, however, the natural

---

28. Longxi Zhang, *The Tao and the Logos: Literary Hermeneutics, East and West* (Durham, NC: Duke University Press, 1992), 27. Zhang quotes and translates the *Dao-de-jing* from the Chinese edition, *Laozi zhu* [The Annotated Laozi], with the commentary of Wang Bi (AD 226–49).

29. Zongqi Cai, *Configurations of Comparative Poetics: Three Perspectives on Western and Chinese Literary Criticism* (Honolulu: University of Hawai'i Press, 2002), 107.

and the supernatural or transcendent-of-nature are actually inseparable and cannot be conceived except in relation to one another.

The Nothing on which even blandness pivots does, after all, have something transcendent about it, though not to the exclusion of immanence, especially not of total immanence. Yet such *total* immanence transcends itself and can no longer be adequately conceptualized as only or exclusively "immanence." The idea of absolute transcendence cannot be excluded from it either. Immanence as such absolutely transcends every possible conception of it. *Total* immanence is without confines and involves or contaminates everything, transcending all limits. Even what the imagination of a transcendent God as Creator is ultimately aiming at cannot be categorically excluded from the infinite immanent-transcendent energy of the *Dao*.

The theistic notion of God is inadequate as a representation of the all-encompassing reality in which we live, but so are all representations. And the theistic notion does arguably serve better than any other images do to capture *certain* nuances of the experience that gives rise to notions such as "God"—for example, the feeling of absolute dependence such as Schleiermacher delineated it in *The Christian Faith* (*Der christliche Glaube*, 1830). A theistic divinity may in some respects express better than any other images can the unconditional contingency of all that exists. One could dispute about whether the attendant doctrine of creation from nothing (*creatio ex nihilo*) is accurate and adequate to describe this experience of radical contingency. But in any case it is not any more adequate to pin the label "nature" to everything, as if that summed it all up and let us know its true and abiding being or essence. All, nature, must rather be admitted to be a great unknown and, as such, to master us and our very thinking together with everything else—hence *Deus sive Natura*. A variety of images and approaches, even ones that in word and expression may be mutually opposed, are necessary. In any case, inconsistent and even incompatible images crop up persistently in our efforts to relate to this unknown. Such plurality proves necessary in Chinese as well as in Western cultures, with each displaying their inexorable and inextricable polarities. Only the multiplicity of perspectives enables us to approach the absolute of having no perspective at all.

MENCIUS, OR THE NATURALNESS OF MORALITY: IS THE ALL WITHOUT TRANSCENDENCE?

In a paradigmatic case that is outstanding for its philosophical coherence and rigor, the thought of Mencius (372–289 BC) is taken by Jullien to be worldly and merely human or as emphatically *without transcendence*.[30] It is based, instead, on humanity in the sense of being connected with others, other humans (85). Nonetheless, humanity and its harmony are connected with the total regulation of the world, which flows from a source beyond any of its manifest forms or phenomena. The connection between—and the order among—all things is not simply one more thing alongside others in the world. It eludes any inventory, however exhaustive, of the discrete items that make up the world. This order and connection among things is necessarily infinite, given the nature of the temporal world as open and evolving. Jullien acknowledges here a connection with "transcendence," which he conceives of expressly as the absolutization and totalization of immanence (173). Yet he insists that this has nothing to do with mysticism or the ineffable (82): as a purely immanent ordering, it has no relation to divinity. I submit that such unlimited connectedness is a perfect incarnation of divinity in the *negative* sense in which no identities or representations can be adequate to the divine—certainly not those of being *a* thing or of being any*thing* at all. And yet, all such representations might serve to bring about or foster unreserved openness to the universe and to life as a whole and as exceeding our comprehension. Such representations contribute through being exceeded themselves by a transcendent principle or instance that cannot be properly conceived at all but can be expressed only in terms of the insufficiency of that which is transcended by it.

The sources of Chinese wisdom, as Jullien expounds them, open up to a dimension of the infinite and inexhaustible that exceeds all human power to understand or even to conceive of it. Such wisdom, in crucial ways, thus approaches the theological dimension that apophasis points to by negation of all propositions concerning God. In Mencius, by Jullien's own admission, morality is an unconditional ideal ("idéal inconditionné," 45) that is manifest only very partially in actual human comportment. Moral sense is the *un*manifest core of our human nature. It never appears in or as itself but always only in tendencies and approximations. Moreover, it is not just a mechanism for regulating our egoisms and their conflicting desires. Morality belongs rather to the fulfillment of our persons, or to the perfection of our natures, and it lies embedded in our natures beneath the level of conscious choice and control.

To this extent, Mencius turns out to be surprisingly close to Rousseau and Kant, inasmuch as he perceives morality as rooted in something anterior to experience—in something innate or a priori. In Jullien's words:

---

30. François Jullien, *Dialogue sur la morale* (Paris: Grasset, 1995), 88. This is the default reference in this subsection for otherwise unattributed quotations.

To found morality is thus to find for it a rootedness that is anterior to and renders it independent of experience—in our natural inclination (Rousseau) or in the a priori of practical reason (Kant). Mencius cannot but be ranged alongside them: he is first in China to define the category of the original [foncier] and innate: "that of which one is capable without learning it is our original capacity"; similarly, "that which one knows without reflection is an original knowing."[31]

There is, for Mencius, a natural disposition to morality, an inherent goodness in humanity. This seems to be an invitation to embrace a purely humanistic ethical ground, and yet by thinking the human radically as without any assumed frame or foundation, this natural disposition becomes not *only* that but turns out to be open to its own Other as well. This interface with alterity is perhaps only more vividly figured by Kant and Rousseau as the divine Voice of conscience. Its equivalent may be lurking unexpressed in the promptings of nature in Mencius.

There is, however, for Mencius, as Jullien reads him, no external or personal "voice" of conscience, as there is for both Rousseau and Kant. And there is in Mencius no moral imperative as such but rather just an inborn feeling. Jullien emphasizes that, for Mencius, moral conscience is manifest in our spontaneous reactions—for example, in the natural impulse to prevent a child from stumbling into a pit or in the emperor's stopping a sacrifice out of pity for the terrorized bull being led as a victim to the slaughter. This is simply a natural prompting of sympathy, not any actual or formal moral injunction. Heaven, in the Chinese classic tradition, does not speak (43–44), however much it reveals. As Mencius famously affirmed, "Heaven does not speak, but simply reveals the Mandate through actions and affairs" (5A5).[32] Jullien interprets this to mean that natural reactions of pity reveal a norm and an absolute in its outer, terminal manifestation or "tip" ("bout"). In fact, the instinctive revulsion from the child's impending

---

31. Fonder la morale, c'est donc lui chercher un enracinement qui soit antérieur à l'expérience et la rende indépendante vis-à-vis d'elle: le penchant de notre nature (chez Rousseau), l'*a priori* de la raison pratique (chez Kant). Mencius ne peut que se ranger de leur côté; le premier en Chine, li définit la catégorie du foncier et de l'innée: "ce dont on est capable sans qu'on l'apprenne est une capacité originelle" (ou "foncière"); de même "ce qu'on sait sans y réfléchir est un savoir originel" (ou "foncier," cf. VII, A, 15). (*Dialogue sur la morale*, 45.)

32. *Mengzi: With Selections from the Traditional Commentaries*, trans. Bryan W. van Norden (Indianapolis, IL: Hackett, 2008), 123.

harm or from the victim's slaughter is only incipient and inchoate, not explicit and articulate: it is just the beginning of a sentiment that needs to be developed and cultivated into full-fledged "humanity" (*rén*, 仁). The impulse as such is inconstant and is soon forgotten, as the Confucian texts show. Yet it alludes to something natural, persistent, potentially all-pervasive, and even, I maintain, transcendent: this shows up in its being coordinated with "Heaven."

Jullien concludes that heaven is a principle of harmonization internal to the cosmos rather than a Will imposed from without by a Creator (*Dialogue sur la morale*, 52). The absolute is conceived simply as a "regulated process" ("*processus régulé*," 53), and Mencius reflects on people's relation to this process. We can correspond to it, but we cannot control it nor even define it. There is indeed an unconditioned and absolute basis for morality, yet it is approachable only indirectly or negatively. Given this predicament, Mencius turns to reflection on human conduct rather than to speculating on the nature of reality per se: like Socrates, Mencius deflects thought from "speculation on the march of the world" to "reflection on his own conduct" (53). It is only through regulating one's own conduct in quotidian life that one gains access to or becomes conscious of the transcendent principle, the Way, that governs all things in their evolution. Cosmic regularity is experienced day by day in ourselves as an inherent normativity of what is good for us.

Nonetheless, Jullien takes all this in a rather one-sided, exclusively humanistic sense. His eschewing of the role of religion in classical Chinese thought can be placed in the lineage of Marcel Granet. Granet's categorical exclusion of theology from Chinese wisdom is summed up in his statement that "Chinese wisdom is entirely human" and "owes nothing to the idea of God" ("La sagesse Chinoise est une *sagesse indépendente* et tout humaine. Elle ne doit rien à l'idée de Dieu").[33]

However, in reality, and explicitly in negative theology, God cannot be made to fit into an idea, and no idea of God can be more than heuristic. Moreover, and for the same reason, it may be inexact and reductive to circumscribe Chinese wisdom as merely "human." Granet may well be right that in China religion is not a "differentiated function of social activity" (*La pensée chinoise*, 476). Indeed, in its most authentic forms anywhere, religion does not "exist" as such distinctly: nevertheless, it informs everything. As Paul Tillich expressed this insight, "Religion is not a special function of man's spiritual life, but it is the dimension of depth in all of its

---

33. Marcel Granet, *La pensée chinoise* (Paris: Albin Michel, 1999 [1934]), 478.

functions."³⁴ The *truth* of religion is never found in a separate institution or in a discrete practice or consciousness but rather in what informs and ties together all aspects of life. This is the subtler awareness of religion that the apophatic approach has all along been trying to foster and restore also in the West. In this spirit, I defend traditional forms of religion as often our best and most revealing poetry³⁵: they can serve to forestall forgetting of the Nothing that is not objectively manifest and yet is the heart of all everywhere. This is the Nothing that, as ineluctable negation, wounds and opens us up and thereby ties us (*religere*) all together.

Like Granet, Jullien emphasizes that Confucian regulation, which is the foundation of this teaching, is without any basis in religious revelation. The coherence to which it is attuned is that of the total immanence of nature (*Dialogue sur la morale*, 276). However, when revelation is nothing positive but rather an opening to what no formulations whatever can grasp, then even revelation is not to be excluded from this vision. Jullien himself emphasizes that every minute particular can "reveal" the general and bind or tie us to totality ("nous relie à la totalité"), whether that of Heaven or of the Sage ("celle du Ciel, celle du Sage," 276). It may be granted that instead of aiming at transcendence, Confucius's words treat things as indices of the ground of immanence ("fond d'immanence," 276). There is an immanence working throughout reality, and this is "Heaven": it has a kind of height of transcendence, but not as exterior to humanity. Instead, Jullien concludes that such transcendence is nothing but "the totalization of immanence on the scale of the whole world" ("la totalisation de l'immanence à l'échelle du monde entier," 280).

Mencius's Sage, like the Sage of Confucius, is apophatic, or without words; in fact, his saying is not a saying ("le dire de Mencius, en fait, n'est pas un dire," 280). His goal is also to be without perspective or bias; only so can he react to the natural course of things by a purely immanent logic and without any arbitrary impositions of his own. Such is his attunement to the natural regulation of the universe. There is a belief here in the harmony of the whole. However, is such belief not already itself something religious in the sense that counts most? Is it not a belief in what binds all together—literally *re-ligio*—in a common world? Granted, such sagacious reasoning entails no figure of God as a personal being. Nevertheless, in an apophatic perspective, it is already clear from the start that no such figures

---

34. Paul Tillich, *Theology of Culture* (Oxford: Oxford University Press, 1964), 5–6.
35. See especially *A Philosophy of the Unsayable* (Notre Dame, IN: University of Notre Dame Press, 2014), 109–10, 130–31.

can possibly reveal the ultimate truth of religion. To this extent, Chinese wisdom discloses, in especially naked and transparent terms, what religion, as understood even in the West in its apophatic core, suggests and portends: an erasure of all our finite figures in order to expose something infinite that they conceal at the same time as they reveal it. This cannot, then, be taken as an exclusion of metaphysics or a reduction of religion to ethics. It rather helps to clarify what the *poetry* of metaphysics and theology are also really about—namely, relating all together in a harmonious, or at least a common, order. The idea that the "principle" of it all, "God," should already be perfect apart from any of his self-manifestations in the world is affirmed likewise of the *Dao* in the *Dao-de-Jing*: the *Dao* was formless and perfect or complete in itself before the universe began (chapter 25).

The perfection of "Heaven" is indeed a cardinal postulate consistently affirmed throughout the Confucian classics, too. *Zhongyong* (中庸), *The Book of the Mean*, chapter 26 is a *locus classicus* stressing the permanence and infinity of the way of the universe. And this is, after all, the essential meaning of divine "transcendence." Not that the divine can be opposed to the world as something else. Yet neither is divinity as such dependent on the world—or conditioned or compromised by the world's imperfections. The *Dao* is also said to exist before and without the world. It exists "before Heaven and Earth" and "stands on its own" (*Dao-de-Jing* 25). And any conception of it in worldly terms, even in terms of the world's own self-transcendence, is also a misconception: Heaven, like God, can only be miraculously and paradoxically *mis*conceived. Zhuangzi, that most worldly of Daoist philosophers, demonstrates this fact in some of its most extreme and paradoxical forms. Our only means of representing the *Dao* are poetic. Then why not represent the principle of things as effectuating an act of Creation—and why not then as a Creator—for good *imaginative* measure? These particular images are not ones that retained currency in Chinese classical wisdom, but as *images* they come from the same *negative* apprehension of unity as do the paradigmatic Chinese figures of interdependent poles—yin (阴) and yang (阳)—and the imagination of a totally inconceivable Way (Dào, 道) in immanent-transcendent terms.

Jullien's point is typically how different this is from Western, transcendentalist representations of moral and religious consciousness. My point is that beyond the representations there is, in any case, a common ground in the *unrepresentable*. "Heaven" (*Tiān*, 天) is ultimately a representation for this Source of regulation, which, however, is not accessible except through its effects. It is not as such an object of knowledge. Like God, it can be described only indirectly. There is a difference in the choice of representations. But it is a difference only within a common basis or "fund" of understanding (Jullien's "fonds d'entente") at the level of the unrepresentable. There are important differences in the way that the governing and energizing Power at the source of the universe is represented, but the representations are in any case only heuristic. What they share in common is pointing beyond themselves and beyond the structural cultural relativity of all images and representations.

A goal of Mencius's reflection is to affirm, as the last chapter of Jullien's book itself announces, that "moral consciousness gives access to the unconditioned" ("La conscience morale donne accès à l'inconditionné," 164) or to what in Chinese tradition figures as "Heaven" ("Le Ciel"). Jullien conceives of this not as a religious and certainly not a theological notion, but again these are differences of imagery—and not of the nature and intellection of the relation to an absolute that relativizes our every thought and action.

What is missing in China is not at all the sense of everything being tied together in one, nor of the perfection of this conjoining of all in an invisible and unrepresentable Way, and thus of all things as existing in relation to All in responsible reciprocity grounded in a common Source. Some such vision and conviction is the basis of religion in almost any culture, and it is every bit as strong in China as in the West. Only the institutional and even conceptual and imaginative forms of religion characteristic of the West are missing from Chinese classics and culture. But all these forms and expressions are only expressions and even disguises, when not outright perversions and betrayals, of a more authentic (apophatic) "religion." Of course, institutional forms and public practices can also be authentic mediations of religion, but they are in their particular determinations and manifestations not necessary and inevitable so much as culturally relative—even in being *about* the absolute. The thesis that Confucianism is not a religion and that religion as such is foreign to Chinese thought and culture is correct if and only if one adheres to a certain positive and external definition of religion. Seen in terms of negative theology, the genuinely religious is always what is not and cannot be explicitly formulated in any of the articulations that are commonly labeled and analyzed as "religious." The essence and inspiration of religion is itself not properly "religious." It cannot be characterized or formulated adequately or properly in any language.

Chinese wisdom is seeking and recommending a more radical commitment to a view of the wholeness of life and of our belonging to the overall process of things. One can take this as a purely ethical commitment but not in a sense that would allow it to be cordoned off from religion. In fact, Jullien remarks that the notion of the "Way of Heaven" (*Tiān-dào*

天道) was first introduced into Chinese thought, during the Shang dynasty in the second millennium before Christ, as a "Lord on high" (*Shàngdì*, 上帝) or high Sovereign—thus in terms very near to those of a personal God. The Way is at this stage a "mandate" or command conceived of as coming from a sovereign (*Dialogue sur la morale*, 54). But Jullien stresses that this "absolute factor" ("facteur absolu") was progressively depersonalized to a function of engendering and transforming. From near the inception of the Zhou dynasty (1046–221 BC), a little more than a millennium before Christ, the figure of a personal God disappeared from the Chinese universe.

This "progress" could be considered one of becoming less beholden to myth, but it can also be considered simply as reflecting a lesser development of—or indulgence in—the powers of the imagination applied to rendering the experience of regulation in the world. This world is imagined as a spontaneous natural process rather than as originating in a personal and willed creative act. Yet these latter, theistic and revealed forms of apprehending and relating to the regulation of the universe might indeed capture other, further possibilities for imagining the mystery of the relationship between the world and its only imaginable source or unity or potential. For Hegel, such theistic imaginings represented "higher," more evolved modes of religious consciousness. In any case, all aspects of reality must be admitted to be subject to this universal regulation.

What seems to be so limited about theism, specifically from the point of view of the imagination, is that it apparently reduces the universe to a human measure by anthropomorphically construing its supreme principle as a divine Person made in the human image. However, theism, when conceived of through negative theology, can also cut in just the opposite direction so as to undercut the human and expose it to a divine measure—that is, to the radically Other. The true person is not fully apprehended in the human beings that we know: these individuals are only a limited and often perverse form of personhood making manifest in a corrupt guise the power or energy that sublimely infuses the universe beyond our comprehension. God is ultimately, in "his" own being or "Godself," the *not*-personal (not, anyway, as we know persons), but this must still be thought of from the basis of, and not as excluding, the attribute of personality. Thus the regulation of the universe, if it is not just a machine or a purely and impersonally vital force, must also be thought through along lines that include rather than exclude personal will, consciousness, etc. And these are all so many invitations to the imagination—ones that can hardly be refused, unless we choose to construe our personal and moral and spiritual beings in purely mechanistic and/or vitalistic terms.

There is a tendency, registering clearly in Jullien, to deem Chinese cosmology to be sublimely free of all the metaphysical, anthropological baggage of intentionality and caring or consciousness. This can be bracing, especially as the antidote to the characteristic strictures and extravagances of Western religious imagination. Yet such a cosmology leaves much of the real in its many possible dimensions still relatively unimagined. The great poetic potential of the personal has been exploited prodigiously in the West, signally in its theological epics ranging from the *Divine Comedy* to Tasso's *Gerusalemme liberata*, from Milton's *Paradise Lost* to Blake's *Jerusalem* and even to Joyce's *Finnegans Wake*.[36] The lack of metaphysical and theistic figures in Chinese classical wisdom is an unambiguous advantage only if one thinks one knows what the universe really is and that it is like a mechanism, or perhaps like spontaneously living nature, but in any case not like a person. However, claiming to have such knowledge is more presumptuous than leaving open the ultimate nature of the universe and rather pursuing imaginatively to their limits all aspects of universal experience. This involves imaginatively exploring the whole panoply of forms, including those that are personalizing in nature, in which various cultures have imagined reality.

Religions are all so many ways of entering into relation with the source of "regulation" envisaged by Chinese wisdom. A fully deconstructed version of Western tradition finds in the Chinese tradition, specifically in its being without epic and revelation (as Jullien stresses), confirmation of precisely what these forms were persistently aiming at and yet always failed to encompass and to reduce to the word: they inevitably failed, notwithstanding all of the West's heroic epic attempts and sublimely rhetorical revelations. The Chinese approach may seem to undergo less extravagant imaginative elaboration and conceptual detour in its illuminating or pointing to what is simply beyond the verbal. Yet in Chinese and in Western apophatic wisdom alike, the purpose of representation is not to lay down or define truth so much as to point as an index to the Way or Truth that lies beyond saying. This, moreover, is the necessary premise for any possible *inter*cultural understanding. This possibility, in which all the particular discursive forms of various cultures need to be bracketed, is based on what Jullien likes to call the "fonds d'entente"—something in the background that "funds" common "understanding," a resource to be drawn on in dialogue, one rendering

---

36. I undertake such a reconstruction of Christian epic tradition in *Poetry and Apocalypse: Theological Disclosures of Poetic Language* (Stanford, CA: Stanford University Press, 2009), part 2.

possible the convergences and especially the divergences between patterns of thinking characteristic of different cultures.

Jullien takes Confucianism to be pure morality without religion (*Dialogue sur la morale*, 91). Nevertheless, its wisdom has served to point beyond the field of representations that he generally identifies as "religion" to the unrepresentable Source or Way in which the separate identities that divide things from one another are abolished or at least are suspended. This corresponds also to what Western wisdom sometimes recognizes as the apophatic. Not any human act of morality, but rather doing nothing on our own initiative and positing nothing that is merely of our own invention is the only principle of morality in this understanding of both Daoist and Confucian ethics. Our part is fulfilled simply in following and enabling the *natural propensity* of things, as flowing from their Source, to take its course.[37]

The hard thing for us is *not* to interfere and thus not to block the flow of energy and life from their source. The basic strategy of Chinese wisdom is to gain access to the source of all by removing human limitations as so many obstacles to its full and unencumbered self-deployment. One does not have to have the truth or the right way oneself, but simply to let the Way (*Dao*) be itself and so become also *our* way. It can be the one and only Way only negatively—as the negation of all of our ways. An echo of this idea—juxtaposed in a spirit of comparative religions—can be found in Isaiah 55:8–9: "For my thoughts are not your thoughts, neither are your ways my ways, saith the Lord." Diverging from Jullien, I present nature in the Chinese conception not so much as a fundamental alternative to theistic conceptions of divinity but rather as a different and more consistently—or at least nakedly—apophatic way of approaching an abyssal mystery or enigma (for finite human understanding) at the source and foundation of all reality. One of these human approaches to value and meaning that transcends our comprehension and summons our capacities to feel out their limits passes through morality and its sovereign dictates or promptings. Another such path leads to the making of poetry in its unaccountable creativity and uncanny inspiration. This is the path we pursue in the next chapter.

---

37. Cf. Jullien, *La propension des choses: Pour une histoire de l'efficacité en Chine* (Paris: Seuil, 1992).

Chapter 2

NOTHING AND THE POETIC "MAKING" OF SENSE

THE ART OF EFFECTIVENESS: DOING OR SAYING NOTHING

In his ambitious book *Detour and Access* (*Le détour et l'accès*), Jullien elicits his central theses concerning China's peculiar wisdom of All as Nothing (nothing definable in static terms or as stable truth) from his reading of the Chinese classics.[1] He uses the perspective so developed as a vantage point for looking at Western tradition and critiquing the inveterate closures of its approach to the world and to life. This culture becomes particularly pernicious in asserting its imperious claims to universal knowledge. Chinese indirectness, on the other hand, enables thought to maintain a relation to the whole that cannot as such be encompassed. It is possible to relate to this whole only indirectly by cultivating the arts of "allusiveness" and "incitation." By such means, Chinese thought in poetry discovers or invents ways of access to an effectually universal sort of cognizance, although these ways are only negative and work rather through the undoing of thought itself so that it can cease to be an obstacle to an undistorted encounter with reality.

---

1. Jullien, *Le détour et l'accès: Stratégies du sens en Chine, en Grèce* (Paris: Grasset, 1995), trans. Sophie Hawkes as *Detour and Access: Strategies of Meaning in China and Greece* (New York: Zone Books, 2004). As with Jullien's other texts, I cite and translate from the French original directly. This text is the default reference throughout this chapter. The terms I use, however, when not in quotation marks, are not necessarily Jullien's own. More than exegesis, my purpose is to assimilate his researches in articulating views of my own.

The art of war, for example, as presented in China's classic treatises on the subject (*bingfa*),[2] is itself not just a technical method for a limited operation geared to achieving a particular strategic aim: it is rather a means of relating to the entire universe. Such martial art proceeds from a kind of global knowing. It envisages conquering not by direct assault but by omission of overt action and by the attunement of oneself rather to the forces at work on the terrain of conflict and in the cosmos generally; this art thus reaches far beyond the scope of one's own conscious aims and powers. For this purpose, our own human activity must become a form of passivity, even though, at the same time, this passivity needs to be intensely active and participatory in what is in act already, even without our having to instigate it willfully. Our part consists simply in getting out of the way of the Way and in orienting ourselves instead to it, so as to allow and enable its stream of creative and sustaining energy to flow unhindered through us and throughout the universe. Whatever we are able to positively accomplish has its source not in us, unless it be in our own self-limitation and virtual self-elimination—hence in apophasis (negation) and in kenosis (self-emptying).

Whether in war or in political discourse or in literature, the arts and techniques of indirection aim to orient us so as to allow the whole, or the overall drift of things, to work in our favor. We stop trying to constrain a part of the whole (the part that we can grasp) to conform to our wishes and rather conform ourselves to the greater All: working in alignment with this All, we can achieve all that is effectively possible for us. By allowing our channeling of events to be guided by the options that they themselves afford, we let the goal itself be given to us together with (and within) a gesture of opening on our part. The *detour* of not trying to achieve our own immediate objective and definable goal, but of working rather in deference to the natural and irresistible flow of things, is the secret of success—or, more exactly, of effectiveness.

More specifically concerning the ways of meaning, Jullien discovers an alternative strategy of sense in the Chinese classics, where consciousness aims

---

2. The most celebrated of such treatises is attributed to "Sunzi" by the Han dynasty historian Sima Qian (145–86 BC). It was offered to the king of the state of Wu in the mid-fourth century during the Warring States period and exercised influence on Mao Tse Tung and apparently even on Napoleon. Another such treatise, authored by Sun Bin, a descendent and perhaps a grandson of Sunzi, and often confounded with his own text, was unearthed in 1974 in Shandong.

not so much to represent the world as to interact with it advantageously. Consciousness does this by modulating itself in a manner that marries it with circumstance ("plutôt à se moduler—pour épouser la circonstance," *Le Détour et l'accès*, 9). This entails no longer doubling the world in consciousness by means of representation and then, furthermore, lending consciousness (into the bargain) a transcendent foundation in the Subject, which is itself founded in turn on Being or on God. Chinese thought and culture do not posit another plane or horizon of sense consisting of essences or spiritual beings, or even simply of meanings. Chinese wisdom envisages, rather, the endless modulation of meaning on a plane of immanence that is infinite and all-encompassing or "global." Jullien explains the central thesis of his book near its outset in terms contrasting the Greek (specifically Socratic) logic of the essentially real with the Chinese (especially Confucian) approach to the ever-fluctuating nature of things:

> . . . à la définition (socratique) s'oppose la modulation (confucéenne), comme à la généralité s'oppose la globalité; et commence à s'imposer cette idée: puisqu'il ne conduit pas vers autre chose (de l'ordre de l'"idée"), ce détour de la parole confucéenne trouve en lui-même sa propre fin; il ne cesse—sur un mode indiciel—d'éclairer la réalité. Car à travers la variation des propos du Sage, je suis en adéquation continue avec le renouvellement des choses; en abordant le réel sous un biais ou sous un autre, j'en épouse constamment la régulation. Et c'est pourquoi ce détour est en même temps l'accès. (12–13)

> . . . to the definition (Socratic) is opposed the modulation (Confucian), just as to the general the global is opposed; and this idea begins to impose itself: since it does not lead to something other (of the order of the "idea"), this detour of the Confucian word finds its end in itself; it never ceases to elucidate reality in an indicative manner. Because through the variation of the lessons of the Sage, I am in a continual correspondence with the renewal of things; in approaching the real through one angle or another, I constantly espouse regulation. And that is why this detour is at the same time access.

Accordingly, Jullien's reading of Chinese classics, right from the *Analects* of Confucius, places emphasis on the Master's reticence, his reluctance to teach in a direct way by positive precepts, and on his refusal of words.

The emblematic passage that might sum up the whole work in its essential import for Jullien ("De tous les propos de Confucius . . . le plus important," 281) is one in which the Master says nothing. Instead, he gets up and leaves the room without replying to those who have come to inquire of his wisdom (*Analects* 4.15). Confucius, Kong Fuzi, or simply Kǒngzǐ (孔子), literally "Master Kung," is the master, before all else, of a certain art of evasion. The Master teaches by what he does not say more than by what he says: he spurs his disciples to probe on their own the void that he forces them to confront. Words, in his minimalist employment of them, have value not so much for accurately representing how things really are but rather for inciting appropriate or productive actions. No verbal formulation is adequate, and words cannot be held on to, for they are only temporary ("toute formulation n'est que temporaire," 237). If held on to for themselves, they become sterile. Words count rather for what they issue in, for what lies beyond them, their "au-delà" (237). They serve like bells to waken and alarm people (238; cf. *Lun Yu* 3.24). They open upon an unsaid ("non-dit," 250) and thus remain incitative or indicative rather than discursive, descriptive, and argumentative.

As with apophatic texts generally, the key to these Confucian texts is always in what they do *not* say, not explicitly or directly anyway. Learning to read this unsaid in and behind their often jejune affirmations and beyond the ostensibly innocuous, if not trivial, matters that they relate is prerequisite to their intelligibility as genuine and challenging works of philosophical thought and wisdom. The *Analects* employs literary genres such as the anecdote or the apothegm and parable that offer merely *seeds* of speech (*semina dicendi*, 251) rather than conclusive discourses.

Confucius produces tautologies, furthermore, which *say* or assert nothing but nevertheless work by allusion from a certain situated angle in order to evoke a global dimension of "all" without exclusions (266). The situated uttering of any enunciation entirely conditions its stated content so that from context to context its meaning is transformed completely and can even be reversed. A placing into evidence of the complexity and elusiveness of this meaning points us beyond any specific, explicit sense that could be fixed to its source in a concrete situation. All particular meaning thus opens into a more general type of significance, but not as if this were another level of meaning: in fact, just such a distinction is what is transcended in this shift beyond the binary logic of exclusion. What emerges instead is a connection of effects to their source. Of course, at the level of *language* and enunciation, a binary logic (the source versus its effects) still inevitably operates. The Master's statements, however, serve only to shift into evidence the silent background factors. The latter are what he brings to bear and avails himself of in order to subtly attune his disciples to what lies before and beyond any message that can be conferred in words.

The humanity (*rén* 仁) or virtue that the Master warmly recommends remains indefinable. He confesses that he knows "nothing at all" about it (5.7).³ It reaches to and connects humans with heaven, as expressed by the conjunction "human nature and the way of heaven." But the disciples add that no one has ever "learned his discourses" about these matters. As they explain, "The Master's *personal* displays of *his principles* and *ordinary* descriptions of them may be heard. His discourses about *man's* nature, and the way of Heaven, cannot be heard" (5.12). Indeed, in the *Analects* such matters are never discussed directly. The sage is himself without character or quality. He is indefinable and without exclusions, like God in apophatic theology. "His only singularity is to have none" ("Sa seule singularité, en somme, est de n'en avoir aucune," 280). This happens to match statements in occidental apophatic authors such as Meister Eckhart and Nicholas of Cusa, who say that God's only distinction is to be wholly without distinctions.⁴

Confucian discourse, in these respects, is close to poetry, and indeed poetry takes a leading role in Jullien's analysis of the ethos of classic Chinese thought and literature. The ways of evading representation are the special pursuit of Chinese poetry as Jullien presents it. Very often Jullien contrasts these ways with the procedures that he takes to be governing paradigms for Western poetry and poetics—namely, techniques serving for symbolic representation of the real. However, the flight from representation and its transcending, particularly through the refusal of modes of representation referenced to a supposedly separate world of objects, have likewise been pursued in highly sophisticated and insistent ways by practitioners of negative poetics in Western traditions. The contrastive logic of Jullien's exposition thus proves to be inadequate to what it actually discloses beyond its own stated aims.

---

3. Chinese text in James Legge, *Confucius: Confucian Analects, The Great Learning and the Doctrine of the Mean,* trans. James Legge (New York: Dover, 1971), originally published by Clarendon Press, Oxford, 1893, as volume I of "The Chinese Classics" series. Translation compared with *The Analects of Confucius,* trans. Lao An (Jingsilu: Shandong Friendship Press, 1992), 85, 81.

4. Cusanus develops this position extensively in *De li non aliud* (*God as Not-Other*).

POETIC APPROACHES TO THE
LIMIT OF EXPRESSION

In his analysis of classic Chinese poetry beginning from the oldest collection, the *Book of Odes* (*Shi Jing* 诗经, eleventh to seventh century BC) and its commentary tradition, Jullien constantly emphasizes that the profoundest level of meaning of the poem is to be found not in what it represents, but in what it "incites." However, to say just what this means requires considerable interpretive investment of our own, and in what follows I will freely interpret the idea of Chinese poetics that this language suggests. Fundamentally, the poem does not represent its object; instead, it intervenes in the world by transforming its readers or hearers into a state of greater awareness or harmony with themselves, promoting thereby, in some ways, a more advantageously regulated relation with the whole at large. The poem is a way, furthermore, of seeing things more clairvoyantly in their relationships with one another through reflecting on the relation that we take up ourselves in their midst. We are incited to seek out and forge specific modalities of belonging to the order of things that surrounds us. Accordingly, Chinese classical poetry enacts not a restrictively cognitive approach to poetry and the world so much as an interactive one. It does not place a prefabricated frame on things but rather adapts to the constantly changing, spontaneous framings and reframings—or, we might best say, immanent framings—of the always-still-emergent order of the world. Poems are privileged places for the emergence of such immanent framings and for reflection on it.

As envisaged in and through the poem, then, nature is not a given object so much as an open, ongoing poetic creation that emerges with and from our involvement in the world. Nature has a kind of transcendence in that it continues beyond our finite minds and lives a life all its own: we never get to the beginning or end of it. This inexhaustibility constitutes its own intrinsic transcendence. It transcends any frame that we can impose on it. Eluding any separate structuring principle or Ground, nature is always only emergent—and in this sense more of the order of what has just been called an "immanent frame." Understood as such an emergent order, nature is not a principle that can be grasped or articulated: it is Nothing, at least nothing that can be named or defined.

Jullien builds up to something like this understanding of nature—which I call "apophatic"—through a detailed reconstruction of the character of Chinese poetics as opposed to the symbolic and allegorical poetics of the West. Western literary hermeneutics, he argues, is driven to erect distinct planes of literal and figurative meaning. A complex interpretive apparatus becomes necessary and is deployed in such a manner as to link these two separate orders of meaning together. The modes of inciting and of allusion practiced in Chinese poetics, in contrast, do not define another, truer sense referring to a higher plane of reality but rather open sense to its intrinsic infinity, releasing it from all limits. This, however, makes of sense ultimately an empty Nothing. As Jullien himself suggests, "This widening-out of the figurative sense does not result in anything, consequently, other than its own emptying. It evacuates that which in figuration is too particular in order to render it infinitely allusive" ("Cet évasement du sens figuré n'aboutit à rien d'autre, en conséquence, que son propre évidement. Il évacue ce que la figuration a de trop particulier pour la rendre allusive à l'infini," *Le Détour et l'accès*, 222). Such indirect, allusive expression, as understood by Chinese poetic theory, is "empty" but is therefore all the more "lively" (223).

Put another way, Chinese poetics are based on "figuration beyond figuration," which is allusive and not symbolic, not geared to mimesis, not serving to represent an idea but rather to expand infinitely in savor—like an enveloping atmosphere. Jullien cites a ninth-century Chinese theoretician Sikong Tu for the phrase "figuration beyond figuration." Yet, such an expression would also be quite at home in the language especially of apophatic writers in Western traditions. A word beyond words, or an image beyond images, has been evoked in verbal conjurings persistently by modern European authors from Eliot and Joyce to Beckett. And already medieval mystic writers like Hildegard of Bingen (1098–1179) or Mechthild of Magdeburg (1212–82) often used figurative language effusively for the God who is beyond figuration.[5] Phrases such as "religion without religion," moreover, are typical of apophatic rhetoric across disciplines very broadly. In our own time, within the postmodern discussion on religion, Jacques Derrida, followed by John Caputo and others, has revived and given renewed currency to this phrase ("religion sans religion"), which derives from ancient sources of apophatic theology.

Jullien's purpose, above all, is to characterize what is peculiar and distinctive about Chinese poetic language. Rather than opening upon another plane of presumably intelligible meaning that would be separate from the sensible, in Chinese poetics figurative meaning achieves a detachment from all particular reference on the immediate or literal plane in order to open a vague space of indeterminate reference and of emotional incitation (*qíng*

---

5. See, for instance, Mechthild of Magdeburg, *Fliessende Licht der Gottheit*, trans. Frank Tobin as *The Flowing Light of the Godhead* (Mahwah, N J: Paulist Press, 1998).

jī) that works rather by "expansion" (209–10). A poetic sense that is vague and evasive liberates meaning from the opaqueness and limitation of literal reference. The indeterminate, allusive nature of language used poetically makes the poetic motif "vibrate with an infinity of situations and captures the possible emotion at the furthest remove" ("le motif poétique vibre d'une infinité de situations et capte au plus loin l'émotion possible," 213), so that it is no longer the language of just a particular emotion but rather of our whole capacity for emotion in its inner or implicit (*hánxù*, 含蓄) richness. Reference becomes fugitive without, however, instituting a new, abstract level of sense.

The apophatic thrust of this formulation is implicitly acknowledged in the thesis that "the Chinese perspective is the relation of the said to the unsaid" ("la perspective chinoise est la relation du dit au non-dit," 225). Crucial here is "the evocative capacity of any poetic motif permitting it to develop itself beyond words" ("la capacité évocatoire de tout motif poétique lui permettant de se developer au-delà des mots," 216). A surplus of meaning ("surplus de sens") exceeds the text as a fixed and finite structure: the poem brings us into contact with the unlimited space of the unsaid. Jullien would undoubtedly insist that there is no further extra-sensory reality, and yet the said and the sensory are exceeded into a dimension reaching beyond all their articulations and differentiations.

One could, of course, cite parallels from Western literature for this speechless "space of literature"—the "espace littéraire" famously explored by Blanchot.[6] When we open to the silence beyond speech, all traditions and their verbal structures are reduced to being merely means of reaching to something beyond them all. Recent postmodern and post-Holocaust poets, eminently Paul Celan and Edmond Jabès, have in their own ways pushed the poetics of silence to what seem to be their furthest limits.[7] Such an apophatic sensibility is not at all foreign to Western traditions in many of their historical manifestations. It is not clear where the boundaries between traditions lie, once we embark on the sea of the undifferentiated and non-identical.

Consider, for example, the aesthetic principles at work in as central, seminal, and canonical a text as Baudelaire's "Correspondances," with its perfumes "having the expansion of infinite things" ("ayant l'expansion

---

6. Maurice Blanchot, *L'espace littéraire* (Paris: Gallimard, 1955).

7. For detailed investigation of this topic, see my "The Singular and the Other at the Limits of Language in the Post-Holocaust Poetry of Edmond Jabès and Paul Celan," *New Literary History* 36/4 (2005): 621–38.

des choses infinies"). Such "correspondences" open upon an unfathomable dimension rather than constituting calculable correlations between definable orders of things and meanings. Correspondences here are not finite, fixed, coded relations but open, evolving, infinitely transformative sensations. In another emblematic example, in his "Ars poétique" Paul Verlaine's poetics of nuance aim not at definite color but rather at "nothing but nuance" ("Pas de la couleur, rien que la nuance"); such writing likewise turns on indirection and avoids any kind of univocal representation of a separate and stable object. Allusivity was made a cardinal principle of symbolist poetics already by Stéphane Mallarmé. In his "Crise de vers," Mallarmé dissolved the referential structure of language and described how words "light up with reciprocal reflections like a virtual train of fires upon precious stones" ("s'allument de reflets réciproques comme une virtuelle traînée de feux sur des pierreries," *Divagations*).[8] His poetry does not represent an object so much as create an elusive play of mutually allusive references among words and sounds.

Jullien is intent on distinguishing the symbolic expansiveness ("l'expansion symbolique," 209) of Western poetics from the kind of allusive expansiveness typical of Chinese poetry and its figures. However, to do so, he takes the "ideas" of Western tradition rather rigidly in a strictly Platonic sense as separate realities. This schema, of course, was already drastically qualified by Aristotle, for whom form exists sensibly as essentially bound up with matter in a hylomorphic union instead of being a separate entity. And much more radically, all through Western tradition, especially in its shadowy and sometimes esoteric undersides, ideas actually remain connected to and in communication with things. To this extent, ideas are themselves forms of allusion. Particularly the apophatic countertraditions within the West build explicitly on such ideal materialities and incarnate thoughts.[9]

Even if ideas have a separate, superior existence, they can be approached and apprehended only in a plurality of material instantiations and in concrete circumstances such as are refracted in the references of symbolic poetry. We have already begun to see this in Baudelaire's programmatic statement of a symbolic poetics in "Correspondances," where exquisitely particular sensations are evoked as the very forms of true experience that "spirit," for

---

8. Stéphane Mallarmé, *Vers et prose: Morceaux choisis* (Paris: Hachette, 2012 [1893]), 192.

9. Provocative essays along these lines can be found in *Silence and the Word: Negative Theology and Incarnation*, eds. Oliver Davies and Denys Turner (Cambridge: Cambridge University Press, 2002).

all its "transports," does not efface.[10] Baudelaire writes of perfumes that are fresh like the flesh of children, sweet like oboes, and green like prairies. He evokes other odors, too, ones that are "corrupted, rich, and triumphant," and he describes them as:

Having the expansion of infinite things,
Like amber, musk, balsamic, and incense,
Which sing the transports of the spirit and the senses.

Ayant l'expansion des choses infinies,
Comme l'ambre, le musc, le benjoin et l'encens,
Qui chantent les transports de l'esprit et des sens
("Correspondances," emphasis added.)

As the price of the remarkable clarity of his exposition, Jullien hardens the Platonic myth of Ideas into the practically universal mode of Western poetics and thought. He attributes stability, consistency, and a logical structure to the symbol in Western poetry and poetics, but this view overlooks how, in their actual employment and rhetorical functioning, all such theoretical postulates are transgressed by the incalculably subtle and ungovernable movement of sense in the poem. This insidious subversion of the paradigm of separate symbolic sense is then brought to keen theoretical reflection in the thinking outside of and beyond the logos proposed especially by writers drawing from apophatic traditions and their poetics of ineffability.

Further indices can be gathered from Jullien's own works that point to this rapprochement between Chinese and Western poetics specifically in their finally apophatic bases and aims. The decisive characteristic of the incitatory and allusive mode of traditional Chinese poetics turns out to be that true value is found *beyond words* ("la tradition chinoise s'accorde à voir dans cet *au-delà des mots* la valeur veritable," 216). The word is "near," but its sense is "far." And its determinable sense is only a small thing in comparison with its very far-reaching "poetic effect" (following the formulations of Qu Yuan in his *Lisao* from the fourth or third century BC, recounting

---

10. I elaborate on this aspect of Baudelaire's symbolist poetics and their implicit linguistics in "The Linguistic Turning of the Symbol: Baudelaire and his French Symbolist Heirs," *Baudelaire and the Poetics of Modernity*, ed. Patricia Ward (Nashville, TN: Vanderbilt University Press, 2000), 28–40, now in *Secular Scriptures: Modern Theological Poetics in the Wake of Dante* (Columbus: Ohio State University Press, 2016), chapter 6.

his shamanistic voyages). This would seem to be what in the West could be called "the expansiveness of symbolic sense": it can be followed from the Romantics through Baudelaire to modernist poets like Yeats.[11] Yet Jullien is determined to insist rather on the differentiating characteristics and the distances between Chinese and Western traditions.

Jullien points to what he takes to be a crucial difference between symbolic and allusive poetics inasmuch as abstract, symbolic meanings tend to define essences that are exclusive of one another, whereas an unlimited range or kaleidoscope of differentiated figures can be used to refer by allusion to a particular situation. Concrete facts contextualize poetry in a way that always leaves space for further symbolic elaboration. Yet this is patently also the case with Dante's prosimetron, the *Vita nuova,* near the inception of Western symbolist tradition. The allusive power of the anthologized lyrics to evoke aspects of the poet's own experience as presented in the prose of the autobiographical narrative is unlimited. Such grounding in existential reality is a prodigious technique, since concrete existence is inexhaustible in meaning. Just this is what funds the meaning of Beatrice as a theological symbol of the infinite and eternal. Against the existential background of Dante's own life story, words are released in their unlimited poetic dynamism and unrestricted symbolic power. I willingly grant that Chinese poetry has developed an incomparably subtle art for referencing extra-linguistic facts obliquely by indirect allusion. It posits images without description or further determination, and this allows the imagination free play to range across all possible approaches to something that remains unsaid. But the use of symbolism does not necessarily exclude such play and can even contribute to it.

According to Jullien, in Chinese tradition symbolic figuration is theorized only exceptionally—particularly by Wang Bi (226–49) in the third century AD. For the rest, as a concrete figure manifesting an abstract idea, the symbol remains almost entirely undeveloped in Chinese tradition. Jullien understands Chinese figuration not as symbolic but rather as incitatory of an emotion and as allusive in the sense of leading back by specific reference to the context in the world from which the poem arises. The expansiveness of the allusive mode operates still in relation to some specific, at some level usually political, reference to the socio-historical context of the

---

11. I examine this expansive working of the symbol on the basis of the philosophical (Hegelian) doctrine of internal relations particularly in relation to William Butler Yeats's symbolism in "The Dialectical Logic of Yeats's Byzantium Poems," *Yeats-Eliot Review* 15, no. 3 (Summer 1998): 23–32, now in *Secular Scriptures,* chapter 9.

poem rather than in relation to abstract ideas. The incitative mode evokes some particular emotion, for example, from a landscape, but as unbound to any particular occasion and as released from the paltriness of the merely particular. Since the emotion is not represented but is rather incited, it has no defined form and can rather metamorphose in reaction to the reader's own dispositions and susceptibilities. Such incitation is only the beginning of a process of evocation that can set into action the emotional resources of humanity as a whole.

Enlightening in this connection is the fact that the art of simply citing poems from the *Book of Odes* was used in ancient Chinese diplomatic negotiations in order to allude subtly to the situation at hand and to suggest one's own position, whether in petition or in response. By use of such strategic deployment of citation, one let the poem work upon the other party's sensibility, hoping to bend their disposition in one's favor, not by arguing coercively, with supposedly conclusive and irrefutable arguments, but rather by allowing the situation itself to do the arguing: as evoked emotionally in the poem, the situation could work within the unpressured spirit of one's interlocutor. Such a neutral and anonymous form of citation is able to work all the more powerfully to infiltrate perception of the specific situation in ways that discourse cannot control but that nevertheless effectively move the heart. This highly refined art, with its rare use of indirectness, in which Chinese tradition shows its remarkable ingeniousness, is analyzed by Jullien as illustrating an alternative to generalizing, rationalizing discourse.

Likewise, historical writing in the *Chronicle of Springs and Autumns* (*Chūnqiū*) is innocent of explicit judgments of praise or blame but, for all that, the more forceful and incisive in its critique by the power merely of mentioning and suggestion. The point of a discourse must be inferred from what remains unsaid and implicit in the context and circumstances. It is made explicit only by the explanatory commentary of the *Zuozhuan* (covering 636–516 BC). This use of indication rather than of explication as an art of not-saying is characteristic, as we have noted, also of Confucius's wisdom in the *Analects*. Jullien analyzes this style of wisdom in chapters IX and X of *Le Détour et l'accès,* having treated similar or analogous techniques as they are used in poetry and history in the earlier chapters (III and IV respectively).

Still, given this account, we are prompted to ask whether the concreteness of the symbol is not in danger of being exchanged for an abstract code of references, particularly with the use of allusion in Chinese poetry. Or is it rather that access to the concrete imagination and emotion beyond the literal, historical sense is better served by remaining bound to a particular (often political) reference and a specific context (typically the court)? It *can* be, if this sort of referencing is itself opened up. Chinese poetics, as construed by Jullien, opens reference to infinity, yet without introducing any separate, superior plane of symbolic meaning. Indeed, specific references occur in poems only as they are interpreted, and this interpreting must always take place in different ways according to how the poem is received in diverse epochs, as the rich commentary tradition on classical poetry attests.

When figuration is used for the sake of incitation to action, the figure must be related concretely to the world outside of the poem and must also avoid becoming an abstract sense, a mere idea. The world, moreover, is connected with consciousness and its emotions: landscape and emotion interpenetrate, bleed into each other, and fuse together. Jullien endeavors to elicit from these concepts the possibility of an infinity of sense that is not symbolic (220). Figuration deploys itself concretely in the "breath" (*qi*, 氣) rather than on an ideal plane. It creates an atmosphere diffused in the landscape of the poem rather than being focused as an idea. Thus, according to Jullien, we must understand poetic figuration in terms of an aura rather than of an idea.

However, is this not finally the case also with symbolism, or in any case with the cult of *symbolisme* to which it leads, in the West? At least in its most radical realizations, for instance by Mallarmé and Rimbaud? For Jullien, there is "no symbolism" ("pas de symbolisme," 221) in the allusive Chinese poetics that he describes, since the atmosphere in question arises spontaneously rather than as directed by authorial command. And yet, Mallarmé, too, aimed to give the initiative to words themselves—and thus to chance, "le hazard"—rather than allowing them to be peremptorily steered by the conscious intentions of the writer. Similarly, the author is effectively abolished in Rimbaud's visionary and linguistically anarchic *Illuminations*. His "Lettres du voyant" say as much with the oracular pronouncement that "Je est un autre" ("I is another").[12] The idea of consciously calculated, systematically controlled representation narrows and rigidifies the amplitudinous practices of symbolic and especially symbolist art. Jullien stresses in Chinese poetry the evanescence of allusive expansiveness, a fleetingness that eludes the supposed solidity of the symbol and remains pure phenomenon, but such evanescence is just as crucial to the doctrine of *symbolisme* as it is elaborated by Mallarmé and, following him, by René Ghil in his *Traitée du verbe* (1886). These qualities are not outside the scope of the symbol per

---

12. Letter to Georges Izambard, Charleville, May 13, 1871. Rimbaud's letters can be consulted in his *Œuvres completes* (Paris: Gallimard, La Pléiade, 1972).

se but only of a wooden and artificial conception of it. They are certainly not out of reach of the scintillating symbols created by the resources of Western poetics pushed to their limits by Mallarmé finally in his "grande oeuvre," his *Coup de dès* (1897).

Jullien describes within Chinese poetics a range of contrasting approaches to allusion as either punctual or indefinite—and open to infinity. But in every case, he reads Chinese classical poetics as working against the representation of an idea and rather as indicating the infinite beyond words. The word is savored only as emanating and disseminating a kind of atmosphere. The relation to the subject, which remains unsaid, is only implicit rather than represented. All this turns out to be a perfect paragon of what I call "apophatic poetics," and it is noticeably close to what Mallarmé forged as his poetics of "suggestion." Apophatic poetics recognize that representations leave only implicit and incipient what they more truly and deeply intend. It is impossible to render the apophatic explicit by representation, since no terms are adequate. In his intense vigilance against any type of access to another plane of being or meaning, Jullien ignores what the apophatic most essentially brings out and exposes—namely, that all such hypostatization of this other plane is a myth and freezes the dynamic functioning of poetic language and thereby falsifies it. He takes the myth for the true teaching of symbolic or symbolist or, in any case, Western poetics. This is one place where I detect a prejudice, a *parti pris,* a sort of atavism that needs to be reflected upon in order that it not be left to operate blindly as an automatism.

Indeed, the "other world," as alluded to in Western traditions, *can* be conceived as a reality that is glimpsed in privileged moments, when the blinders of our perception of this world are suddenly removed and the scales fall from our eyes. The otherworldly vision of Dante appears as such an epiphany, a momentary "unmasking" ("Poi, come gente stata sotto larve / che pare altro che prima, se si sveste," *Paradiso* 30.91–92). It is the world *as other,* but not as actual, objective, and known—thus neither this world nor any other known world, but a possible and a projected world that paradoxically is more real and true than the world that we ordinarily (mis)know. Such is the reality prophetically known in this visionary tradition of prophetic poetry. As Blake announces: "If the doors of perception were cleansed, everything would appear to man as it is, infinite" (*The Marriage of Heaven and Hell,* plate 14, "A Memorable Fancy").[13]

---

13. *Complete Writings,* ed. Geoffrey Keynes (Oxford: Oxford University Press, 1957).

Now Chinese poetry is perhaps not often or not obviously visionary, at least not in the sense of the Western prophetic poetry produced by Dante, Milton, and Blake. China's decision *not* to elevate the immediacy of *sight* to the status of the model of true knowing is one of the major premises of Jullien's argument. We have seen that Jullien emphasizes, furthermore, that the Chinese poem exists for the sake of transformation rather than of representation. He argues also in *La propension des choses,* anticipating the theses of *Le Détour et l'accès,* that in China art is geared not to mimesis but to a "process of actualization" (71). Jullien's main point is constantly the fact that figuration in Chinese tradition, even in evoking a beyond of figuration, a beyond of the image, does not presuppose some other plane other than that of *this* world of sense. Instead, figuration liberates from all types of reductive reference: it figures what becomes thereby no longer merely particular but rather vague and diffuse and charged with expanding emotion. Above all, Jullien wants to avoid positing any kind of other world: the "world that is born beyond figuration" ("naît au-delà de la figuration,") in a phrase Jullien quotes from Liu Yuxi, the Tang dynasty poet and essayist, is "not an other world but this world—the only one—purged of its opacity and rendered available to be enjoyed" ("pas un autre monde mais ce monde-ci—le seul—décanté de son opacité et rendu disponible à la jouissance," *Le Détour et l'accès,* 222).

This position expresses a deep-seated conviction—not to say an article of faith—typical of French laicism and of Western antitheism generally. Rather than consolidating as another world or level of sense, figuration points beyond the figure and so to a self-emptying of sense ("son propre évidement," 222). Figuration, to this extent, is indirect expression and is "empty" ("vide"), or we might say "kenotic." Nevertheless, as already remarked, such empty expression turns out to be the "liveliest" form of expression.

For the most part, this is all very congenial to an apophatic outlook, but Jullien does not rest content just to make such kenotic constatations. He goes on to assert something of a certainty about there being only one world, this world. And here I suspect that he is producing a counter-dogma motivated by a determination to reject all otherworldliness, perhaps especially all *Christian* otherworldliness. For decades, if not centuries, there has been widespread ideological agreement among French leftist intellectuals—for all their zeal to disagree with one another in almost every other respect—about this specific rejection. Recent signs, however, announce a possible breaking down of such simple opposition. Jean-Luc Nancy, for instance, in his language of kenotic self-emptying, is notably close to Jullien. Yet Nancy uses such deconstructive patterns of thought in order to open to questioning some of his own secularist presuppositions through an infinite self-critical movement that breaks with Enlightenment ideology and with his own earlier unilateral opposition to Christianity.[14] Both Jullien and Nancy are philosophers of "sens," but whereas Nancy traces the inevitable dissolution of sense, emphasizing how meaning is realized only in its own dissolution, Jullien attempts to establish unequivocally the different regimes of "sens" in Greece and China. The "intelligibility" of the enterprise seems to force him to embrace the fiction of sense as definable in different ways according to the respective cultures rather than seeing sense as intrinsically ungraspable and as finally confounding all such attempts at any stable differentiation.

Indeed, stripped of its ideological commonplaces or *convenues*, the critical part of Jullien's analysis describes also the way that apophatic thinking and poetics perform *within* Western traditions. Meaning opens upon an abyss that cannot be properly objectified as another world or even as another plane of significance. Rather than representing meaning in terms of another ontological sphere, Chinese poetics, in some of the later developments of its theory of the incitatory mode, envisages an inarticulate dimension of emotion and sensation beyond words. This makes for an indirect poetics in which sense is liberated from all exclusivity. The poetic motif is opened to all possible perspectives and surpasses all their differences. The totality of perspectives is thus embraced without abstraction. This is a world of "non-duality." Jullien himself employs this quintessential technical term from apophatic thought in the tradition of the Vedanta.

Whereas the symbol, according to Jullien, defines a sense beyond the concrete and claims to deliver a spiritual intuition, allusion savors the sensory as its only aim and result. However, savoring sensations is also very much in the spirit of Baudelaire's symbolist poetics, as we have seen, right from his manifesto poem "Correspondances." We can concede that this approach leads to self-affirmation of the poet as seer (*voyant*) in Rimbaud. In contrast with this centering on vision, Jullien describes a process of osmosis in which the reader is impregnated by the aura of the poem. Blanchot, too, for not dissimilar reasons, rejected vision and, with it, the chief paradigm or cardinal metaphor of knowing in Western epistemology.[15] However, vision

---

14. See in particular Nancy's *Déconstruction du christianisme*, vol. 1: *La Déclosion* (Paris: Galilée, 2005), vol. 2: *L'Adoration* (Paris: Galilée, 2010). I argue that this is Nancy's "Kehre" or turning point in *The Philosophy of the Unsayable*, chapter 4.

15. Blanchot, "Parler . . . ce n'est pas voir," in *L'Entretien infini* (Paris: Gallimard, 2003 [1969]).

in Western poetics can also be only a metaphor for consciousness. It can even become explicitly *blind* vision, for example, in Milton's *Paradise Lost*, where the poet "sings darkling" (3.39) and where imagery is allowed to dissolve as a self-consuming artifact, so as to suggest a sense beyond any that can be distinctly formulated in words pertaining to objects of perception.[16]

As such, "vision" in Western poetics seeks and approaches the dimension of globality, which Jullien discovers at the motivating sources of Chinese philosophy. Reaching beyond limited, partial perspectives, such global multilaterality becomes especially programmatic and self-reflective in Chinese classics, both in the Confucian tradition, with *Mencius*, and in the Daoist lineage, with *Zhuangzi*. But Western art and poetics are also centrally concerned with the recursive *negation* of their own explicit founding principles, and this is the reason why they come especially close to Jullien's Chinese models. Of course, the processes by which each literature comes to envisage similar possibilities of thought are peculiarly its own, yet these common possibilities are illuminated by showing the extremely diverse ways in which they can be realized.

NEO-DAOISM AND NEOPLATONISM: AN UNCANNY HISTORICAL PARALLEL

In chapter 12 of *Le Détour et l'accès* (319ff.), Jullien himself expounds this apophatic mode of thought characteristic of classical Chinese wisdom in explicit and extended parallel to the apophatic thought of ancient Neoplatonist philosophers. Initially, he compares Laozi's *Book of Dao* (*Dao-de-jing*) with Plato's most metaphysically challenging dialogue, *The Parmenides*. Both works in some sense present universal philosophies of the All, which itself turns out to be, in the most essential respects, the Nothing. Jumping forward in history, Jullien then intriguingly juxtaposes the classic third-century AD interpretation of the *Book of Dao*, Wang Bi's *Laozi zhilüe*, with some key sections of Plotinus's *Enneads,* passages in which Plotinus is occupied specifically with interpreting Plato's *Dialogues*. Wang Bi (226–49) elaborates

---

16. I develop this interpretation in "Blind Prophecy: Milton's Figurative Mode in *Paradise Lost,*" in *Through a Glass Darkly: Essays in the Religious Imagination*, ed. John Hawley (New York: Fordham University Press, 1996), 87–103, now in *Secular Scriptures*, 103–19. Stanley Fish, *Self-Consuming Artifacts: The Experience of Seventeenth-Century Literature* (Berkeley: University of California Press, 1972) treats this motif more broadly in seventeenth-century poetry.

a Neo-Daoist vision contemporaneous with and analogous to the Neoplatonism of Plotinus (205–70). Both philosophical reincarnations develop interpretations that accentuate the mystical side of their respective source texts. Both cases, moreover, represent a sort of religious turn in philosophy. Each commentary helps us to chart the development of the core revelation given in the Ur-text of its respective tradition by registering the effects in a philosophical reappropriation produced several centuries later. Wang Bi writes in the wake of the demise of the Han Empire (206 BC–AD 220). His period thus coincides chronologically with the decline of the Roman Empire that is experienced by Plotinus and refracted in his work. Both cases suggest, therefore, how apophasis flourishes precisely at moments of historical crises in which a venerable, traditional discourse begins to founder—when the order of things, as established by a triumphant word or logos, shows signs of fragility and incipient collapse. Curiously, both authors receive a vital impulse from India. Plotinus registers the Upanishads' infiltrating across the Hellenistic world from the East, while Wang Bi at the same time evinces the influence of Buddhism coming to him across China's frontier to the West.

Placing the original vision of the *Laozi* in parallel with the foundational apophatic reflections on the One in Plato's *Parmenides* highlights, furthermore, the fact that both of these source texts in their own traditions affirm the priority of non-Being as more originary than Being, indeed as the origin of Being. Plotinus brings out clearly the identification of the One with non-Being in his commentary on the *Parmenides* in *Enneads* 6. 9, 5, and this (dis)identification will be extended further and become even more programmatic with the later Neoplatonist Damascius (AD 480–550). Paralleling this Hellenistic development, on the Chinese side Wang Bi likewise highlights the implicit privilege of non-Being in his commentary on the *Dao-de-Jing*, most unmistakably in chapter 14.[17] Thus, both the Neoplatonic and the Neo-Daoist revival movements bring out especially the apophatic or negative underpinnings of the corresponding revelations of which they become the renewers—of Being, in one case, and of the Way, in the other. For both, only the relentless negation of all differences and qualifications is able progressively to approach unity or the ineffable. Such is indeed the so-called way of negation (*via negativa*) in all its radicality. This negativity is rendered explicit and is emphasized at this later stage in each cultural tradition reflecting more deeply upon its founding principles with the phil-

---

17. *Commentary on the Lao Tzu by Wang Pi,* trans. Ariane Rump (Honolulu: University of Hawai'i Press, 1979), 43–44.

osophico-mystical interpretations of Plato elaborated by Plotinus and those developed by Wang Bi interpreting Laozi, respectively.

It is not too difficult to discern a motif of the negative that is universal in Western mysticism and that joins together Sufis, Kabbalists, and Christian mystics, all of whom share the Neoplatonic heritage in common. However, these Western streams are matched and should be joined also by Eastern currents in their recognition of the secondariness and inadequacy of whatever can be said to be, beginning with Being itself. Apophatic mysticism in Eastern traditions such as Daoism, the Advaita Vedanta, and Buddhism, similarly rises above the inevitably divisive effects of articulate discourse and points towards what different discourses presuppose in common, or are motivated by, without being able to say it. All are spurred from somewhere beneath or before all that they can say.

In the face of ultimate mystery, all such anti-essentialist currents of thought tend to meet one another in the common impotence of their languages to say the unsayable. Jullien even asks whether such discourses, in their aspiration towards the One as the unconditioned, are not led to surpass their cultural conditioning ("le conditionnement culturel," *Le Détour et l'accès*, 323). This is a question that we will pursue later under the rubric of universality in chapter 4. But already we can affirm that in this apophatic vision everything must surpass itself and its limits in order to be more truly and deeply itself, even while still remaining open to the All. It must have nothing of its own, no fixed essence, but rather be entirely in evolution, and that without limits. Only so can it *be* all things and be made not to abide within any unsurpassable bounds or to countenance any insuperable exclusions.

The universality of Nothing for Jullien is that of immanence itself. Still, however, this must be an immanence that does not exclude transcendence. It begins for him with the *self*-transcending of every particular thing in its never-ending changes. Jullien identifies the empty Nothing of the *Dao* as a "source or fund of immanence" ("fonds d'immanence"). He makes this disclosure of immanence the central realization at the origins of Daoism:

> In every determinate use of things in their actualized state, it is this immanence that I capture in a particular mode. Such an evacuation of the impediments to the progress of things constitutes the principle intuition of the *Laozi*.
>
> Dans tout usage déterminé, au stade actualisé des choses, c'est cette immanence que je capte sur un mode particulier. Une

telle évacuation des entraves à la marche des choses constitue l'intuition principale du *Laozi*. (*Le détour et l'accès*, 328)

Jullien takes his leitmotif or the keynote of his overall argument from a line of Laozi's *Dao-de-jing*, poem 41: "The great image has no form" ("La grande image n'a pas de forme"). The principle expressed in this line negates form, yet not *simpliciter*, since form is negated only *within* the dimension of the image, which never exists apart from a continuum of form. In Jullien's words, "Form is denied but *within form*; the sensible is surpassed but *without being abandoned*" ("La forme est niée mais à l'*intérieur de la forme*, le sensible est dépassé mais *sans qu'il soit délaissée*," *Le détour et l'accès*, 336). What is negated is virtually present in any and every particular form, but the negation is performatively realized in an ongoing, open-ended production of proliferating, never definitive forms. While every specific form is negated, the element of form constitutes itself through this continual metamorphosis of any given form into endlessly many others. This is not abstract negation that cancels out what it negates, and is thenceforth done with it once and for all, but rather a *process* of negating taken to infinity. More specifically, it is an infinitely ongoing process of the *self*-negation of every successively achieved and simultaneously superseded form.

I have been working here from Jullien's comments in *Le détour et l'accès*, especially chapters 12 to 13, where he deals with literary and philosophical expressions of this principle that "the Great Image has no form." He also treats it in relation to the art of painting in *La grande image n'a pas de forme*, where he defines the great image as the one that does not get stuck in any one form ("ne s'enlise en aucune forme") but keeps "compossibles" in play so as to display the availability of what lies at the bottom of them ("la disponibilité du foncier," 16) and grounds them all.

Jullien's discussion of the "Great Image" that is without form in the *Dao-de-Jing* is supposed to present an alternative to the apophatic negative way (the so-called *via negativa*) as a way of approaching the ineffable in the West, beginning from the ancient world. This brings it within the parameters of his project as a whole, which aims at differentiating the strategies of sense developed in China from those practiced in Greece. The nuances of difference are crucial, of course, and yet the apophatic tradition in the West is also persistently seeking for an escape from sense and an evasion of its logic by turning upon and twisting away from any paradigm that might otherwise govern and enforce a regime of sense or stable meaning. Whether as two levels of reality (sensible and intelligible) or as two stages of a process (such as actualizing differentiation and harmonizing dis-individuation, *yǒu*

有 and *wú* 無), any form of representation making sense can be no more than heuristic and must in the end be discarded or released. Perhaps such release is more natural to Chinese thought; perhaps it is normative there rather than being only the exception. Still, it is not without parallel nor unattainable in Western thought, certainly not categorically.

The countercurrent represented by apophasis in Western thought turns self-critically in directions similar to those pervasively present in Chinese tradition. It is questionable whether differences taken by Jullien (and commonly by others, too) as characteristic and paradigmatic are not rather differences in degree. And it is further questionable even how any differences at all can be more than relative markers of convenience for what in absolute terms is wholly without differentiation. Jullien characterizes "the ineffable" as entailing a categorical refusal of all discourse ("un refus catégorique de tout discours—et saut dans l'Ineffable," *Éloge de la fadeur*, 16) in contrast to "the bland," which remains "concrete." But he neglects the fact that the discourse of the ineffable is itself a highly developed, intricate, and concrete discourse articulated in various registers, even in visual and sonic media, and that what is denied is only that such discourse can ever be *adequate* to the ineffable "nothing-definable" toward which it aspires. By associating ineffability with abstraction, Jullien ignores the vast Western traditions of ineffability that do attend to its concrete, sensory, bodily, and material modes.[18] Even abstract expressionism in modern painting (for example, Mark Rothko's) works essentially with the concrete, with texture and color, in order to evoke their removal and erasure, as in the plain black square of Malevich's suprematism.[19] In this regard, so central to the radicality of its quest, Western apophasis is comparable to the Chinese discourse on the motif of blandness.

Jullien does adroitly compare Chinese thought with the Neoplatonic speculation from Plotinus to Damascius that builds on interpretation of

---

18. *Apophatic Bodies: Negative Theology, Incarnation, and Relationality*, eds. Chris Boesel and Catherine Keller (New York: Fordham University Press, 2010), pursues this specific orientation in apophatics. Keller's essay, "The Cloud of the Impossible: Embodiment and Apophasis," in this volume demonstrates "the potential of the apophatic tradition to support re-symbolization of materiality" (38).

19. See *On What Cannot Be Said*, vol. 2, chapter 13. More broadly, see the apophatic aesthetics of Amador Vega, *Arte y santidad. Cuatro lecciones de estética apofática* (Pamplona: Universidad Pública de Navarra, 2005), or in summary form, Vega, "Estética apofática y hermenéutica del misterio: elementos para una crítica de la visibilidad," *Diánoia* 54, no. 62 (2009): 1–25.

the initial hypotheses of Plato's *Parmenides*. He lights with sure instinct and precision on the generative source of programmatic Western apophaticism, where Western thought is closest to the Chinese. Yet he generally seems nevertheless (though he later denies it) to be looking for the irreducible difference—or more exactly the gap (*l'écart*)—that makes them definitively strangers to one another.[20] Their lack of historical contact before modern times is his constant point of departure. And yet the spirit of the *Dao*, not to mention that of apophasis, might well direct us to focus more naturally on the *indifferentiation* from which both discourses and their respective vocabularies hail. Jullien's procedure marks itself in this respect as typically Western, according to his own schemas. He is concerned with differentiating and defining more than with surrender to experience reaching beyond all articulation. Both traditions of apophaticism, East and West, aim at discerning this undifferentiated source and background as prior to the determination of any discourse and so also as prior to all cultural characterization. And in this regard, Jullien's concern with defining for us what is so distinctive about Chinese thought should in principle, on this subject above all—or rather on this non-subject, this subject under erasure—yield and grant precedence to what is not discursive nor perhaps even differentiated.

Jullien does consistently play up the undifferentiated ground or background, the "fond indifférencié," as prior and as a resource of life and of transforming renewal in painting and in all other aspects of Chinese culture. However, he does not apply this perspective or emulate this approach in his own scholarly endeavor. His own method aims at an articulate philosophical analysis rather than at ineffable wisdom: it turns on conceptually stated and elaborated distinctions between culturally defined objects rather than on seeking, above all, their indefinable sources in indifferentiation. His method proves to be strategically opposite to and stands in a kind of performative contradiction with the burden of his thinking, as the latter turns on expounding and valorizing the typically Chinese privileging of the undifferentiated ground ("fond") from which all forms arise.

Jullien's virtuoso exposition of different regimes of "sens" in China and in Greece is itself tributary to the characteristically Western belief in ultimately distinct senses or essences that he so ably demolishes through revealing comparison with the classical wisdom of China. This is the irony

---

20. In *L'invention de l'idéale et le destin de l'Europe* (Paris: Seuil, 2009), 168–69, Jullien treats this theme, attempting to differentiate the European fascination with a structure of non-being from the functional void recognized by Chinese, particularly Daoist writings.

of his project, subtitled *Stratégies du sens en Chine, en Grèce,* as itself based on and subject to what it portrays as typically Western habits of thought that it effectively undermines. Jullien sometimes denies that sinophilism is in any way integral to his project. Yet his method nevertheless relies on such a partisanship in order to give his discourse its motivation as an intervention inspired by insights gained from frequenting Chinese wisdom that are then used for critiquing Western philosophy from an outside perspective and exposing its inveterate blind spots.

There is a discourse in the West, just as in the East, aiming beyond discourse and piercing through all of its determinations. As discourses, they can be differentiated, and Jullien's work is valuable for helping us to make pertinent distinctions. Nevertheless, the agreement in aim and intent—or, more incontrovertibly, in effect—of diverse apophatic discourses transcends such cultural differences. This transcending is the pivot upon which the dimension of the universal opens up and offers itself to all, to Greek and Chinese alike, and to all others as well—beyond the limits of language. This is a universality beyond the usual, declared universalities of discourses of enlightenment East and West. It is the universality of what cannot be declared or even said, of what can only be suggested and suspected by use of indirect means that cut against the grain of saying and stating.[21]

WESTERN APOPHATIC POETICS

Jullien brings out how the negation of form in Chinese classics does not yield simply an abstract Nothing but rather issues in an infinite, or at least open-ended, series of transforms. However, neither is apophatic discourse in the West merely negative and abstract, leading inevitably into an empty desert. It, too, involves an opening into infinite indetermination that plays itself out in endless *re*determination.[22] John of the Cross, to

---

21. Another current and parallel approach to eliciting this inarticulate dimension of universality, one that proceeds especially by theorizing community, is William Desmond's *The Intimate Universal: The Hidden Porosity Among Religion, Art, Philosophy, and Politics* (New York: Columbia University Press, 2016).

22. Denys Turner, *The Darkness of God: Negativity in Christian Mysticism* (Cambridge: Cambridge University Press, 1995), especially emphasizes the hyperbolic and inextricably kataphatic side of discourse as indissociable from the apophatic in traditional Western sources.

take just one eminent example, elaborates a richly sensual imagery of night as an inexhaustible, erotically charged plenitude in "O noche oscura," the emblematic expression of his dark night of the soul.[23] This dark night is enflamed with love's urgent longings ("con ansias enamores inflammada") and scented with cedar ("el ventalle de cedros aire daba"), even as it suspends the senses ("todos mis sentidos suspendía"). John's poetry builds on the Rhineland apophatic mysticism flowing from Meister Eckhart as transmitted via Johannes Tauler (1300–61) and Heinrich Seusa (1297–1366).[24] It also bears marks of contact with the Sufi mysticism of Ibn al-'Arabi, which is consummately expressed in the equally sensuous apophatic poetry of Jalal al-Din Rumi (1207–73).[25] This mystic poetry is akin, furthermore, to the seventeenth-century English metaphysical poetry of John Donne, Henry Vaughan, Richard Crashaw, and George Herbert.[26] Their poetry, too, most notably Donne's, is likewise erotically inflected. Among this last group of poets, Thomas Traherne (1636–74) in particular opens a rich vein conveying late medieval apophatic mystical traditions concerning *docta ignorantia*. His poem "Eden" celebrates "a learned and Happy Ignorance."

Still closer to us in time, another eminent practitioner of this vein of apophatic poetry, one who strikingly makes Jullien's overarching point about access through detour, is Emily Dickinson:

> Tell all the Truth but tell it slant—
> Success in Circuit lies
> Too bright for our infirm Delight
> The Truth's superb surprise
> As Lightning to the Children eased

---

23. I discuss Western aesthetic expressions of apophasis generally in "Apophatic Paths: Modern and Contemporary Poetics and Aesthetics of Nothing," *Angelaki: Journal of the Theoretical Humanities* 17/3 (2012): 7–18. John of the Cross in particular I explore in "Un díptico apofatíco: Juan de la Cruz y Samuel Beckett" ("An Apophatic Dyptich: John of the Cross and Samuel Beckett"), *Despalabro. Ensayos de Humanidades* 6 (2012): 179–88.

24. J. Orcibal, *St. Jean de la Croix et les mystiques rhénoflammands* (Paris: Desclée, 1965).

25. Luce López-Baralt, *San Juan de la Cruz y el Islam* (Madrid: Hiperión, 1990).

26. R.V. Young, "Ineffable Speech: Carmelite Mysticism and Metaphysical Poetry," *Communio: International Catholic Review* 17 (1990): 238–60. This area of research is developed in groundbreaking ways on the basis of seventeenth-century Cambridge Platonism by Chance Brandon Woods in his Vanderbilt dissertation, *Transfiguring the Ineffable: Mysticism and Conversion in Seventeenth-Century England* (2017).

> With explanation kind
> The Truth must dazzle gradually
> Or every man be blind.[27] (Franklin, 1263)

The blinding truth of religious revelations such as the epiphany to Moses on Mount Sinai cannot but be beheld indirectly. It can be perceived only by means of negations: taken in itself, it is characterizable only as Nothing.

Concrete apophatic figures for Nothing abound in Dickinson's poetry: they have the infinitely expansible blandness of "esoteric sips / Of the communion Wine" (1452), in which the common and sensory flows into the transcendent and indescribable. Particularly nature and its forms are perceived and communicated apophatically through recursive negations (the anaphora "Nay") of every attempt to find words for them:

> "Nature" is what we see—
> The Hill—the Afternoon—
> Squirrel—Eclipse—the Bumble bee—
> Nay—Nature is Heaven—
> Nature is what we hear—
> The Bobolink—the Sea—
> Thunder—the Cricket—
> Nay—Nature is Harmony—
> Nature is what we know—
> Yet have no art to say—
> So impotent Our Wisdom is
> To her Simplicity. (668)

Sensuous form is employed by apophatic poets to suggest something that has no form and that reaches altogether beyond form but that can nevertheless be experienced in all forms, given their changeableness. Such forms can be *trans*formed across the whole spectrum of natural phenomena, from animals to atmospheres. Dickinson's "Nothing" plays the universal role of blandness in allowing things of every imaginable color or flavor or tone or nuance to communicate with one another. Nature, as Nothing, is also the force that through broken words and poetic emotion renews the world.

---

27. Helen Vendler, *Dickinson: Selected Poems and Commentaries* (Cambridge, MA: Harvard University Press, 2010), 461. This poem is found also in *On What Cannot Be Said*, vol. 2. The source is *The Poems of Emily Dickinson*, Variorum Edition, ed. R. W. Franklin (Cambridge, MA: The Belknap Press of Harvard University Press, 1998).

> By homely gift and hindered Words
> The human heart is told
> Of Nothing—
> "Nothing" is the force
> That renovates the World. (1563)

Sensual expression without limit, such as is found in many modern poetic texts, especially since James Joyce's *Finnegans Wake,* breaks the regime of saying as a conveying of meaning.[28] Jullien analyzes this phenomenon as consisting in negation only of the complement of the verb rather than of the predicate per se. The activity of the verb is preserved—only its object is removed. Action, which becomes generically an act of "savoring," thus continues and does so infinitely—but without the exclusiveness imposed by having a particular, finite object. Open without limit and without barriers, such as are imposed by divisions between this world and another, the *Dao* is completely free to realize itself fully in its infinite nature. This overcoming of all exclusion by infinite expansion that embraces all sensible forms of expression as always non-definitive, as always opening infinitely into further expressions, however, can be envisaged also in the West: it is indeed envisaged—in ways paralleling the Way of Chinese wisdom—eminently in Western apophatic traditions.

Jullien admits that the complete reversal of discourse is common to Laozi and to Damascius, who is positioned at the culmination and turning point toward the demise of ancient Neoplatonic apophasis. He maintains, however, that the reversal (*peritropé*) in Greek philosophy is only logical rather than open to the full range of possible experience. He remarks, furthermore, that in Western religion the movement of negation is based on faith in another world rather than emerging from an immanent development. In *Laozi,* by contrast, the sense of reversal is strategic, and its benefits are reaped in immediate and spontaneous experience. Reversal engenders an augmented efficaciousness that follows from giving up one's self-will and self-imposed limits so as to be more effectively borne along by the infinite, unstoppable energy of the *Dao,* which works wonders with and for us beyond what we ourselves can imagine or intend.

For Jullien, the logic of reversal characteristic of apophasis has to be put in a context of the quest for efficaciousness, if one is to understand it the way ancient Chinese tradition does.[29] Reversal has an internal logic

---

28. I pursue this thesis in *Poetry and Apocalypse*, part 2.

29. See Jullien's *La propension des choses*—for example, 80, 149, and also his *Traité de l'efficacité* (Paris: Grasset, 1996).

and comes about by itself, without need of intervention from any power or instance transcending the sphere of immanence. Jullien does tend—and sometimes even seems to *in*tend—to create a clean contrast with all thinking that appeals to a transcendent God or to metaphysics. Not infrequently, he represents Chinese thought as a clear-cut alternative to this drive towards transcendence.

However, this stereotyping of Western thought as metaphysical and transcendental in contradistinction to Chinese thought of immanence is more characteristic of the kind of dichotomous thinking that stands under critique in his work than of the alternative to it that Jullien discerns in Chinese classics and works so resourcefully to deploy. He contrasts "immanent regulation" ("une régulation immanente") with "religious vision" ("la vision religieuse," *Le Détour et l'accès*, 347). We are to imagine, for example, the Daoist Sage as one whose reward is immediate and immanent. There are no promises of salvation or future paradises on his horizon: ethical action is its own reward. At the heart of Western literary tradition, in contrast, the *Divine Comedy*, following especially biblical precedents, institutes a system of punishments and rewards in an afterlife sanctioned by a transcendent divinity. What could be clearer?

And yet, if one examines the punishments and rewards assigned by God in the universe of the *Divine Comedy*, they turn out always to be nothing but the projection to infinity and into eternity of what the soul already of itself has chosen as its lot. The soul's state in eternity simply embodies and illustrates, as projected into an afterlife, the decisive act by which it here and now commits itself to a certain form of ethical or unethical existence. There is always an *intrinsic* logic that justifies damnation or blessedness. In fact, the souls persist in doing whatever it is that they are damned or blessed for in eternity, even as Dante encounters them. They are doing it still, even as *we* its readers encounter them in Dante's text. Capaneo (one of the famous "seven against Thebes") says so explicitly: "Such I was alive, so am I dead" ("Tal fui vivo, tal sono morto," *Inferno* 14.51). And Brunetto Latini ironically boasts that he still lives eternally in his book, his *Tesoro* (literally his "Treasure"), even as we see him eternally dying in his continuing effort to *"make himself* eternal" ("come l'uom s'etterna," 15.119, 85) by his own humanistic achievement in letters rather than acknowledging the one true Lord who alone can confer life, indeed eternal life. The literary ingeniousness of the *Divine Comedy* contrives to show precisely that the final Judgment of God is nothing but the soul's own choice for a certain quintessential act defining its existence: it becomes irreversible through repetition beyond the point of no return—symbolically and spiritually, death. Such is the self-chosen destiny that is being eternally reenacted in the afterlife of the text. This afterlife is the revelation of the soul's own intimate truth in the immanence of this life—and even immanently to the reader's own life in the present moment of reading.[30]

There are similarly secularizing interpretations of apocalyptic religion going all the way back in Western tradition. They work to demythologize the otherworldly images in terms of their pragmatic and existential value. Such interpretations can be read, moreover, trans-historically as intrinsic to (or as participating in) the "original" meaning of the texts in question. Just such this-worldly deployments of evangelical promise are the constant emphasis of certain currents of interpretation of the Gospel message, beginning even within the canonical Gospels themselves, especially the Gospel according to John but also the others, emblematically in the declaration in Luke 17:21: "Behold, the kingdom of heaven is within you." The miraculous cures in the Gospel of physical infirmities, like leprosy, for example, are presented only as ratification of the more significant healing that has taken place already inwardly in the person who is transformed by belief and becomes incandescent in love. The attempts to delimit Western tradition so as to keep it from arriving at the type of ethical insight reached by the Chinese are inevitably based on exclusion of crucial elements of Western texts and traditions. Apophatic writers in particular are typically at pains to bring out what other strands of the tradition exclude.

Jullien insists that even where Plotinus, in his Neoplatonist interpretation of Plato's *Parmenides,* and Wang Bi, in his Neo-Daoist commentary on the *Laozi,* seem to say the same things, the real intents of their respective discourses remain worlds apart. For Jullien, Greek apophatic or negative theology is about predication, whereas Chinese Daoist discourse concerns efficaciousness at work. The latter is not theoretical, ontological, or theological. It is not concerned chiefly with contemplation or truth, but rather with effectiveness in action (350). Instead of inventing distinct planes and dividing reality into the transcendent and the immanent, as in Greek thought, Laozi works without any such distinction: he renders the sensible insensible and brings out the dimension of emptiness at work in the midst of sensuously dense things. There is no access to any higher kind of hypostasis but rather liberation from being stuck in the particular and concrete. This is what grants access to the free and spontaneous development of nature and its inclinations. However, this is not quite as completely foreign to

---

30. I develop these interpretations of the *Inferno* in chapter 5 of *The Revelation of Imagination: From Homer and the Bible through Virgil and Augustine to Dante* (Evanston, IL: Northwestern University Press, 2015).

Western thinking as Jullien makes it seem, not at least when we include Western tradition's own internal reversal by apophatic thinking—that is, by the negative theological tradition that shadows the thinking of the logos all through its history.[31]

Jullien explicitly rejects negative theology in many of his works—for example, in *La Grande image n'a pas de forme*. He is evidently taking negative theology narrowly (as Derrida sometimes did and as his followers, such as John Caputo, often do) as a method of abstraction to some sort of super-being or hyper-essence. He is ignoring the concrete ways that it operates in Western apophatic discourses in which "God" is incarnate and embodied and manifest only fleetingly in the vanishing of what "he" is not. Such apophatic discourses in their descent from negative theological matrices include such practices as abstract expressionist painting and certain kinds of postmodern architecture that evoke an infinite emptiness materially and concretely.[32] They include musical approaches to silence by the likes of Arnold Schoenberg, John Cage, and Vladimir Jankélévitch (see *On What Cannot Be Said*, vol. 2, chapters 14, 16, and 17). Modern phenomenological expressions of apophasis are effectively connected with ancient theological sources by Emmanuel Falque.[33] This rediscovery of apophatic wisdom in the West has been the work also of authors such as Michel Henry and Jean-Louis Chrétien, protagonists of the so-called theological turn in French phenomenology—to be dealt with further below in the subsection on "Metaphysics as Poetry."

ONE AND OTHER, ALL OR NOTHING, EAST AND WEST

In his effort to categorically differentiate Greek and Chinese approaches to the constitution of sense, Jullien seems himself to be playing the game of oppositional thinking rather than to be overcoming it. He seems not to be

---

31. In *Si parler va sans dire: Du logos et d'autres ressources* (Paris: Seuil, 2006), taking Aristotle as exemplary, Jullien deals in a focused way with this logos tradition, and he does deal here with some of its own internal reversals.

32. See Mark Taylor, *Disfiguring: Art, Architecture, Religion* (Chicago, IL: University of Chicago Press, 1992).

33. Emmanuel Falque, *Dieu, la chair et l'autre: d'Irénée à Duns Scot* (Paris: Presses universitaires de France, 2008).

allowing that deeper than either culture's characteristic forms of expression is the undifferentiated Nothing (sayable) from which both arise but which both inevitably fail to interpret adequately. This polarizing approach is surely nothing but an effect of a strategy of exposition required by discursive handling of what in itself evades articulation—what is, thus, a heuristic to be discarded—and not Jullien's own intimate way of understanding those traditions. The deeper aim of Jullien's work cannot be to differentiate Chinese from Western thought at the level of first-order description, as if there really were essential differences between cultures that could be described in general terms.[34] What Jullien clearly believes, instead, is that cultures develop by their own internal logic and that the Chinese expression of each idea or apprehension comes as an organic growth from a certain Chinese world and its own intrinsic resources. However, understood thus, culture does not form a stable or distinct object susceptible of adequate or detached description. Such description proves impossible as more than a superficial and not ultimately valid characterization. Contrasts between cultures are not finally valid as defining distinct general paradigms but rather as specific interventions bringing about their mutual delimitation and their reciprocal setting into relief and transformation.

The upshot of Jullien's research and thought is rather to show that the key to our access to other cultures, as well as to our own, is *self-negation*. It is in and through self-criticism that we are able to open ourselves to a transforming interaction with another culture and even with what we call our own (which is always also other). Otherwise, we end up distancing ourselves by objectifying the other culture and thereby making it something *for us* rather than letting it be what it naturally or independently is. This presumable (or at least imaginable) intrinsic reality proper to the other culture itself is what it reveals only if it is not framed as our object by our alien and externally imposed parameters. More fundamental than just a two-worlds or two-levels model of meaning, the epistemological pitfall that we need to be on guard against is the hypostatization of the other as object. Of course, we cannot attain to the other in itself apart from all framings, but we can attempt to critically negate or neutralize our own externally imposed enframements. This is an essential part of the task of comparative philosophy, as Jullien, too, understands it.

By avoiding hypostatizing objectification through a self-critical movement, we can open ourselves to what irremediably transcends us, to what

---

34. As we have noted, Jullien programmatically refuses just such a method in *L'écart et l'entre: Leçon inaugurale de la Chaire sur l'altérité* (Paris: Galilée, 2012).

we cannot make commensurable with ourselves. The openness created in and through this act of self-negation constitutes the sense of transcendence for us. It places us in relation to a radical otherness. This strangeness can assume the form of something, or perhaps even some*one* other than, and quite beyond, ourselves. It does so quite radically in certain theological imaginings in the West. But just as a sense of the irrecuperably or insuperably *other* is at the source spring of Western apophatic thinking, so also it is near the generative source of inspiration of Chinese thought, as Jullien, a determined thinker of alterity, constantly emphasizes. Each tradition, working from its own cultural base and resources for reflection, makes a self-critical, self-delimiting movement in order to open itself to the Other and the All as nothing that can be grasped or said.

Thus, there is really no warrant for choosing immanence in preference to transcendence. Jullien should not in principle privilege immanence over transcendence but should instead prefer thinking that breaks down the opposition between them and settles for no definitive exclusions. This is indeed the drift of his discourse, when it is understood beyond the letter of certain of its headlines. It is not that his partisanship for immanence and for Chinese culture—and his contrasting it with the Greek—should not be allowed to function as an expedient for his discourse. But these prejudices belong to his own strategies for making sense, a *certain* sense that is situated and that has its validity in an evolving historical context, which is his own. These *partis pris* need to be surpassed in opening to the totality of sense, the global vision that is the ultimate aim—Jullien's own, as well as that of his Chinese models. It is the aim also often of the Greeks, at least at their most radical, when not obstructed by a certain metaphysical-scientific narrowing of their apophatic outlook.

Jullien summarizes his book (*Le Détour et l'accès: Stratégies du sens en Chine, en Grèce*) on the different "strategies of sense" in China and Greece as developing a contrast between representation and correlation. Instead of two planes, sensible and ideational, the one mirroring the other through symbolic expression, the allusive mode in China establishes a correlation between realities on the same plane of immanence constituted by continual exchange between what is latent and what is patent, between the implicit and the explicit. Chinese thought is based on relationality and on the interdependence of its poles (heaven and earth, yin and yang), without anything that is categorically external to anything else; nothing in particular is able to be correctly considered in isolation from everything else (345).

This relational mode of thinking that refuses to abstract from the plane of immanence can be observed operating at the level of the very words of the

Chinese language. For example, the word for "landscape" is the compound *shān-shuĭ* (山水)—"mountain-water" (435). The Chinese word does not make abstraction from its concrete components but rather coordinates and stays on a level continuous with the elements that it encompasses and gathers into the comprehensive, all-inclusive notion. This contrasts strikingly with the essence or the "in-itself" or the "what it is" (τὸ τί ἐστι, *to ti esti*) that is constitutive of Greek thought and its ontology. Such essences exist on another plane of reality, an intelligible one doubling that of the immediate phenomenological appearing of things (436). The universalizing notions that Western languages indicate by abstractions and often by negations are conveyed in Chinese rather by amalgamation of component parts.[35]

This linguistic example encapsulates Jullien's argument concerning the technique of allusion (and incitation) as the key to Chinese poetics in contrast with representation (mimesis) as the operating principle at the foundation of Greek poetics. And here, too, Jullien emphasizes that allusion is itself a way of bringing out "the importance of the un-said in relation to that which *is* said and the pertinence of the bond between the one and the other" ("l'importance du non-dit par rapport à ce qui est dit et la pertinence du lien entre l'un et l'autre," *Détour et l'accès*, 434). The said is there in order to awaken ("éveille") the idea of that which is not said. And all this is quintessentially apophatic in its leading insights. It can and should be applied to interpreting certain outstanding Western poetic models as well. For if the "other plane" of Western poetics is recognized as one that cannot be represented, as one that defies conceptual thought and language, then the barrier and division that Jullien imagines between the planes of immanence and transcendence does not actually constitute itself. To the extent that reifying language is used, it is also relinquished and given over as inadequate, as mere imagery—a heuristic or a propaedeutic, a vehicle for initiating a searching relation to an Unknown.

The ontological constitution of the "other world" was often taken very seriously in tradition, but that was not the only way to take it, and it is not even clear that Plato himself might not have invented it in an ironic spirit in order to playfully express the partial perspectives of the characters that speak by turns in his dialogues. However, even if we take it quite seriously, such an other world can best be considered serious as poetry is serious: that

---

35. This characteristic use of part-whole logic instead of type-token (or abstract-universal and concrete-instance) reasoning in Chinese is elucidated by Chad Hansen, *Language and Logic in Ancient China* (Ann Arbor: University of Michigan Press, 1983).

is, as offering images that guide our imagining and channel our relation to what lies finally beyond our representational faculties. That "beyond" is the realm of the apophatic, and it cannot be properly constituted by language as a field of objective entities. Instead, it is made to perform rhetorically, for example, by Kenneth Burke through his use of "beyond" as a verb—"to beyond." Burke suggests that the catharsis effected through pity and fear in tragedy brings about a kind of "beyonding" that transcends the miseries of the world as displayed in tragic hero-victims like Oedipus.[36] Thus, even in the paradigmatically mimetic art of Greek tragedy, representation needs to be considered in relation to the *beyond* of representation. This apophatic perspective places the differences between Greek and Chinese sense in a larger ambit of non-sense, which envelops both cultures and which both are subliminally aware of in their different ways and languages.

Jullien pursues his discussion of Daoist (apophatic) thought in chapter XIII of *Le Détour et l'accès*. He shifts the focus from the *Laozi* (*Book of Dao*) to the *Zhuangzi,* a fourth-century BC work by "Master Zhuang" that develops the mystical-poetic vision of Master Lao (Laozi) in a mode of critical and even of skeptical philosophical reflection and in open polemic against the conventional pieties of the Confucian school of thinking. *Zhuangzi,* in many and various ways, explores further the paradoxical and unsettling modes of apophatic expression. They are found in the hollow or in the shadow of failed direct expression vis-à-vis something that proves to be inexpressible. It becomes even clearer that this ineffable "something" is not any remote hypostasis. It can be quite simply the globality or full reality of anything whatever, since any expression in words works by opposition and takes up therefore only a restrictive point of view. The *Zhuangzi* explores philosophically the full range of possibilities and critiques all merely partial points of view, all particular perspectives.

What is needed, then, is a word that can divest itself of all its particularities so as to metamorphose potentially into other words without limit and hypothetically into all other words, overcoming their ostensible mutual exclusivity. This word is figured as a pivot, "the pivot of the *Dao*," turning in all directions and never ceasing to change in its orientation.[37] This mobility,

---

36. Kenneth Burke, *Language as Symbolic Action* (Berkeley: University of California Press, 1966), 299.

37. This image is central in the *Zhuangzi,* for example, in 2:16 in *Zhuangzi: The Essential Writings with Selections from Traditional Commentaries,* trans. Brook Ziporyn (Indianapolis, IN: Hackett, 2009).

through remaining open to and responding to all occasions, is an image of the global vision that corresponds to the *Dao* and lies beyond language, with its distinctions and differential logic and restrictions, and with its inevitably enclosed point of view. To achieve such a *non*-perspective, words must speak against themselves and undo themselves: above all, they must undo their constitutive definitions with all their limitations and mutual exclusions.

Jullien brings forward suggestive examples that begin from the opening story of the *Zhuangzi*. The extravagant image of a gigantic (and elastic) fish named *Kun* ("fish egg") that becomes a bird is used to make language strange, so as to turn it back against its tendency to differentiate and to sort everything out into separate categories. However, such a gambit of defamiliarization is not wholly unlike strategies used by many Western writers. Particularly the mystic tradition of apophasis has evolved techniques of transgressing the boundaries of linguistic sense-making in order to gesture indicatively to what lies beyond the bounds of sense and its exclusivities and differential logic. Many modern avant-garde writings, too, invite comparison with the Daoist discourse of the *Zhuangzi*, which draws language out of its functional specifications into free evolution that reaches infinitely beyond the artificial boundaries set up by determinate demarcations. Jullien welcomes and celebrates this excess of meaning as rendering to the world its ecstasy or "jouissance" (*Détour et l'accès,* 371).

It is the word's unlimited capacity of variation and always further nuance that delivers it from partiality and consigns it to the global dimension that makes it an instrument of vision (or non-vision) without exclusions. Is this global "vision" incompatible with imagining another plane of sense? Might not such another plane be understood as itself a detour for gaining access to a reality that is inherently non-coincident with itself? Is Jullien endeavoring to exclude what he takes to be the Western way as less commensurable with the truth? But, then, which truth? He should surely take to heart the *Book of Dao*'s teaching of the underlying, inexpressible unity of all things. And he must surely include in this unity the ways of both the Occident (*xī* 西) and the Orient (*dōng* 東), no matter how determined he is to distinguish them. These words combined—*dōngxī*—form the compound word in Chinese for "thing"—that is, the common noun for any and every thing. This word *dōngxī* (東西) itself again exemplifies how inclusiveness rather than conceptual definition by exclusion of not-A from A is engrained into the Chinese language itself and is constitutive of its own peculiar way of thinking.

Jullien's argument constantly seeks to differentiate a Western metaphysical, allegorical approach to the unsayable, or to what is beyond verbal grasp, from the strategies he finds deployed in the Chinese classics, perhaps most provocatively and philosophically in the Daoist text of the *Zhuangzi*. He stresses how in the *Zhuangzi* the very excess and extravagance of discourse lead it out of the unilateralism of having just a certain point of view. Logic, with its specifications and compartmentalizations, is overrun or collapses. The difference with respect to the Western theological and allegorical tradition, for which Jullien pertinently cites Origen, Clement of Alexandria, Proclus, and others leading up to Latin Christian Scholasticism, is that the latter posit another world, a separate plane of intelligibility, whereas the *Dao* does not imply any such other plane; it posits no other—spiritual or theological—world or reality. It remains focused, instead, on individuals in their particularities—but as infinitely variable.

It could be pointed out, however, that the doctrine of the resurrection of the body in the Christian religion likewise preserves this focus on material particularity. The body's being "glorified," furthermore, opens it to endlessly variable metamorphoses beyond any set limits of form. Jullien argues that in the West the image is cancelled out by the reality that it images. In the logic of allegory, the veil must be stripped away in order to uncover reality, the truth, its meaning, or in order to ascend the ontological ladder from the sensible to the intelligible. He emphasizes always this "doubling" of appearance and reality (*Le Détour et l'accès*, 376, and 13, sec. 3). Whereas the "net" ("nasse") is "purely instrumental" and does not consolidate itself (or anything else beyond it) as a separate plane of reality, the allegorical veil supposedly hides a wholly other, spiritual or intelligible reality behind sensible images. While in Western metaphysics and its corresponding allegorical poetics the intelligible is the contradiction of the sensible, creating an opposition and a gap between the image and its transcendent meaning, the *Zhuangzi* reabsorbs all such exclusions within the globality of the real. There is thus no rupture between nature and the supernatural. The enlightened view of the Daoist sage presents not another reality but rather reality without limits or oppositions.

However, this is actually what the West, too, proposes, at least implicitly, in its lesser-known apophatic counter-traditions. And Western apophatic tradition does this, to boot, in such a way as not to exclude even otherworldly visions, notably those of Christian revelation. Jullien compares Chinese wisdom with certain standard myths and images of Western religion and its metaphysical underpinnings but strategically overlooks the latter's deeper apophatic logic.

The self-critical movement annulling hypostatization of the uncanny dimension of the infinite transformability of everything into everything else as separate from the world of sensible experience is found in the West as well as in the East. Images recognized as only images are no longer different from reality, except provisionally, since they do not claim to possess ontological independence.[38] Even Dante discovers that the appearance of phenomenal beauty, eminently in Beatrice, is not ultimately anything independent of the reality of God's glory. And the ultimate reality of God is known and approached never directly but always only through representations. Even when we say "ultimate reality" that is but another representation, and this is well recognized in negative-theological traditions.

Strategies of consciously extravagant representation as means of access to unrepresentable reality are common to both Eastern and Western traditions. And in both, only an indirect, allusive saying without saying can attain to the real. For only such *un*saying (and unnaming) allows "the infinite deployment of sense by reality itself: only by not claiming to name reality (in any exclusive and static way) but rather by the sense itself deploying its own sense indefinitely, can we speak of reality" ("Car c'est seulement si l'on ne pretend pas en parler nommément [c'est-à-dire de façon exclusive et arrêtée] que, le sens se déployant alors indéfiniment de lui-même, on peut effectivement parler de la réalité," *Le Détour et l'accès,* 384).

Jullien develops a perfectly apophatic theory from his Eastern sources by contrasting them with Western stereotypes, but these same stereotypes are themselves reversed by Western apophaticism. The idea of a verbal activity without an object, which he stresses in reading the *Book of Dao,* is frequently found in Western poetics of the unsayable, and such activity is undecidedly immanent *and* transcendent. The overcoming of partiality by a word and image pivoting in every sense and direction, yet without deserting the plane of sensible experience for any other or intelligible world, is also a fecund direction of development of thought in the apophatic West and its poetics of ineffability. Jullien has articulated his own thought in opposition to a certain Western metaphysical paradigm: the coherence of his exposition undoubtedly required this. We always make sense in language only by the principle of difference, and Jullien's philosophical method is indeed discursive, turning on subtly detailed and delineated comparisons and contrasts. However, in the end, coherence demands not rejecting the model that he

---

38. The problematic is treated broadly in relation to medieval tradition by Olivier Boulnois, *Au-delà de l'image: Une archéologie du visuel au Moyen Âge (V^e-XVIe siècle)* (Paris: Seuil, 2008). For postmodern permutations of this theme, see Jean Baudrillard, "La précession des simulacres," in *Simulacres et simulation* (Paris: Galilée, 1981), 9–68.

has used as his foil but rather showing how it, too, can be folded back into the dynamism of the *global* reality without exclusions by which this thinking is animated.

The imagery of another world or plane of meaning, like the imagery of transcendence—of a Creator God, for example—and the imagery of immanence, or of the mutual and perpetual metamorphosis of all forms, constitute different languages, but they belong to a common reality and issue from a common endeavor to relate oneself to and within that reality. They express different orientations improvised in responding to different dominant exigencies in their own epochs and cultures of origin. If Jullien is right, they should not be hypostatized into separate cultural worlds—except perhaps heuristically. We saw that from its very first poem the *Book of Dao* differentiates between the secret and the manifest, and this differentiation is enough of an axis on which to open up the dimension of the apophatic as a space of retreat and a movement of critique with respect to what presents itself at first as evident and real. With regard to the *Dao*, we were instructed:

> Hence always rid yourself of desires in order to observe its secrets;
> But always allow yourself to have desires in order to observe its manifestations.
>
> These two are the same
> But diverge in name as they issue forth. (*Laozi*, 1, Lao, trans.)

Thus, not two worlds but two approaches diverging in their naming as language fetches the real from a secret order that is unveiled only to the desireless. Jullien rejects over and over the two-worlds model that is prevalent in Platonism and in Christian New Testament imagination alike. But what ensures that this image is the bottom-line reality rather than just another allegorical image for a reality that cannot as such be represented—precisely as apophatic thinkers have all along insisted? In this case, there is no bottom-line image—and no graspable reality independent of images either. It is the very vanishing of the sensible and its multiplication in fleeting images that allude to this unrepresentable dimension that can also be called—as it is by Arthur Rimbaud—"L'éternité." In his exquisitely visionary poem of an epiphany at sunset on the Western horizon, "eternity" occurs precisely as a plunging into indistinction at the moment when "the sun is gone with the sea" ("c'est la mer allée / avec le soleil") and all instantaneously becomes invisible, or simply neutral. This apocalypse of the world becoming suddenly dark at nightfall is imagined as an ontological or metaphysical and, at the same time, a purely sensory sunset. In either case, the loss of all distinction between sun and sea, symbolically between transcendent source of order and amorphous matter of chaos, is experienced as an event of absolute presence—as "eternity." The transcendent resonances with which this word rings can hardly be filtered out of the sensory event of time that enshrines it.

THE ABSOLUTELY OTHER AND THE MOVEMENT OF TRANSCENDENCE

Remaining fixated upon the different paradigms characteristic of Chinese and Western cultures respectively answers to the demands of scientific typology but not to those of working through and undoing oppositional binaries and their inevitable exclusions, with their invidious, hierarchical valuations. Whole vision is attained, in the vocabulary that Jullien derives from ancient Chinese wisdom, through the "fluctuating word" ("parole fluctuante"), which is in unceasing evolution: it follows the contour of things themselves in reality and as free of artificial constructions in language. By exceeding all fixed and merely partial sense, by never ceasing to be an allusive variation, the word is able "to rejoin the spontaneous coexistence of things and grant us access to the natural" ("rejoindre la coexistence spontanée des choses et nous fasse accéder au naturel," *Le Détour et l'accès*, 385). It is telling that Jullien, following classical Chinese usage, speaks of the "natural" by translating the character for "heaven" (*Tiān* 天) as the horizon of the real as a whole. However, there is also another important clue to the meaning of nature present in the common Daoist word for it: *zì rán* (自然). Literally meaning "self so," this notion for nature envisages the "such as it is," things as yet unconstrued by human language and culture but simply such as they are *in themselves*.

As is brought out by use especially in literary contexts, a word is capable of turning on itself and opening in all different directions. This gives it infinitely open possibilities of sense. Another plane of significance would presumably be a closure and a limit, assigning one true meaning. The other plane of meaning is hierarchically superior in that it assigns a definite, definitive, "higher" sense and significance. This is how Jullien understands it in his dismissal, or at least surpassing, of the allegorical mode of signification, which he takes as characteristic of Western literature and culture. However, Longxi Zhang vigorously contests the usual thesis (as propounded also by Jullien) of the inapplicability of allegorical interpretation in Chinese tradition by showing how this supposedly Western paradigm is far from lacking in counterparts in the East and in Chinese poetics in particular.[39] Haun Saussy, furthermore, furnishes a case in point by reconstructing the allegorical program of the traditional Chinese *Book of Odes*.[40]

Indeed, such allegorical meaning can also be just part of the *game* of generating every possible alternative sense with no exclusions. Another plane of meaning does not necessarily put a stop to this activity of generating always further sense but can itself play into and even enhance it. Another plane can heighten the meaning to another apparently higher, and in any case heterogeneous, level. This is, after all, part of the connotation of "heaven" (*Tiān*), which Jullien sometimes translates from the Chinese by "nature." The fact of recognizing a dimension of height and even of transcendence is not nearly as lethal to the infinite allusiveness and endless proliferation of sense within immanence as Jullien generally presumes. The "higher" plane itself is apt to be indeterminate and so to unsettle all meanings, suspending them on an empty Nothing—or at least on one knows not what.

The connotation of something absolute and categorically different from all things immanent is, in the end, not contrary to Jullien's own assumptions about what makes the world what it is. He and Chinese culture alike can, after all, acknowledge the absolutely other, as long as it is not definitively formulated in language. He and Chinese culture are, in fact, ineluctably committed to such an absolute. Chinese classical wisdom articulates itself not as a refusal of the dimension of transcendence. Such a refusal has been a quintessential gesture typical rather of numerous currents within the West. It might even be taken as the defining or inaugural move of modern Western culture as a whole, at least since the Enlightenment. It is by the complete assimilation and absorption of "heaven" into the thinking of change within the universe, not by its elimination, that Chinese classical thought obviates the need to speak explicitly of "the transcendent" and of other such attendant abstractions. "Heaven," with all its unmasterable, even unthinkable, transcendence is concretely lived out in the self's experience of being infinitely surpassed through its relation to the real already in nature.

In this (day)light (of *Tiān*), the polemic against transcendence needs to be qualified. It is really only *reified* transcendence that is problematic in

---

39. Longxi Zhang, *Allegoresis: Reading Canonical Literature East and West* (Ithaca, NY: Cornell University Press, 2005).
40. Haun Saussy, *The Problem of a Chinese Aesthetic* (Stanford, CA: Stanford University Press, 1993).

Jullien's terms.[41] Transcendence, as an openness to the absolutely other and unfathomable, is a necessary ground-principle for the cultural perspective that Jullien represents as authentically Chinese. However, such an open approach to something unknown and ungraspable, something neutral in the Blanchotian sense of the "neuter," can also be found as the sense of transcendence at the heart of the Western canon—for example, in Dante's *Paradiso*. Unfathomable transcendence does not work as a limit or a barrier that stops thought so much as a gap in its very midst that cracks it open to its own abyss.[42]

Recent theological treatments of transcendence, particularly in feminist theology, can help us to avoid overly monolithic thinking and its inevitable amalgams by developing a more differentiated understanding of transcendence. The reified transcendence rejected by Jullien lines up with what Catherine Keller pertinently treats as *separative* transcendence. Keller contrasts this with what she envisages as a "double or self-negating transcendence" that "moves beyond the breakaway transcendence" or "separative transcendence" that hardens and petrifies into just itself and blocks "any possible self-transcendence."[43] The infinitely self-critical movement that I describe as apophatic is epitomized by its unlimited openness to and availability for all ways and possibilities of self-transcendence. I allow that these possibilities may include even being reached by a grace that transcends all one's own self-transcendings and willful strivings.

When Jullien strongly separates Eastern and Western modes of apophasis in order to define what proved unattainable in the West, in contrast with the East and its natural feeling for continuities free from dichotomous logic, one senses that he is understandably biased, at least for strategic reasons, in favor of the (to us) little-known world of Chinese thought that he wishes to open up in its hitherto mostly unsuspected richness to a Western

---

41. Jullien still treats this as *theological* transcendence in "Essai: "Fonder" la morale, ou comment légitimer la transcendance de la moralité sans le support du dogme ou de la foi (au travers du Mencius)," *Extrême-Orient, Extrême-Occident* 6/6 (1985): 23–81.

42. I argue this specifically in "Transcendence and the Sense of Transgression," the concluding chapter of *Dante and the Sense of Transgression: "The Trespass of the Sign"* (London: Continuum [Bloomsbury], 2013), as well as in chapter 3: "At the Limits of Language or Reading Dante through Blanchot" and chapter 5: "The Neuter—Nothing Except Nuance," 29–46.

43. Catherine Keller, "Rumors of Transcendence: The Movement, State, and Sex of 'Beyond,'" in John Caputo and Michael J. Scanlon, eds., *Transcendence and Beyond: A Postmodern Inquiry* (Bloomington: Indiana University Press, 2007), 141.

NOTHING AND THE POETIC "MAKING" OF SENSE   77

audience. For all the acuteness of his contrasts between what is characteristic of Daoist thinkers and Neoplatonists respectively, he sees less in Western forms of apophasis than he could. This is a natural consequence of a certain (disavowed) partisanship for the Chinese tradition of which he makes himself the philosophical interpreter and cultural ambassador.

This hermeneutic partisanship is inevitable: it is what gives his whole project its point. But Jullien attempts to mask (or at least moderate) it by highlighting deficiencies in Chinese thought—for example, its inability to cope with human responsibility for evil.[44] Even in *Le détour et l'accès*, he does not fail to convey also certain common depreciations of Chinese culture—for example, in chapter 6 on "The Impossibility of Dissidence." There are moments in which he sharply critiques China's ideological immobility and compares the traditional authoritarianism of the Chinese Empire unfavorably with the open democracy of the Greek polis. Freedom and truth are all too easily traduced in conformist Confucian culture, which ostensibly requires one to please the powerful. In *L'écart et l'entre* (74–75), Jullien lucidly explains his strategy as not one simply of embracing Chinese culture but rather as undertaking to work between it and the West. He is naturally selective and one-sided in order to make his point. He ignores myriad qualifications and counter-examples for the sake of seeing something broadly characteristic of whole cultural continents. Admittedly, there does seem to be a broad difference in character along the lines he suggests. Still, to define and set limits to what can be attained by one culture or the other belongs more typically to the categorizing, taxonomizing mentality of the West that Jullien so effectively critiques by contrasting it with the classical Chinese model of knowing.

There is in other works, like *L'invention de l'idéale et le destin de l'Europe*, a nuanced acknowledgment that nothing is impossible for either culture but that certain resources remain relatively unexploited in one or the other. Such a divergence can be seen, for instance, in the West's choice of pursuing a theoretical point of view set alongside China's relative indifference to theory (75–105). Or again, it is not that the vision of a fundamentally allusive type of discourse is altogether lacking to and beyond the reach of Western thought. There are simply different approaches and different accents in the East and in the West that bring out specific aspects of apophasis with greater or lesser effectiveness.

Jullien's tendency to elevate the approach or method of one culture over the other is ironically what he says is typical of Western thought and

---

44. See *Dialogue sur la morale*, 95–109, and passim.

what the radical valorization of blandness at least in theory undermines. Blandness is eulogized for its perfect indifference and impartiality towards all competing tastes. In fact, the lowliest and most insipid form turns out to be the richest, reversing the obvious, conventional valuation and power hierarchy. Jullien's thought, in becoming partisan, betrays itself as belonging very much to the Western mold rather than exemplifying the virtues he is praising as typical of Eastern, specifically Chinese, thinking. Not that it necessarily should be anything else: Jullien's discourse is expressly Western and for a Western audience. But he needs to allow also for Western discourse's achieving, in its own original ways, species of insight and wisdom that are akin to those modeled by the Chinese. Such insight is not hermetically sealed up in one cultural world or another. In fact, Jullien himself frequently repeats and undertakes to demonstrate just this in his recent book delineating an intercultural philosophy of the universal (see chapter 4).

I believe that it is possible to derive from Western sources, specifically from Western apophatic traditions, essentially the same principles of thought as those that Jullien praises in works such as his *In Praise of Blandness*. These sources also develop ways of thinking from the not-yet-differentiated ground *from* which differences emerge but *in* which they are not yet mutually exclusive. From Porphyry, Dionysius, and Damascius to Maimonides, al-'Arabi, and Gregory Palamas, non-Aristotelian logics are tried out to purposes not unlike those evidenced in Chinese source texts that refuse or evade the logic of the excluded middle.[45] Poetry in these texts, even if in very different ways, is paramount. Jullien reads Western poetry as if it were inevitably a deployment of a metaphysics with two separate realities, one sensible and the other intelligible. I would rather read metaphysics as metaphor, or as a form of poetry: the sensory is not conceived as a separate reality but as dependent on and expressive of true reality. In poetry, intelligible sense or meaning is inseparable from sensation as experienced in the sounds and shapes of words. Such interpenetration of sound and sense is characteristic of the "poetic function" as theorized by Roman Jakobson.[46] Both Jullien and I emphasize the artificiality of discourse and aim at its undifferentiated "fond" or ground, but in different ways, or from opposite directions.

---

45. See corresponding chapters (3, 13, 5, 15, 17, 24) on these figures in *On What Cannot Be Said*, vol. 1. Jullien treats the Chinese sources from this specific perspective in *Si parler va sans dire*.

46. Roman Jakobson, "Closing Statement: Linguistics and Poetics," in *Style in Language*, ed. T. Sebeok (Cambridge: MIT Press, 1960).

Strategies of indirection, Eastern or Western, aim in their interventions at a stage anterior to that of the manifest effects of events. Once events have occurred and are construed, determinate objects all stand in oppositional relations to one another. One needs instead to accede to a stage of indifferentiation before the outbreak of conflict between parties constituted by reciprocal opposition in order to begin to nurture solutions to their still future disputes.

(NEGATIVE) METAPHYSICS (OR PRE-PHYSICS) AS POETRY

Following his chosen path through the thought of classical China, Jullien finds a common inspiration for Daoism and Confucianism in their discretion, in their reserve, in what they do not say, in their promotion of simple "blandness" ("fadeur"), *dàn* 淡. In *Le Détour et l'accès*, Jullien produces practically a manual of apophatic logic, rhetoric, and semantics, comparing and contrasting Western (Greek) models with (classical) Chinese. He contrasts Greek metaphysics with Chinese strategy, devoting special attention to the Chinese classics on the art of war, in which strategy rather than force is seen to triumph even against superior power.[47]

But metaphysics, too, can and indeed needs to be viewed as a *strategy*. Beyond its discourse of truth, there are motivations that are not and cannot be fully articulated, ones in which strategic interests operate behind the scenes in erecting metaphysical systems. Nietzsche, as is well known, endeavors to unmask such strategies as the "will to power" lurking behind all claims to metaphysical "truth." Paradoxically, this same strategy could also serve to *redeem* metaphysics and enable it to metamorphose. Indeed, any philosophically speculative word can be turned around on itself so as to mirror everything around it and, as a consequence, metaphorically metamorphose without limits.

What Jullien seems not to consider is that the metaphysics of the other world *taken as poetry* can tell us something important and perhaps, in a sense, "true." I am not unwilling to defend in certain regards the doubling of worlds at the level of representation; such doubling expresses and renders metaphorically conspicuous the lack of univocity of any language that we might invent for objectively describing the world. As Derrida, for one, has

---

47. Jullien treats this subject further in *Traité de l'efficacité* (Paris: Grasset, 1996).

insisted, a certain equivocity inheres in the very nature of representation: poetry proliferates in *fabulae*. Against a certain smugness of maintaining that there is only one world and that it is *this* one, the one we know, the metaphysics of the other world preserves the mystery of this world or of any world that we can know and articulate. It points beyond our grids and systems designed for taming and categorizing the elements of our experience. Paradoxically, the prescriptive and indeed proscriptive gesture of eliminating other (metaphysical) worlds can itself become like a metaphysics dogmatically asserting knowledge of the one and only world (supposedly the known one). Jullien seems still to be claiming to have a more accurate, a more realistic, or at least a less self-deceived, description of the world, one more adequate than that of any metaphysician, whereas the assumptions of such a direct realism have been undermined and placed on a different footing by negative or apophatic critique.[48] Jullien perceptively detects and marvelously expounds such critique of dogmatic realism as practiced in its pervasive Chinese expressions, but he has sometimes been selectively blind to such critique when it occurs subtly and implicitly in Western sources.

Marking certain nuances of difference between Neoplatonist and Neo-Daoist or Confucian styles of approach is a vital contribution of Jullien to comparative philosophy. But to circumscribe Western thought as "metaphysical" and to proclaim Chinese thought to be sublimely free of it is to forget that the essentially wordless or apophatic insight that he is seeking can be reached through any culture and is indeed envisaged in different ways by each one. Cultures attain to apophatic insight specifically through their self-reflective capabilities of turning on themselves in self-critique, often with a strong dose of self-irony. Such insight is reached in Western culture, not least in the apophatic self-critique and reversal of naïve forms of faith in Catholic Christendom, eminently in the thought of John Scott Eriugena, Meister Eckhart, and Nicolas Cusanus.

In a typically French, anti-clerical, lay spirit that has a long and venerable pedigree but that may now find itself out of sync with a post-secular age, Jullien excludes the traditional discourses of faith as dogmatic. He

---

48. Theologians reconsider the meaning today of traditional Christian teachings concerning the other world and show how this meaning has been transformed in *Ewiges Leben. Ende oder Umbau einer Erlösungsreligion?* eds. Günther Thomas and Markus Höfner, Religion und Aufklärung series (Tübingen: Mohr Siebeck, 2018), forthcoming. My contribution, "Unsayability and the Promise of Salvation: Apophatics, Literary Representation, and the World to Come," demonstrates how apophaticism remains realistic in orientation but ungrounds reality, making it other to itself in any of our ready-made codes or languages.

writes disapprovingly even of Paul Verlaine's turning or being "converted" to "transcendence" on his deathbed (*Éloge de la fadeur*, 126). Yet Verlaine verisimilarly found faith at the end of his life as another kind of (non)language for the mystery that he had attempted to approach during his writing career through the self-subverting, self-withdrawing language of poetry and its peculiar species of implicit faith. Verlaine, as the poet of the imprecise and indecisive, "l'imprecis" and "l'indécis" ("Art poétique"), preferring to all realist description of things "nothing but nuance" ("rien que la nuance"), perfectly expresses, albeit poetically, the neuter. This is what Blanchot and Levinas and Barthes, as already evoked, would later do theoretically.[49] And theology is not fundamentally an impediment to this enterprise: it is indeed a preeminent language of the unsayable, notably in the often-heterodox tradition that I have repeatedly cited.

Jullien's portrayal of Verlaine's death scene sets up a strict dichotomy between the fluid indetermination of sensible experience ("l'indétermination sensible") and the hard-edged certitudes of a revealed Christian faith (*Éloge de la fadeur*, 126). But this is a false dichotomy to the extent that it ignores the possibility of apophatic theism (as it is found in Dionysius the Areopagite, Meister Eckhart, John of the Cross, Silesius Angelus, etc.), where precisely the transcendent is the indeterminable.

The now famous "theological turn" in phenomenology testifies to such possibilities from within the crucible of French philosophical thinking today as represented by the likes of Jean-Luc Marion, Michel Henry, and Jean-Louis Chrétien.[50] Such thinking as that developed particularly by Michel Henry in *L'essence de la manifestation* (1963) is invoked by Isabelle Robinet *against* Jullien's insistence on immanence as the foundation of the world; for in so emphasizing immanence instead of and *without* transcendence, Jullien overlooks or at least underplays the invisibility of this immanence, thereby

---

49. I cannot but note with keen interest that in his later *Si parler va sans dire*, Jullien himself quotes Verlaine, as well as Mallarmé, much as I have done, to provide parallels to the poetic principles that he finds especially in Daoist texts (160–62). *Le détour et l'accès* in closing also concedes the exception of Mallarmé and the late nineteenth-century "révolution poétique" (432).

50. The work of reference here is Dominique Janicaud, *Le tournant théologique de la phénoménologie française* (Combas: L'Eclat, 1991). For representative texts, including ones by Henry, Chrétien, Marion, Jean-François Courtine, and Paul Ricoeur, translated into English, see Dominique Janicaud, et al., *Phenomenology and the 'Theological Turn': The French Debate* (New York: Fordham University Press, 2000). For probing commentary, see J. Aaron Simmons and Bruce Ellis Benson, *The New Phenomenology: A Philosophical Introduction* (London: Bloomsbury, 2013), 99–136.

erasing the ontological difference of appearing from what appears: in so doing, he folds all reality into one seamless envelope of immanence.[51] Paradoxically, recognition of a discontinuous, heterogeneous element of ontological difference is necessary in order to realize the unity and continuity of all. Making differences at the conceptual and linguistic level is necessary for us so as to allow all to be one beyond all our perceptions and articulations, since we cannot see this oneness as such. In order to avoid the illusion of sufficiency, our conception of the world must recognize itself as incomplete and as opening upon and oriented to the absolutely other.

It is much more true to the spirit of Jullien's own contribution not to set up a dichotomy between Eastern and Western apophasis but rather to underline the continuities between them as deriving from a common basis that is properly nowhere, neither East nor West: it is a basis that neither culture can possess or confine. Even the much-maligned Rudyard Kipling (and certainly not all that he wrote is ethically palatable today) stated as much with disarming simplicity in an apocalyptic image of overcoming a seemingly insuperable divisiveness between peoples inhabiting opposite ends of the earth:

> OH, East is East, and West is West, and never the twain shall meet,
> Till Earth and Sky stand presently at God's great Judgment Seat;
> But there is neither East nor West, Border, nor Breed, nor Birth,
> When two strong men stand face to face, tho' they come from the ends of the earth![52]

Kipling's "neither-nor" rhetoric happens to be one of the principal resources also of apophatic thought and writing as used, for instance, in the Upanishads ("neti neti") for overcoming dichotomous thinking through nondualism. Today, he might further extend this logic by continuing, "But there is neither man nor woman when two true singularities meet face to face in the fray of the oldest war in the world."

---

51. Isabelle Robinet, "Une lecture du Zhuangzi," *Études chinoises* 15/1–2 (1996):109–58: "Insister comme le fait F. Jullien sur l'immanence du fondement du monde et ne pas percevoir que la nature de cette immanence est d'être irréductiblement et à jamais invisible, c'est s'arrêter en chemin (c'est ce que montre bien M. Henry, *L'essence de la manifestation* [Paris: Presses universitaires de France, 1963])," 125n27.

52. Edmund Clarence Stedman, ed., *A Victorian Anthology 1837–1895* (Boston: Houghton Mifflin, 1895).

Only in cultural non-identity can this elusive non-entity or Nothing be glimpsed so as to be remarked at all. It is proper to no culture: it is found only where each and every culture tends to lose—or to escape from—itself. This empty space of the *inter* is where identities—whether geographical, national, racial, or sexual—and the wars they engender all come from, although it is itself unidentifiable and has no contrary to oppose it. As the humanly universal, considered apophatically, it turns out to be indistinguishable from the divinely transcendent.

CODA ON CHINESE EXPRESSION OF NEGATIVITY

The apophatic cast of Chinese thought has been well appreciated quite apart from and long before Jullien's interventions. In fact, he is often making many of the most traditional points about Chinese thought, albeit in his own philosophically suggestive and probing language. The originality of his own discourse consists not in its saying something unheard of before—any more than the originality of Chinese thought consists essentially in something that it alone can say or that is categorically different from all that Western thought can think, as if its singularity were susceptible to being identified by criteria that could be made fully explicit and be stated in discourse. The respective characteristics and traits of cultures are means of individuating their distinctive and original approaches to what are, after all, common aspirations and intuitions and not exclusive realities or materials naturally accessible to any one culture alone.

For Confucius (551–479 BC), the basis of human nature, *rén* 仁, was nothing that could be defined. Asked about this founding quality of "humaneness," Confucius reportedly said that "you have to feel the meaning of this virtue. You must never put it into words."[53] Nor can the whole or the all be otherwise securely grasped. The hand cannot grasp itself, just as the mouth cannot chew itself. Whatever it can chew is not the mouth itself, in the same way that "the *Dao* that can be expressed is not the true *Dao*." *Wú Wéi* (無爲), literally "not doing" or not forcing, is the apophatic practice par excellence. We are not in control of nature, not even of our own. All our efforts at cogitation cannot control the growth of nerves and tissue in our brains. We can at best only work with rather than against what nature

---

53. *Analects,* cited by Alan Watts, *What Is Tao?* (Novato, CA: New World Library, 2000), 30–31.

does of itself: only so can we apprehend nature as *zì rán* or "by itself so." We need to get out of our own way and stop being an obstacle to our own instinctive motion in order to let our activities flourish with natural grace and effectiveness. We are within nature and must harmonize with it rather than foisting our agenda upon it, as if we could stand outside of it and determine by ourselves our own overall direction and purpose.

Alan Watts lucidly expresses this fundamental point about nature that Chinese tradition has so vividly illustrated and so beautifully embodies. In his own very different style, he anticipates many of Jullien's emphases, including that placed on "jouissance" in the indirect ways of knowing by which alone nature is susceptible of being known:

> we have to come to terms with nature by wooing her rather than fighting her, and instead of holding nature at a distance through our objectivity as if she were an enemy, realize rather that she is to be known by her embrace. . . . Do we trust nature, or would we rather try to manage the whole thing? Do we want to be some kind of omnipotent god, in control of it all, or do we want to enjoy it instead? After all, we can't enjoy what we are anxiously trying to control. One of the nicest things about our bodies is that we don't have to think about them all the time. If when you woke up in the morning you had to think about every detail of your circulation, you would never get through the day. (91–92)

Watts is making some of the same points as Jullien, yet without the presumption of teaching the West lessons that China knows better. Jullien often shows that he knows better, too, but their polemical posture and argumentative edge have sometimes made certain of his discourses sound a little moralizing towards his Western audience. He has also made some strenuous efforts to counter this interpretation of his thought, but that also tends to confirm its inevitability: critique of the West through comparison with China underlies the very intelligibility of his discourse and its raison d'être. Yet in the end he renounces all pretensions to be able to accurately characterize Chinese thought and admits to being incited by it only to pursue his own thinking. The striking virtue of Jullien is that he thinks actively along with his Chinese sources rather than only elucidating them as his object of study. This distinguishes him and often sets him at odds with traditional sinology. Still, it is by interacting with these sources in an original way that he or anyone else can most authentically respond to the solicitations and incitations of Chinese thought and tradition, as his *oeuvre* so powerfully demonstrates.

Chapter 3

IMMANENCE
The Last Word?

FROM FIGURES OF IMMANENCE TO FORMLESS TRANSCENDENCE: THE *YIJING* AND NEGATIVE THEOLOGY

The question of immanence versus transcendence is among the most controversial and has become, in many respects, the key issue in comparative or intercultural philosophy in our time. On this question, the most authoritative interpreters find themselves in sharp and seemingly irresolvable disagreement. Minds simply divide ("die Geister gehen auseinander," as German says). Something more is at issue here than just accurate reading, sober reflection, and level judgment. Our most basic decisions concerning who we are, what it is to think, and the fundamentals of our worldviews are at stake. My aim in addressing this topic is to show how when transcendence is reinterpreted apophatically, as I think it implicitly is by those who defend it in its application to Chinese thought, it stands no longer in opposition to immanence. I contend, in fact, that apophatic transcendence recuperates the essential insights also of those advocating immanence as an indispensable key to interpreting Chinese thought. Either apophatic transcendence or apophatic immanence captures what both apparently antagonistic parties are trying to express as fundamental and distinctive about Chinese thinking, even while coming at it from different angles and opposing directions.

Both factions are trying to individuate what is specific and perhaps in some ways unique about Chinese thinking. Yet this project can be carried through in apophatic terms not by direct description of the Other but only by critique of one's own limits in light of Chinese alternatives. An apophatic way of understanding either transcendence or immanence brings the type of insight characteristic of China, furthermore, into close correlation with some of the deepest and most elusive strands of thinking that have persistently asserted themselves also in the West, often by indirect means, since antiquity. The concepts of transcendence and immanence, accordingly, lend themselves to serving as axes for cross-cultural comparisons.

In this chapter, I begin from François Jullien's analysis of the *Yijing* as a way of raising some key issues regarding the apophatic reinterpretation of transcendence in Chinese philosophy. What Jullien means by immanence is not easy to grasp or encompass with a concept, but he endeavors to explain it with regard to the *Yijing*, the *Book of Changes,* the Chinese classic par excellence. This work, on Jullien's reading of it in his *Figures of Immanence*,[1] is not in its core a book in the usual sense, for it is constituted not by words but by diagrams: solid or broken line segments stacked on top of one another to form trigrams, which are then combined by pairs into hexagrams. This system of combinations of broken and unbroken lines is not a language nor even a code bearing a discernible sense or meaning. Yet it does somehow correspond to the world in its incalculably complex dynamic as deriving entirely from the interaction between two simple alternatives or poles, yin and yang, earth and heaven, the unbroken and the broken. What is the nature of this correlation? Jullien contrasts it with myth.

Myth is a history (literally a "story," *muthos* in Greek) that is determined by a beginning and an end. It gives a comprehensive sense to things that is fixed by an origin (*arché*) and a goal (*telos*). Myths aim to define the overall purpose and purport of things from beginning to end, from creation (Genesis) to consummation (Apocalypse). What Chinese thought, by contrast, aims to represent, starting from this foundational divination text, the *Yijing,* is rather the idea of transition or transformation without beginning or end. Simply the play of opposites (broken / unbroken) and their transforms across the sixty-four combinatorial possibilities of the hexagrams (made up *in toto* of 384 lines) constitutes a system for describing the ongoing changes in which nature consists. This combinatorial grid does not have a sense or meaning, as a myth does, but rather embodies a mechanism for producing unlimited transformation beyond all bounds of sense. Such is the transformation that is effectively produced by nature in its endlessly continuing alternations and in its unceasing cycles of life and death. The hexagrams embody in an abstract schema the alternative combinations of yin and yang that result in all the complex changes of phenomena throughout

---

1. *Figures de l'immanence. Pour une lecture philosophique du Yiking* (Paris: Grasset, 1993). This work is the default reference throughout this section.

the universe. The *Yijing* maps the coordinates of the infinitely complex process of change that is uninterruptedly underway in all natural occurrences: all are propelled by the working of simple polarities analogous to various combinations of continuous and discontinuous lines. These operations can be applied recursively to produce infinitely complex variations of combinations of the same simple elements—in effect, just the digital one and zero.

This original classic equips Chinese thought with a very different way of adhering to the nature of things than what we find in the West. This way does not work by attributing a purpose through a static image of origin or end-goal, which imposes a sense from without on the whole process, but by entering into the dynamic play of the world as it constantly shifts and transits between poles in phases of systole and diastole. In this manner, we are able to live in correspondence with the way things really are—with things *such as they are* (*zì rán*, 自然), which is one crucial way of saying "nature" in Chinese. The trigrams of the *Book of Changes,* taken as such (and without the accumulated interpretations of the ages), do not express a meaning or sense. They are not like ideograms or pictograms that are supposed to refer by resemblance to objects in the world, and they do not constitute any meaning-bearing code or language. Their constitutive traces (broken or unbroken lines in combinatorial groups and sequences) are not exactly just given things, but they are not quite meaningful signs either: they are ambiguously intermediate between the orders of logical form and natural things.

Jullien draws the consequence that China is without a founding epic and without a divine revelation—that is, without a myth of beginnings. Instead, in the *Book of Changes* (易经, Yì Jīng), China has a system of diagrams consisting in simple traces corresponding to the changes that constitute life and the universe. "In China, there is neither divine Word nor epic; consciousness is born rather from something traced. And the *Yijing* is the work par excellence of the written trace, which is primordial in it" ("Or, en Chine, il n'y a ni Parole divine ni épopée, la conscience naît du tracé. Et le *Yi king* est l'œuvre par excellence de la trace écrite, qui en lui est primitive," 15).

A trace bears no sense; it is not rounded into the wholeness of a meaning that can be extracted from universal flux and be defined. Instead, it is a vector of movement, a tendency toward one pole or the other—hotter or colder, more or less, up or down, greater or smaller, tending toward birth (*dàn shēng,* 诞生) or toward death (*sǐ wáng,* 死亡). Without pretending to concretely grasp the sense or meaning of any of these phenomena, we nevertheless perceive them, and we can trace their tendencies. All natural processes are constituted by very numerous intersecting and overlapping trends of continuing change. All changes are of this same nature and consist in moving between poles of yin and yang along intersecting axes in incalculably complex ways. For example, temperature, pressure, precipitation, wind-chill factor, etc., are constitutive of weather as one exemplary system of change. Like meteorological phenomena, all reality proceeds only from such complex interactions of yin and yang. The complexity, however, is further multiplied by the fact that there are innumerable systems of determination simultaneously operating in any given concrete situation. Since there is no overarching system envisaged as enclosing all the others, what emerges from their interaction is indeterminate or even *the* indeterminate ("l'indéterminé"). As in nature, so in the *Yijing*, the interplay of these different grids superimposed on one another is responsible for the constant improvisation of what Jullien calls "immanence" (39).

The diagram, unlike the myth, is the mark of a *transformation* rather than of a story or drama. It is made of factors rather than of actors. It is indicative of a tendency, even of an inexorable trend (for example, of the body towards aging and death), instead of being an etiological explanation in terms of origins and causes. It is used for purposes of detection and divination and avoids resorting to the invention of a fiction. It adheres to and immanently corresponds with the continual transformation of reality rather than imposing any transcendent sense on it all from a position outside (16). Such a simple, yet infinitely complex, indexing of reality constitutes the founding text for a civilization that has no need of an epic poem such as the *Iliad* and *Odyssey,* or the *Mahabharata*, at its literary origins. Neither does it need a divine Word of revelation such as the Bible. It needs no word at all. Below or before the threshold of language, this less-than-discursive pre-text opens upon an infinite, always yet-to-be-explored *space* of literature. This space, like the *Dao* (but also like Banchot's "neuter"), is other to every word that can be said.

The thinking of transcendence, as it can be found in apophatic thinkers from Plato to Franz Rosenzweig and Emmanuel Levinas, likewise opens itself to this proto-verbal alterity (called with inevitable impropriety *khôra*, "space," "interval," or "receptacle" by Plato) and endeavors to explore this wholly unfamiliar territory. Such thinking refuses the closure of any achieved sense. The thinking of immanence, too, in its way, strives to remain infinitely open but does not readily acknowledge any absolute otherness—understandably, since even this expression, like any other, is ridiculously inadequate for what it intends and can indicate only by its failure. Such an absolute otherness would seem to put a stop or set a limit to the absolutely infinite unfolding of immanence. By focusing on the correlations between all things, the thinking of immanence aims to be a revelation, instead, of the internal coherence of a process that englobes us together with everything else—just as nature does (17). And yet, even this immanence is not seamless, as might be thought: it, too, is not without negation or heterogeneity. It opens infinitely from within and unfolds towards no fixed ground or anchor. It opens upon a void.² By its relating to what is not, it takes on a shape homologous to the *quest* for transcendence. If it is not self-enclosed and complete, a totalized sphere of immanence, it cannot exclude what is other than it, nor therefore what in this sense transcends it. Thus immanence, being without the foundation of a beginning or an end, itself becomes practically a figure of transcendence and metamorphoses into a way of relating to absolute otherness. It does not posit the other as existing separately and outside itself but evolves from within in such an internal self-unfolding as cannot refuse or avoid unlimited relation to all and even to its own negation, to what it cannot define or encompass in any way as identical or as itself. Otherwise, immanence would become a reduction of all to sterile self-identity.

One interesting feature of the hexagram, as made up of two trigrams, is that there is no line (either broken or unbroken) at its center but rather a space. The center is empty. This embodies the spirit of the *Yijing*, for which true centrality is not occupied by any thing or substance but rather situates an ability to move and evolve in all directions: "Ripeness," in the sense of adapting to occasion and circumstance, "is all," we might say, echoing Edgar in *King Lear* (5.2.11). Each hexagram renders intelligible a phase in an ongoing process and so is essentially linked with all the others. However, there is no overall fixed or formal order. Instead, responding to a complex and always changing situation forms our spirit. The true reality is change itself and not the states that can be defined along the way by abstraction from the process as a whole. In this logic of renewal without end, nothing transcends the great process itself. The responsibility of humanity is to respond harmoniously to its summons and to solicitations within this irresistible process, which will be for us felicitous or pernicious (*faste* or *néfaste*, in Jullien's French) depending on our ability to effectively play our part in the great process of the real.

Here, too, Jullien draws very strong contrasts between the Chinese and the Greek/Christian worldviews (especially 53–54). The interaction of

---

2. Gilles Deleuze, *Le pli: Leibniz et le baroque* (Paris: Minuit, 1988) elaborates an analogous reflection on immanence opening upon the void in baroque aesthetics.

two principles, earth and heaven, yin and yang, which are contrary but nevertheless complementary poles, is the origin of all in China, as against the myth of the Creator with a personal Will in Western monotheism. The idea of a "Lord on high" (*Shàngdì* 上帝) akin to a personal God, disappears early on from Chinese tradition, towards the end of the second millennium before Christ with the advent of the Zhou dynasty (end of eleventh century). At this stage, anthropomorphic representations of God are replaced by *Tiān*, the sky, while ancient chthonic deities condense into the earth. From this point on, in Jullien's view, the entire effort of authors producing the Chinese classics is governed by a "coherent vision of reality as founded on reciprocity and immanence" ("une vision cohérente de la réalité, fondée sur la réciprocité et l'immanence," 54).

This way of differentiating Chinese from Western (Greek-Christian) thought is very clear and may seem incontrovertible; nevertheless, it still makes the difference consist in their controlling myths and images. Even if a certain layer of first-order, anthropomorphizing myth has been stripped away, the yin-yang duality still functions to some degree as an explanatory representation. Such representations, however, even by Jullien's own acknowledgment, cannot be the deepest and truest stratum of Chinese thought. Even just in terms of its traditional myths and figures themselves, the originary duality in Chinese thought has a remoter origin in non-being: "Non-being is the origin of heaven and earth" we learn already in the first chapter of the *Dao-de-jing* (1.3; cf. chapters 2, 11, 40). But this happens to be exactly what negative theology similarly informs us is the true sense (or non-sense) of Western creation myths as well. Critical apophatic philosophy insists that, for the West, too, the explicit stories, the narratives, are negated and reversed by their unsayable origin in the non-sense beyond any and every stated or representable sense.

I am willing to concede that the different mythologies are highly significant and define different cultural continents, but they do not finally determine different logics or realities so much as different ways and means of expression of common possibilities of thinking a common reality and even something beyond the reach of every culture's definitions, something "absolute." In other words, they point to that for which there is no word and yet that to which all alike remain related—indeed, to that *in* and through which all are related to one another. To this extent, what is most deeply intended by one culture is not simply out of reach for the others. And thus cultures are not inaccessible to—or exclusive of—one another. What is aimed at in common by both Chinese wisdom and Western apophatic thought is not fully expressible in either culture's vocabulary or in any encultured vocabulary whatsoever. In the end, only the failed attempts at expression are there as markers of the unsayable. Thus what is ultimately at stake in intercultural philosophy is not defining one culture or the other, whether comparatively or contrastively, but rather opening a dimension beyond culture—whether as ethical, religious, or metaphysical. These forms of expression and significance are so many registers of transcendence or so many ways of sounding what can be encountered at the limits of culture and language.

What both Chinese wisdom and Western apophatic thought alike succeed in doing is effectively to escape, or rather to neutralize, the sphere of immanence that culture creates. Culture tends ineluctably to become a self-referential system—another or a second-order realm of immanence separate from nature. Consequently, the task of apophatic thinking is to circumvent culture and all its concepts so as to expose what remains unsaid by—and unconceived in—them all. Logical thinking or critique, in contrast, by creating a sphere of immanence, is designed to exclude the ineffable Nothing of nature (even as Parmenides banishes non-being) and therewith also the ineffable relation to the All. This logic-based type of immanence is actually the abandon and suppression of nature as being beyond the range of the concept, and this disconnection and consequent self-enclosure of a thenceforth purely immanent nature is what apophatic thinking is called upon to reverse.

I bring Daoism and Western negative-theological thinking together in their critique of the logos and of the consequent loss of touch with nature as All. Jullien would presumably (at least in a first moment) resist this rapprochement, since he is loath to embrace and sometimes even to approach anything with an odor of theology. Many, if not most, philosophers today, in our secular age, are likely to share this view. But I aim to show why theology should, after all, be part of this conversation and why excluding it mutilates our tradition and drastically diminishes the resources with which we work. We need, now more than ever, to reappropriate theology at a critical historical juncture that evinces powerful propensities driving toward self-transformation into a post-secular age. This has been recognized even by staunch defenders of the secular project of modernity like Jürgen Habermas.[3] Our entering into post-secularity means that the secularist paradigm, which has dominated modern culture in its planetary expansion, will no longer be able to impose itself hegemonically—to the

---

3. Jürgen Habermas, "Ein Bewußtsein von dem, was fehlt," in *Ein Bewußtsein von dem, was fehlt: eine Diskussion mit Jürgen Habermas*, eds. Michale Reder and Josef Schmidt (Frankfurt a. M.: Suhrkamp, 2008), trans. Ciaran Cronin as *An Awareness of What Is Missing: Faith and Reason in a Post-Secular Age* (Cambridge, UK: Polity Press, 2010).

suppression of all the religious faiths and expressions that also make up such an important part of the cultural heritage of humanity. Culture is, after all, also a call to confront radical alterity. Humanity has, in this perspective, a vocation to imagine and to seek its other, and it has done so typically through imagining divinities.

Jullien sometimes insinuates that Chinese thought is free of theology or of onto-theology and, consequently, of the illusion of transcendence, and that it therefore offers a better model of thinking, one that the West inevitably fails to match.[4] This view, I submit, reflects a typical Parisian prejudice, a crypto-credo of the left bank (*rive gauche*). For what Jullien actually finds in Chinese thought is essentially the apophatic, which on my analysis is the hidden core of theology in its limitlessly self-critical form as negative theology. The most subtle and penetrating thinking of precisely the insights that Jullien is pursuing is to be found not by exclusion of theology but rather by following it without limit or reserve in its own self-critique, which becomes even self-erasure or self-exclusion at certain radical extremes such as may perhaps be represented most movingly by Simone Weil.[5]

As Derrida once pointed out, negative theology is a kind of thinking that, by its own account, does not exist. If negative theology does exist (and this remains always doubtful, since no positive assertion whatever regarding negative theology can be unambiguously warranted), it does so only as its own self-subversion and self-annulment. I read Jullien against himself in order to bring out what, for me, too, are the most important philosophical insights for us today, ones that are richly, even incomparably, expressed in traditional Chinese classics and wisdom literature. But this is, at the same time, also the deeper wisdom of the Occident in its negative-theological, apophatic traditions, or rather counter-traditions.

The strategy I recommend is to let onto-theological tradition deconstruct itself from within rather than pounding on it from without, like Nietzsche, with a hammer. This is what Jean-Luc Nancy, in effect, does in his *Deconstruction of Christianity*, taking crucial cues from the insights of Marcel Gauchet.[6] There is an embryo of this appreciation of Christianity's intrinsically self-deconstructing propensity already in Derrida, particularly in

---

4. One of many such pages is found in *La Grande image n'a pas de forme*, 139.
5. See chapter 12 of *On What Cannot Be Said*, vol. 2, 202–08.
6. Jean-Luc Nancy, *Déconstruction du christianisme*, vol. 1, *La Déclosion* (Paris: Galilée, 2005), vol. 2, *L'Adoration* (Paris: Galilée, 2010). Marcel Gauchet, *Le désenchantement du monde: Une histoire politique de la religion* (Paris: Gallimard, 1985).

his teasing encounters with negative theology.[7] But Jullien's usual construction of theology confines it practically to a cliché or catechism and is far from exploiting the unlimited potential inherent in its subtly profound and virtually inexhaustible archive.[8]

I enthusiastically follow and embrace Jullien's development of apophatic thinking on the basis of the Chinese classics. It is only the largely implicit meta-narrative about overcoming the hang-ups of our Western theological transcendence-obsessed civilization through an eradication of theology and/or onto-theology that I wish to contest. Theological thought belongs to our richest, most sophisticated, and most generous heritage. Precisely in the form of negative theology, critical theological reflection has anticipated and paralleled virtually every type of insight and intellectual maneuver that Jullien discovers in ancient Chinese tradition and elaborates in his own original ways. In its most radically apophatic representatives, negative theology is what we have to offer that can best complement the untold treasures of Chinese thought as Jullien discovers and uncovers them for us.

In culture at large, theology tends to be treated only in terms of the myths that it proffers for the masses, and especially for children, rather than in terms of its deep and subtle philosophical logic—which actually springs logic open to what cannot be logically comprehended. The nursery myths of religion are, of course, what are best known because, on the whole, we the people are childish. Consequently, it is these myths—most often rendered into the form of dogmas—with which we tend to be most familiar under the rubric of theology. This level of comprehension, moreover, is not to be spurned, since in certain respects the wisdom of children is the purest, the most whole and intact; it is not necessarily improved on but may in some ways even be diminished by increasing dialectical sophistication and philosophical reflectiveness. Nonetheless, mature thinkers cannot abide simply within the confines of these myths and their translations into dogma but are called upon, instead, to think critically beyond them.

---

7. See especially Jacques Derrida, "Comment ne pas parler: Dénégations," in *Psyché: Inventions de l'autre* (Paris: Galilée, 1987), 435–95, trans. as "Denials: How Not to Speak" in *Derrida and Negative Theology*, ed. H. Coward and T. Foshay (Albany: State University of New York Press, 1992).

8. Some qualification is due here in light of Jullien's recent work (especially *De l'intime*) in which Jullien does draw positively from theological insights found in Augustine, Gregory of Nyssa, and others.

IMMANENCE AND THE INEFFABLE

These conclusions can be confirmed with respect to another overarching structure of Jullien's *oeuvre* that also bears on articulating the relation between the manifest and its apophatic ground or *un*ground. In *Les transformations silencieuses,* Jullien expounds the silent transformations that are going on continuously and much more profoundly than any of the events and manifest movements that we identify with and foster (or resist) by our conscious and willful activity.[9] In order to profit from life's situations rather than being frustrated in our willful efforts, we have to learn to relate all our own conscious activity to this unarrestable, irresistible, natural change that is always underway within us no less than around us.

Jullien's *Silent Transformations* argues persuasively against all hypostatizations of a *subject* that undergoes this constant change. Between the poles that change into one another, all positing of metaphysical essences, identities, or substrates proves vain. However, it should also be acknowledged that such vanity is the predicament that comes along with language *tout court.* To pretend that these particular terms are false, as if there could be others that would be true, is a way of encouraging the delusion that there could be a language adequate to this reality of change. And just such an assumption should in reality find itself undermined by this analysis. Jullien deploys his powerful and accurate analyses of the pitfalls of the language of ontology as if it were about only the type of language generated by the special destiny of thinking the logos in Greece. Yet, more exactly, there is something about the predicament of human language per se in its relation to what we have called "nature" that is being revealed here.

Jullien sometimes seems to make it easy for us to choose the right way rather than a wrong (or ineffective) one. Chinese thought seems to be by and large in the right. However, this is so only relative to what stands in need of correction in Western thought. The very structural falsifications inhering in Western thinking, with its penchant for hypostatizing, are simply specific instances and incarnations of the inescapable erroneousness of thought and language as such. They may even be the more valuable for the conspicuousness of their error, for making obvious the fact that the truth of things *cannot* be what is literally said in language. A more metaphysically charged language, one which reifies and objectifies, may also be more poetic, more naïve and uncritical, and therefore also more illustrative of

---

9. *Les transformations silencieuses* (Paris: Grasset, 2009). This text is the default reference throughout this subsection.

the profound and mysteriously creative power of language in its relation to the real. Such language might be apt to reveal a dimension of ontological depth beyond that which is grasped by a merely pragmatic or taxonomical categorization of things.

Jullien warns against interpreting the *Dao* in a "mystical" sense, which would be to attribute some superior type of being to an object of mystical experience supposed to be standing behind all phenomenal appearances (52). But what of the apophatic mysticism, the mysticism of the *un*sayable that escapes ontology and, finally, even the categories of "experience"? Jullien seems to assume here that discriminations in words can make the difference between valid and invalid thinking. However, it is not finally words that determine the reality of the *Dao*. The reality envisaged by Chinese wisdom is beyond words—or at least is never exhausted by them. This is what negative theology, too, has maintained all through Western tradition.

Jullien sometimes takes precisely negative theology as his target, since it appears to be the way in which Western thinking recuperates its sense as the Unnameable ("l'Innommable"), even beyond all ruptures at the surface of the system of totalizing sense. As a system, *were* it that, negative theology would indeed be the apotheosis of metaphysical thinking. However, it can be—and more radically *is*—also just the opposite; namely, the most radical critique of metaphysics, and not least because it is an internal critique. If we take it as a fixed paradigm, it is the culmination of all that Jullien wishes to escape. He sardonically mocks the pathos of positing some great nothing to which we are beholden and perhaps devoted—and that may inspire apocalyptic dramatizations. His "silent transitions" are not to be confused with something ineffable ("Non qu'il y ait là quoi que ce soit d'ineffable," 78): they are rather constantly at work as the pure process of things, like aging, which takes place pervasively, ineluctably, without a word, in absolute immanence. And this, for him, is the marker of an essential difference from Western thinking.[10]

---

10. Although qualified by critical reflections elsewhere, the language of "la différence essentielle" is used by Jullien to differentiate between Greek and Chinese thought, for example, in *La propension des choses*, 194: its transforms include "divergence essentiel dans la conception de la nature" (222–23) and "se distinguent essentiellement" (228). Jullien critiques such oppositional language, but at the same time he needs it for the intelligibility of his discourse, which is based, finally, on comparison. This is comparison, of course, not of fixed entities or objects: it situates itself rather in the "between" of the "gap," that is, in the *entre* of the *écart*.

Nevertheless, to see Chinese thought portrayed as superior and as a better alternative to Western thinking, I believe, is a wrong way to read Jullien, even though admittedly his texts (especially some of the earlier ones) often seem to encourage such a *parti pris* or bias in favor of the East. Indeed, such a polarizing approach is typical of the binary way of thinking that is actually under relentless critique in his works. What Jullien's thought more profoundly recommends is not just another paradigm, the Chinese in place of the European, but rather a method of thinking in the gap (*écart*) between paradigms and so with a relative freedom from all paradigms rather than simple adherence to any one. This is the space, or rather the non-space, of the apophatic. Chinese thinking is not to be taken as the superior way of thinking but as a heuristic for helping us to move beyond the impasses inherent in our own traditional and habitual frameworks, whatever they may be.

We have seen that an "apophatic" or literally a negative way (*via negativa*) is articulated from the opening verse of the *Book of Dao*. This thinking is also accessible to the West, to the extent that the West is willing to release *itself*. No country or culture has a monopoly on such thinking: it resists and evades all identities whatsoever. There might even be some advantages to the reifying language of Western metaphysics, provided that we take it poetically. It, too, can be read as elaborately indirect. Its speaking of another world and of another (an allegorical) plane of meaning, different from the literal one, is not necessarily the end and goal of this thinking: it can also serve as a means of forcing thought beyond its acquired notions about "this world"—beyond all its complacencies and into the beyond, or the other, of thought.

Jullien himself places certain Western thinkers such as Heraclitus and Hegel outside the typical metaphysical framework of Occidental thought, which ignores the fact that opposites themselves pass directly into one another rather than successively occupying a third thing—namely, a subject—as it changes from young to old. The Platonic model of contraries-plus-being adds a third element in which all must participate in order to exist. But Heraclitus comes before the definition of Platonic and Aristotelian ontology, "the reign of Being and predication" (112) set in, and he recognizes that contradictories coincide: not just that hot and cold determine a changing subject, but that they are themselves identical or at least continuous, indeed without a third term—viz., the thing. Hegel, with his dialectical logic, comes at the end of this same history of metaphysics, and he, too, steps beyond it. He sees contraries themselves as changing into one another and therefore not only as successive determinations of an underlying thing or changing substance. Actually, even in the middle of this trajectory, the notion of *coincidentia oppositorum* was never forgotten by key apophatic thinkers of the West—signally Eriugena, Eckhart, and Cusanus.[11]

Alongside the myth of the freestanding subject—and, in fact, as just another transmogrification of that myth—stands the Western notion of time. In Jullien's interpretation, we make time artificially into the subject of the silent transformations that govern our lives and world. Yet time, like the thing, is but an invention of language, particularly of European language, through reification or hypostatization ("je crois que le 'temps' est une construction du langage, et plus particulièrement de la langue européenne," *Transformations silencieuses,* 125). We assign a fictive personage to these processes so as to give a name and face to the unthinkable—or at least unthought—process of silent transformation.

Even in Heidegger's destruction of Western metaphysics, dissolving being into time in *Sein und Zeit* (*Being and Time*), time becomes another myth and metaphysic replacing—but thereby only relaying—the myth of Being. This is, in fact, still of a piece with the mythical apotheosis of time that is imagined magisterially by Proust in his *À la recherché du temps perdu*, especially with its culminating volume *Le temps retrouvé* and literally with its *last word*: "temps." Giving time a consistency or existence of its own and a capacity to produce itself introduces a break into the continuity of change in nature, and precisely this discontinuity is what constitutes an event (*Transformations silencieuses,* 144).

Accordingly, the vocabulary of the *event*, so dear to the likes of Alain Badiou and Gilles Deleuze, appears as complicit in the same sort of mythmaking. It focuses on an explicit, evident manifestation of what in its full reality is a groundswell that, more authentically and efficaciously, calls to be apprehended in its deep, subterranean movement. It is the unbroken continuum of slow but relentless change that the crisis of the "event" makes visible only by privileging some specific point of view and assigning a meaning. The myth of the Last Judgment as the end of all is, in one way or another, recycled in all these Western conceptions and imaginations of time. The theology of the event (for example, John Caputo's) is meant to be a completely demythologized form of thinking, but it shows up in this light as in the grip of exactly what it strives to escape and negate—the mythological.[12] Thus the production of philosophical conceptualities such as that

---

11. See corresponding chapters of *On What Cannot Be Said*, vol. 1.

12. John Caputo, *The Weakness of God: A Theology of the Event* (Bloomington: Indiana University Press, 2006).

of the event, however steeped they may be in a deconstructive analysis of time, proves nevertheless to be still the perpetuation of a myth.

Jullien's notion of silent transformation models, instead, what I have tried to indicate under the rubric of the "non-concept." Typical Chinese wisdom urges acting by induction and working with the underlying tendencies of things rather than attempting to impose one's own will on them against the course of nature or the direction that things take in and of themselves. To be efficacious one has to intervene discretely "upstream," at the level of the antecedent conditions, in order to nudge a situation in the desired direction ("d'intervenir discrètement en amont, *au niveau des conditions*, pour infléchir la situation dans le sens souhaité," *Transformations silencieuses*, 190).

Jullien writes of a strategic use of concepts, since it is not exactly what they can comprehend as such, but only what they allude to without grasping it conceptually, that is their most potent content. Decisive is the concept that is lacking—lacking as an explicitly formulated and determinate content. This "concept which is lacking" ("concept qui manque") is the concept that remains and perdures at the bottom of things ("concept 'de fond,'" 192).

Taking Chinese thought as the paradigm of the true or right way to think, over against the Western model, with its postulates of creation, God, transcendence, etc., is not exactly what Jullien wants to recommend in the end either. As already noted, he proposes rather to think in the gap or interval (*écart*) between cultures. This, as I see it, is the apophatic space that cannot be definitively or adequately determined by any cultural vocabulary. It cannot be simply that change is the true nature of things, while transcendence is merely a false illusion. All such determinate approaches to conceiving the All are inevitably inadequate attempts. The various conceptualities invented by different cultures need to be evaluated as to what aspects of the All they endeavor to articulate or convey and which ones, in contrast, they suppress or ignore. Something can be learned from all of them in our effort to survey the territory of human culture and thought oriented to the *all* that is and is not. This All is the origin of inexhaustibly original approaches or ways—to the extent that any of them do aim to relate to the all in their own ways and out of the singularity of their own situation and experience. Apophatic thought is committed to the attempt to think this all.[13]

---

13. I make this argument concerning Western tradition in *A Philosophy of the Unsayable*, chapter 2: "In the Hollow of Pan's Pipe: Unsayability and the Experience of Truth and Totality."

THE MATTER OF METHOD IN INTERCULTURAL PHILOSOPHY

Jullien's construction of an intercultural dialogue between Western philosophy and classical Chinese wisdom runs parallel in crucial respects to the work of David Hall and Roger Ames in the Anglo-Saxon world. They voice many of the same objections to imposing Western notions of metaphysical transcendence on Chinese thought. Their objections are directed, in the first place, against the purportedly misleading use of words such as "heaven," "truth," and "freedom" for translating key characters (hànzì, 漢字) of the Chinese classics. The principal objection is that this introduces a wholly inappropriate "transcendental pretense" into a type of thinking that thoroughly ignores such transcendence.[14] Chinese thought is then presented rather as an alternative to the dominant metaphysical tendencies of Western thought that have seemed to so many in postmodern times to have led the West into a cul-de-sac. We stand to gain a richer perspective on the peculiar virtues and liabilities of Jullien's work through comparison with such English-speaking and English-writing counterparts, who are also in some ways competitors with him in pursuing what is in many respects a common project. The powerful motivation and necessity of such a project, as well as the limits of its validity as determined by certain subtle yet crucial nuances, can be made to stand out in relief by such comparison.

Hall and Ames have retranslated some of the Chinese classics into a more philosophically critical language that avoids what they consider to be the pitfalls of the earlier translations. For instance, they translate *dao* not as "way" but as "way-making."[15] This is an interesting and ingenious translation that usefully brings out certain essential emphases of the *Dao*. It avoids the static fixity of the nominative case, employing instead the gerundive to convey an actively verbal meaning. Nevertheless, this is but one aspect of the *Dao*, and this translation is but one possible interpretation among many. Somewhat perversely, such critically interpretive translations of key terms can steer the reader by the specific critical vision of the philosophers who are doing the translating even more peremptorily than is the case with the more traditional translations. A.C. Graham, in effect, reproves Hall and Ames for failing to clearly distinguish translation from

---

14. David L. Hall and Roger T. Ames, *Anticipating China: Thinking through the Narratives of Chinese and Western Culture* (Albany: State University of New York Press, 1995), xiv.

15. Roger T. Ames and David L. Hall, *Daodejing: Making This Life Significant* (New York: Ballantine Books, 2003).

exposition.[16] The earliest, most obvious and traditional translations have the merit at least of directly presenting the concrete poetic images like "way" or "sky" that correspond most literally to the sensory content of the Chinese word-characters: they thereby open an unrestricted range of further associations without arbitrarily imposing controls on interpretation.

A competent reader has to understand that, in reading words coming from another culture, their own usual assumptions do not wholly apply, not at least in quite the same way: the very same words are liable to operate rather differently. For any cultivated reader of English, a word such as "heaven," as used in anything but a specifically biblical context, is already automatically placed within quotation marks. Such a reader knows that the word "heaven" can mean "sky" just as well as an eschatological kingdom of the blessed. Its acceptation as "sky" is a common meaning in many Western traditions, including the Greek, for example, in astronomical treatises *De caelo*—"On the Heavens"—beginning from Aristotle's work on the subject, which spawned countless commentaries under the same heading all through the Middle Ages. Of course, taken as the inanimate physical region conceived by modern physics, neither is "sky" adequate to the Greek sense of οὐρανός. Used as a poetic and a sensory image, "heaven" can in effect be more open to the multiplicity of interpretations than is a carefully crafted philosophical concept designed to guard against certain presumable misinterpretations. In fact, such an expression as "heaven," laden with both sensible reference and metaphysical resonance, is vague and open to very different ideas and interpretations hailing from many diverse cultural contexts. That is its virtue. Hall and Ames themselves, and Graham alike, often call attention to the characteristic vagueness of Chinese characters. Any particular translation is thus already an interpretation, and in the end the work of reading has to be left to the reader. The pretension to define exactly what such a word means—inevitably according to a certain philosopher's understanding of it—may be more dangerous and deleterious to the spirit of Chinese thought than simply letting the concrete poetic image play freely, without attempting to interpret and delimit it.

Hall and Ames are dedicated to the mission of freeing sinology from what they take to be its history of Jesuitical hijacking. They substitute a pragmatist, process-philosophy framework as more appropriate and in tune

---

16. A.C. Graham, "Reflections and Replies," in *Chinese Texts and Philosophical Contexts: Essays Dedicated to Angus C. Graham*, ed. Henry Rosemont Jr. (La Salle, IL: Open Court, 1990), 288.

with the classical Chinese culture that they are attempting to preserve and convey. By such means, they claim to overcome the distortions of past, especially ecclesiastical mediations of tradition. This is the kind of narrative that gives academics a purpose and a mission, yet this precisely raises the question of who is really the missionary here. Hall and Ames impose their own assumptions about which assumptions contemporary English-speaking readers are going to make. This is not without pretenses and risks of its own. However much one would like to objectively represent the hermeneutic horizon of one's own culture, there are inevitably ideological biases that play into one's interpretive acts.

Thus, I would myself express the same reservation or question in relation to Hall and Ames's work that I do with regard to Jullien's. Both projects are based largely on descriptive typologies defining differences, or, to be more precise, "contrasts" (Hall and Ames) and "gaps" ("écarts," for Jullien) between two types of thought and their respective supporting worldviews. But such description is itself never free from the presuppositions of at least one, if not both, of the cultures being described as objects, and it tends to set them up as exclusive alternatives. Such description remains culturally and historically determined, and it is only within a movement or dynamic interaction that the two cultures can reciprocally disclose one another. Hall and Ames (like Jullien) realize this and, accordingly, they renounce all pretensions to "transcendence." But once the vocabulary in question is appreciated as mobile and dynamic, it is not clear how any terms, including "transcendence," can be excluded as having no applicability at all. Other researchers and translators find that this particular term *is* applicable and even essential from their own angles of approach. One could definitively exclude such vocabulary, furthermore, only if one securely possessed the finally correct vocabulary to put in its place. One could, of course, maintain that such vocabulary is in any case incorrect because it cannot possibly mean in China what it means in the West. But that is true of any terms whatsoever. Even within a given culture, sameness of sense for any given expression is impossible to determine absolutely or unequivocally.

What (I fear) is being excluded in excluding transcendence is also at least certain expressions or evocations of a dimension of the unfathomable and incalculable—even of the "formless," which, as Hall and Ames and Jullien concur, most certainly does have its place in Chinese thinking. What the exclusion actually succeeds in discarding is only a flat and unself-critical Western notion of transcendence. But this notion is itself a construction that misrepresents a very large portion of the Western thinking that has taken place under the aegis and inspiration of "transcendence." Levinas and Heidegger and Kierkegaard, for example, are each in their own ways philosophers of transcendence, and they have predecessors among the most radical of philosophical thinkers all the way back in the tradition, notably in Plotinus as thinker of the good beyond being (for Levinas) and in Parmenides as thinker of being itself in its transcendence of all worldly beings (for Heidegger).[17]

The method of Hall and Ames, like that of Jullien, threatens to eclipse a crucial aspect of Chinese wisdom because the vocabulary for it is compromised by its status in certain Western debates. In the last analysis, these approaches must rely on the apophatic, which proceeds from and is anchored to the source of truth or wisdom beyond words and beyond all possibility of classification and description. Instead of putting all our effort into disputing which is the right term or the better description, as if we could legislate what is or is not appropriate, we should concern ourselves with how to take all terms and descriptions as partial and provisional. Surely, this is closer to the spirit of Chinese wisdom and also to its nearest Western analogues in vision and method and to their implied theories of language. Keeping open the possibility of further choices as occasioned by other angles of approach and (inevitably) appropriation is more decisive than the choice of one current English expression over another. Even the traditional Confucian "rectification of names" (*zhèng míng*, 正名) is read by Hall and Ames themselves as entailing continual readjustment and fine-tuning of language, rites, and music.[18]

This methodological point is inextricable from the issue of orientation to transcendence versus immanence as underlying the vision of one culture or the other. Are we simply translating forms specific to one culture versus another, or is the object of translation ultimately the formlessness that many types of thinking, including Chinese classical thought, intend? Immanence versus transcendence has all along been the underlying issue and overriding concern of Hall and Ames in their "contrast" between Western and Chinese mentalities.[19] Western interpretations, in their view, have systematically

---

17. These thinkers, together with others such as Kierkegaard, are presented very acutely as philosophers of transcendence by Merold Westphal, *Transcendence and Self-Transcendence: On God and the Soul* (Bloomington: Indiana University Press, 2004).

18. Roger T. Ames and David L. Hall, *Thinking through Confucius* (Albany: State University of New York Press, 1987), 268–75.

19. One of the best and most comprehensive treatments of the whole debate on transcendence and its relevance to Chinese thought is part 3 ("Transcendence and Immanence as Cultural Cues") of Hall and Ames's *Thinking from the Han: Self, Truth, and Transcendence*

distorted Chinese thought by importation of transcendental schema into a type of thinking that ignores them and that in its own nature is worked out entirely on a plane of immanence. This alternative between transcendence and immanence, moreover, they deem to be in important ways a transform of the polarities of unity and plurality, or of oneness and multiplicity. According to the self-styled revisionary narrative of Hall and Ames, the West has typically given priority to the former and China to the latter term of each of these pairs in their cosmologies and in their ethical approaches to acting within the world. Accordingly, the irreducible duality of yin and yang resists being brought under any overarching structure of unity that would transcend difference. Such a synthetic, unifying type of thinking for Hall and Ames is characteristic of the West and its inveterate transcendentalism and has no place whatever in classical Chinese thinking. However, Ames is also a formidable critic of Western secular, individualistic culture, which is condemned in comparison with the holistic thinking and communitarianism of Confucian role ethics. So it seems that not oneness per se but only misguided and restrictive applications of it are rejected as problematic.

In fact, wholeness (or what Jullien calls "globality," "*la globalité*") *is* crucial to Chinese thinking. However, it is not conceived of by Hall and Ames as transcending the play of relations between things: it cannot be encompassed and grasped from the outside. Yet, likewise, even in the best Western models, the transcendent wholeness in question is not to be represented as something *else*, another *thing* alongside the set of all things: its transcendence is more subtle than that, not really a "thing" at all. In the classic theistic, transcendentalist model, which Hall and Ames insist must be rejected in approaching China, true unity and wholeness are found only in God, who is the inconceivable par excellence. God is not a *thing* over and above others: God cannot be positively conceived at all, neither as one nor as many, neither as *an* individual (distinct from others) nor as something *wholly* other than an individual. God is other with respect to all representations, whether of individuals or of anything else—and even this statement is nothing but another way of representing "him"! For Hall and Ames, "That God should not be contingent upon the world entails that he be disjoined in some way from the world" (*Thinking from the Han*, 225), but this is erroneous in its conceiving of God as standing alongside other entities and thus, nevertheless, as on the same ontological plane, however distant and "disjoined."

Eriugena, Eckhart, and Cusanus, together with Maimonides and Ibn

---

in Chinese and Western Culture (Albany: State University of New York Press, 1998).

al-'Arabi along with many others among the profounder Christian, Muslim, and Jewish theologians, explicitly correct this inadequate, catechism view that God could be conceived of as an Other or as separate with respect to the world. Yet, "he" cannot be conceived of simply as one and the same as the world either, certainly not if the world is taken just as a univocal "thing." The (negative) theological truth is that God cannot be conceived in any adequate way at all but only analogically through the relations that human beings construct with one another and with the universe. However, these constructions are not necessarily humans' own alone; nor can such constructions fully grasp themselves: they may also be conceived as given from beyond any calculable human capacity. That God should not be contingent on the world entails rather that the world relate to God (or the Dao) as Other. This is to relate to a Dao that is absolute and in relation to which alone it makes sense to understand the world as contingent.

Hall and Ames are only comparing world pictures, and their comparison is valid only within the frame of the age of the world picture (to employ this Heideggerian designation for the modern age). Yet, what is truly transcendent about thinking, including theological thinking, is not its commitment to one world picture or another but rather its capacity to transcend and transform every picture of the world, including its own, and thus to renounce, or at least to relativize, the very representational mode itself that consists in picturing the world.

Even Hall and Ames's talk of "a concept of divinity as a direct extension of the spirituality of particular human beings" (*Thinking from the Han*, 280) pretends to know too much about divinity: it erases the dimension that transcends conceptualization, the dimension from which representation and conceptualization of divinity draw their indefinite sense, allowing for the aura of the numinous. Hall and Ames attempt to define divinity in terms of human being as "theomorphic" (265). This is not without parallel in Western religiosities, notably in the Christian intuition of God as incarnate in humans and especially in Christianity's numerous gnostic and theosophical elaborations and spin-offs. Yet the pretense to reduce divinity to the immanent and familiar works against the spirit of the deeper apophatic wisdom of both the East and the West. This wisdom refers us and our immanence, instead, to the unknown that transcends our powers of conceptualization. Fundamentally, Chinese philosophy is not concerned with representing divinity or the world, but with relating to all that is and without restrictions—and thus to transcending all fixed and finite representations.

Comparative philosophy is at an impasse over transcendence because it deals with *representations* of transcendence, whereas what is really at stake in the question of transcendence is the unrepresentable. No representation of transcendence is appropriate to Chinese thought, and yet nothing is so important to this wisdom as what transcends representation. And this goes for Western thought, too, especially when it is considered in its wholeness and thus as including heterodox and esoteric currents, as well as orthodox formulations, of the apophatic. The predicament of philosophical—and, indistinguishably, religious—thinking across cultures is played out in the inexhaustibly productive impasse of apophasis. This experience of the limits of verbal expression belongs irrevocably to the human predicament and to philosophical reflection on it.

Hall and Ames draw the same contrast between transcendence-oriented and immanence-based worldviews also *within* Western tradition. They take the postulate of oneness, or more exactly of a "single-order cosmos," to be characteristic of what they call the "second problematic thinking" that arises with Plato and Aristotle. This kind of thinking becomes dominant, even "orthodox," in Western philosophy, giving it its cast as "rational," "logical," and "causal" in character. This cast of thinking is responsible, according to Hall and Ames's narrative, for the inability of Western students to understand Chinese thought in an appropriate manner: often Westerners are prevented thereby even from being able to recognize Chinese thought as essentially philosophical. Hall and Ames maintain that the pre-Socratic philosophers, in contrast, particularly the *physiologoi,* followed by the Sophists, were receptive to the irrationality or anarchy of nature, as well as to its irreducible plurality. This "first problematic thinking" in their jargon, is rather "aesthetic," or "analogical" and "correlative," in character. Such thinking was suppressed, they maintain, early on in the West, with the ascendency of the Platonic-Aristotelian paradigm, but it presents a discarded alternative that, by virtue of its inherent affinity, is apt to allow a much more satisfactory intercultural approach to Chinese philosophy in its own proper intent and meaning. Pre-Socratic philosophy thus serves as a "bridge tradition" purportedly enabling Hall and Ames to come much closer to understanding classical Chinese philosophy than is possible when our attempt to approach it is based on the assumptions of mainstream Western rationalism.

My method agrees entirely with that of Hall and Ames in finding neglected strands within one's own cultural tradition (for me, these are especially apophatic strands) that bear affinities with the foreign tradition that the researcher is attempting to engage: such strands can serve as bridges for cross-cultural understanding. However, Hall and Ames's schema privileging plurality over oneness and difference over unity does not seem to me necessarily to allow us to approach Chinese thought in a more engaging way than is otherwise the case. Surely, unity or oneness, as manifest in the harmony of a whole, is just as important as plurality in a Chinese perspective. The unity in question, naturally, is unity in the sense of globality, or the potential unity of unlimited further relations, and thus unity that cannot be grasped and mastered by thought in a unitary concept. Neither can it be defined in a formula. Yet it is unity that is real and efficacious in determining one's whole orientation within a constantly changing world. It can be experienced and must be played along with in order to help harmonize the whole process of things. Thus, there seems to be something that is, if not arbitrary, then at least one-sided about pitting multiplicity against unity rather than accepting their inseparability as poles in the process of determining the whole of the real beyond our ability to conceive it by either the one conceptuality or the other—or indeed by any conceptuality at all.

The drive to demonstrate that one has the best *description*, or at least a more accurate one, belongs to a sort of competition perfectly typical of Western academics, but not of Chinese sages. It seems, at moments at least, to have blinded the Western philosophers to a deeper insight into the ultimate impossibility—from an apophatic point of view that is at least as Chinese as it is Western—of adequate description and representation. After all, the real per se asserts itself most unmistakably only in overturning and belying our representations, even the most accurate ones—in fact, especially those, and all the more radically. This is, after all, well known to Hall and Ames, since they programmatically renounce the pretension that they could "get it right" and propose, rather, simply to "get on with it." They do so above all *pragmatically*, with explicit appeal to American pragmatist philosophy, especially in the form in which it has been transmitted by Richard Rorty. Their aim, they say, "is not to *tell it like it is*; we merely wish to present a narrative which is interesting enough and plausible enough to engage those inclined to join the conversation" (*Anticipating China,* xix–xx; 119).

I wholeheartedly agree with Hall and Ames that being interesting is a crucial criterion for our selection of philosophical theories and narratives to adopt—and one that is hardly separable even from the question of truth. I understand myself to be concerned, above all, with forestalling the elimination or reduction to unintelligible nonsense of what is most interesting in our own intellectual tradition, starting from metaphysics and theology. For me, theology is at the head of the list of discourses in danger of extinction today because they are no longer appropriately understood and are commonly replaced by impostors. Hence my agreement with those many scholars who do find subtle types of thinking of transcendence to be present in and often even to be indispensable keys for access to Chinese wisdom.[20] There are even some, such as Yong Huang and those whom he cites, including Julia Ching, Kelly Clark, P.H. Huang, and the Cheng brothers (Hao and Yi) in the Song and Ming dynasties in the eleventh century, who find in Confucius and Confucian tradition serious forms of "god-talk" or theology. This begins in pre-Confucian sources, the Book of Documents and the Book of Poems, and can be found in many places in the Analects themselves.[21]

CHINA AND THE SENSE OF TRANSCENDENCE

Beyond simply deciphering the canonical texts, Benjamin Schwartz sifts the anthropological and archeological archives in order to discover a sense of transcendence—of straining beyond the actually realized and objective world—in classical Confucianism and even more strongly in Daoism. This "strain toward transcendence" entails "critical, reflective questioning of the actual and a new vision of what lies beyond."[22] Schwartz proffers this enactment of transcendence as the spiritual-intellectual revolution that in different forms characterizes the epoch-making cultural breakthroughs of the "Axial Age." He thus adopts Karl Jaspers's famous notion of a decisive historical pivot in the middle of the first millennium before our era, around 500 BC but also in the broadest terms between 800 and 200 BC, to a new stage and level of civilization, particularly in the most highly developed of the world's cultures in Israel, Greece, India, and China. A communication with the gods is characteristic of this age of extraordinary cultural effervescence

---

20. An interesting sampling of such scholarship is found in the special issue of *The Journal of Chinese Philosophy* 29/1 (2002) devoted to "God and the Tao." It includes pieces by Chung-Ying Cheng, Joseph Grange, Robert Cummings Neville, Michael Lafargue, James Behuniak Jr., Linyu Gu, and Masato Mitsuda. More recent contributions of Wolfgang Kubin and Eske Møllgaard and others are discussed in the next-to-last subsection of this chapter, the one on "New Debates."

21. Yong Huang, "Confucian Theology: Three Models," *Religion Compass* 1/4 (2007): 455–78.

22. Benjamin I. Schwartz, "The Age of Transcendence," *Daedalus* 104 (1975): 1–7, citation, 3. See, further, Schwartz's *The World of Thought in Ancient China* (Cambridge, MA: Harvard University Press, 1985).

and advance to a higher conception and consciousness of life, with which humanity, as we know it, is born.[23]

In the case of China, Schwartz argues that the mythic past has not survived, not as well as in Mesopotamia, with *Enuma Elish* and the *Epic of Gilgamesh*, or in Greece—with Homer and Hesiod, the pre-Socratics, and the tragedians—or in India, with the *Rig Veda*. Yet in China it is still possible to discern a mythic past that has been largely suppressed in the earliest canonical literature, specifically in the *Book of Documents* (*Shu Jing*) and the *Book of Odes* (*Shi Jing*). Just behind Confucius and Laozi and this classical literature of China lies a transcendent vision expressed mythically as interaction between gods and humans.[24]

The starkly anthropomorphizing modes of representation typical of Western mythology are not very much in evidence in the classic Chinese texts as we have them. Yet a correspondence of the human order with the heavenly and divine is undeniable and indispensable to the whole cast of Chinese thinking. The Chinese rational order of things is non-reductive; it includes rather than supplants the gods. As Schwartz writes in a companion article, "What we have is the image of an all-embracing and inclusive order which neither negates nor reduces to some one ultimate principle that which is presumed to exist. . . . It is a synthetic rather than an analytic conception of order. The spirits of nature and the ancestral spirits are not banished."[25] The fact that "the gods of mountains and winds, the presiding deities of the constellations and of the earth, are ever present," even without achieving the degree of anthropomorphization familiar, for example, from Greece, indicates that they are less subject to objectification. They remain closer to their apophatic inspiration as figures for mysteries that transcend representation.

Thus, taking this apophatic sort of transcendence into account, it becomes clear that China should be viewed not in isolation or as funda-

---

23. Karl Jaspers, *Vom Ursprung und Ziel der Geschichte* (Munich: Piper, 1949), trans. Michael Bullock as *The Origin and Goal of History* (London: Routledge and Keegan Paul, 1953). For multiple perspectives on the current relevance of this topic, see Robert N. Bellah and Hans Joas, eds., *The Axial Age and Its Consequences* (Cambridge, MA: Belknap Press of Harvard University Press, 2012).

24. This hidden past is illuminated revealingly from archeological evidence anew by David N. Keightley, *These Bones Shall Rise Again: Selected Writings on Early China* (Albany: State University of New York Press, 2014).

25. Schwartz, "Transcendence in Ancient China," *Daedalus* 104 (1975): 57–68, citation 59.

mentally different and incommensurable but rather alongside other cultures, particularly those of the Axial Age, as contributing to illuminating the human adventure in history.²⁶ Such comparison brings to light the capacity of humanity to re-create itself in relation to another world or order of existence, and thereby to achieve a kind of heightened or transcendent life in imagination or in ritual and religion. This approach to affirming transcendence in Chinese tradition has had considerable resonance.²⁷

Heiner Roetz, *Die chinesische Ethik der Achsenzeit,* supports this view through philologically exacting studies. He attributes the epoch-making and humanity-founding capacity of self-reflectiveness eminently to Chinese philosophy of the axial period. In China, as elsewhere, a sense of transcendence is a precondition for any nonconventional ethics ("Mit der Transzendenz ist eine Instanz eingeführt, die für eine nicht nur konventionelle Ethik unverzichtbar ist").²⁸ Roetz, furthermore, excavates the intellectual roots of the still widespread refusal among sinologists, including neopragmatists such as Hall and Ames, to acknowledge the role of transcendence in ancient Chinese, and particularly in Confucian, philosophy. He traces this attitude to Hegel's and Max Weber's "misconstrual of the basic character of ancient Chinese philosophies such as classical Confucianism" ("Sowohl der weberianische als auch der neo-pragmatische Diskurs verkennen den Grundcharakter der alten chinesischen Philosophie wie des klassischen Konfuzianismus," 12). According to Roetz, these interpretations wrongly answer in the negative the question of whether ancient China knows transcendence in the form of context-transcending reflexivity ("ob das alte China Transzendenz oder kontextüberschreitende Reflexivität kenne," 12). For Roetz, classical Chinese thought takes precisely this step and does so as one of the leading cultures of the axial time. Roetz writes, therefore, of the "universalistic potential"

---

26. See Eric Ziolkowski, "Axial Age Theorizing and the Comparative Study of Religion and Literature," *Literature and Theology* 28/2 (2014): 129–50, special issue on "China and the West in Dialogue," eds. David Jasper and Wang Hai.

27. From the beginning of his "Introduction: The Axial Age Beaktroughs—Their Characteristics and Origins," Shmuel Eisenstadt acknowledges Schwartz's work and focuses on the "strain toward transcendence" through "reflexivity." S.N. Eisenstadt, ed., *The Origins and Diversity of the Axial Age* (Albany: State University of New York Press, 1986).

28. Heiner Roetz, *Die chinesische Ethik der Achsenzeit. Eine Rekonstruktion unter dem Aspekt des Durchbruchs zu postkonventionellem Denken* (Frankfurt a. M.: Suhrkamp, 1992), 42, trans. as *Confucian Ethics of the Axial Age: A Reconstruction under the Aspect of the Breakthrough toward Postconventional Thinking* (Albany: State University of New York Press, 1993).

of ancient Chinese culture of the axial time (17). Roetz does underscore, however, that "transcendence is not to be understood primarily in a *formal* sense" (" 'Transzendenz' nicht primär *formal* zu fassen ist," 43), not therefore in terms of representations.[29] Transcendence is not only signaled in primordial Chinese culture by the idea of "heaven's mandate" (*Tiān míng*) in the *Book of Documents*. The transcendence that Schwartz finds, for example, in Confucius is especially a "transcendence inward" that brings a subjective focus to moral and spiritual life ("Transcendence in Ancient China," 63). The concept of the Confucian superior man or gentleman (*jūn zǐ*, 君子) and the virtue of *rén* (仁, benevolence) are based on interiorized forms of absolute value that can give a normative orientation to the world of human affairs and conduct. All these representations are, of course, provisional and not adequate as representations: they serve, rather, to indicate a mystery that they cannot encompass or exhaust. There can be no definitive interpretation of such ultimate values. Discussions and even disputes among scholars can be fruitful for calling our attention to the innumerable aspects and nuances that inevitably escape us in one approach or the other. But a blanket proscription on employing terms such as "transcendence" insinuates the kinds of pretensions to scientificity and objective knowing that are actually being targeted as needing to be undermined by detractors and proponents alike of transcendence.

The error I am pointing to in Hall and Ames's and in others' polemic against transcendence as it relates to Chinese thought is simply that in campaigning for its exclusion they fall back into the delusion of objectively discriminating between right and wrong forms of imagery for the formless. They take language as able to truly describe things as they are—or, at least, as they *are not*. In doing so, such researchers are working only at the level of representations. Again, in his most recent (re)statement in chapter 5 of *Confucian Role Ethics: A Vocabulary*, Ames still identifies transcendence with "some underlying permanent structure" rather than with the formless, the

---

29. Roetz has extended his views with extensive critical reference to Jullien and also to some of his critics more recently in "Die Chinawissenschaften und die chinesischen Dissidenten. Wer betreibt die 'Komplizenschaft mit der Macht,' " *Bochumer Jahrbuch zur Ostasienforschung* 35 (2013): 47–80. While acknowledging that Jullien sometimes achieves subtle analyses, for example, of Chinese aesthetics, Roetz condemns the compulsiveness of his binary system of interpretation, which wins out in the end. A translation of Roetz's essay is now available in *Transcendence, Immanence, and Intercultural Philosophy*, eds. Nahum Brown and William Franke (New York: Palgrave Macmillan, 2016).

structureless, the unrepresentable.[30] He reiterates his and Hall's definition of "strict transcendence" as asserting "an independent and superordinate principle" that is "irrelevant for an understanding of classical Chinese cosmology" (212). He stresses that the Way is rather always thoroughly "interdependent" with human activity and relations. However, while all representations of the Way are certainly drawn always only from human experience, how can this entitle us to deny the possibility of its transcendence of the human? We run the risk in that case of implicitly assuming the Way to be *merely* a human representation (or to be produced by human representations) and that all that can be known about it can be known by knowing the human. This entails the further risk of treating the human as some kind of known quantity, in effect, turning it into a sort of substance, which is typical of the sort of secularist treatment that Ames is determined to avoid and convincingly critiques.[31] In fact, the interdependence of humanity and the Way, as expressed in Chinese classics, is key to opening the dimension of the Unknown that is effectively explored by various vocabularies of transcendence in Western philosophical and theological tradition. Likewise, such words as "Dao" and "heaven" in Chinese tradition are essential for pointing to what remains always still unexhausted and is elicited by the metaphorical languages drawn from empirical, finite, human life.

Under Hall and Ames's influence, Steven Burik embraces the logic that denies the pertinence of metaphysical transcendence to classical Chinese thought, and he turns to metaphor as an alternative to transcendence (rather than as an expression of it, as in my view):

> In principle, the possibility of a transcendent creator or creative principle is denied in the classical Chinese worldview. In its place, or rather as some other way of seeing things, we look for generation of meaning from the inside. The birthing metaphors abundant in Daoism are one way of seeing the emergence of meaning. These metaphors also imply that there are always

---

30. Roger T. Ames, *Confucian Role Ethics: A Vocabulary* (Hong Kong: Chinese University Press, 2011), 211.

31. In *Confucian Role Ethics,* Ames emerges as an eloquent advocate in the name of Confucianism of a "human centered religiousness as the highest expression of personal cultivation" (92). On this account, and in defiance of typical prejudices of secular modernity, Ames fervently affirms that "religiosity is not only the root of the flourishing community and the seed from which it grows, but is most importantly its matter and its radiant flower" (92).

traces of otherness in the self, each and every mother is also a daughter; the process is continuous.³²

Burik (and he is representative in this regard) does not consider that talk of a Creator can be based theologically on nothing but traces or effects in creatures. This is the reason why Robert Neville argues against Hall and Ames's "strict transcendence" that none of their examples, including God, the Unmoved Mover, Platonic Ideas, and the atom in classical physics can be "explained in itself" but only in its "explanatory function" because "one can say nothing about them apart from their functions in founding the cosmos."³³ Thomas Aquinas's *Summa Theologica* begins by explaining that there is no knowledge of the Creator but only of his creatures as bearing the trace of the divine otherness and the nothingness from which they are created. By the apophatic logic of *Summa Theologica,* question 13, the Creator is a figure for this trace of otherness. The formless can exclude no form or figure as in some way its image or disguise. As Pseudo-Dionysius the Areopagite insisted, the best analogies for God are things such as mud and worms, since they make the radical disanalogy on which all analogies for God are based the more evident (*Celestial Hierarchy* 141b). Greater accuracy of description is in this case paradoxically self-defeating.

When Hall and Ames translate "*Dao*" as "way-making" rather than simply as "way," this serves to bring out some crucial aspects of "*Dao*," but even they would not want to assert that this is the *right* translation. They can argue only for its usefulness in a certain cultural context, which is itself susceptible to different and changing interpretations. So rather than rejecting the "metaphysical" views, it would be more accurate to speak of supplementing them. There is no one correct view, but only an open series of approximations. Even as they come closer in some respects, Hall and Ames inevitably end up further removed in others. And we must ask: to or from what or whom? This, too, is all conjectural and relative. But the experience of absoluteness and of hierarchical ordering is to be respected just as much as are other experiences. No determinate hierarchy and no formulation of the absolute can last definitively, but neither can the absolute exclusion of such determinations. That what is right is relative to context is

---

32. Steven Burik, *The End of Comparative Philosophy and the Task of Comparative Thinking: Heidegger, Derrida, and Daoism* (Albany: State University of New York Press, 2009), 164.

33. Robert Cummings Neville, *Boston Confucianism: Portable Tradition in the Late-Modern World* (Albany: State University of New York Press, 2000), 149–50.

only a partial and provisional truth, too, and hardly valid as an interdiction against *seeking* the absolute—even absolutely: such seeking can itself become in its own right a kind of realized absolute of will or desire.

To acknowledge that "all language and thus all reference is situational" (Burik, 122) must not blot out the vision of an unspoken, unspeakable language that is suggested by Daoist and Western source texts alike. A language that does not as such exist may, from another point of view, be more in existence than any language that is empirically manifest. Saying that "there is nothing other than transformation" (124) can be correct within the limits of a certain interpretation of "there is" that makes everything come under the sway of transformation from the moment that it "is." But the greater challenge of comparative philosophy is to relate to what no "there is" or "il y a" or "es gibt" or "yŏu" (有) can get a grip on in any cultural terms. And indeed this is what the founding texts of traditions both East and West are gesturing toward: that which exceeds cultural categories and language, metaphysical language no more nor less than empirical language.

Burik does say that he is against metaphysical or negative theological interpretations only when they claim to be the only or the right interpretations, but that is exactly what "negative theology," as the relentless and unconditional *unsaying* of itself, is designed to avoid. Beyond this, negative theology is the originary thinking of *Ereignis* (to speak like Heidegger), of what happens beyond and apart from all linguistic artifices. Intended here is an event that is more originary in belonging already to being's self-unfolding before any classifying, categorizing logos gets a hold of it. Exposing it can be sought by subtracting oneself or one's own (almost inevitably linguistic) activity from the situation that unfolds around one. As Maurice Blanchot, from his angle of approach to the absolutely original, put it in *L'Arrêt de mort* (1977): "The extraordinary begins the moment that I stop myself" ("L'extraordinaire commence au moment où je m'arrête"). The Dao, too, is a way of decrease to a zero point of artifice—a negative way to what is also commonly designated as "nature." At this point, all one's doing is original in the sense that it springs directly and spontaneously from the very origin of being or from the course of things itself. Such a gradual and progressive erasure of self is envisaged in *Dao-de-jing* 48:

為學日益, 為道日損. 損之又損, 以至於無為. 無為而無不為. 取天下常以無事, 及其有事, 不足以取天下.

If you take up studying, you increase day by day.
If you take up the Way, you decrease day by day.
You decrease and then decrease again.

> In this, you reach the point of nonfabrication:
> Nothing is fabricated, but there is nothing left undone.
>
> Taking up the affairs of the world
> Is always done without meddling.
> If there is meddling,
> It will not be sufficient to accomplish the job. (Wilson, trans.)[34]

Like Jullien, so the American interpreters illuminate Chinese language and thought brilliantly because of being attuned to its apophatic aspects. Ames and Hall emphasize just such aspects about the Daoist art of naming: "Such knowing is dependent upon an awareness of the indeterminate aspects of things. The ongoing shaping of experience requires a degree of imagination and creative projection that does not reference the world as it is but anticipates what it might become."[35] Being aware of indeterminacy and participating creatively in its self-manifestation is constitutive of living the apophatic. All the chief Daoist ideas about the fluidity of language and its provisional nature—its relativizing of reference to one function among many, and not the most important one, since the non-predicative uses of language come first—are ideas that are developed also in Western apophatic tradition. The provisionality and dispensability of language are imaged emblematically, for instance, in Wittgenstein's kicking away the ladder after climbing up it.

There is something obviously right in pointing out the relative lack, in classical Chinese wisdom, of representation of transcendence, which is left rather formless, yet transcendence is not for that reason absent or irrelevant. Instead, the case is in fact just the opposite. Yin-yang and the *Dao*, as unrepresentable, are at least as thoroughly and irresistibly in command of the universe as any anthropomorphically represented God ever was. To exclude transcendence is to reduce thought to the measure of a this-worldly mentality that may correspond to the mindset of the majority of readers/consumers in the materialistic culture of world capitalism, but this consensus is precisely what most needs to be challenged in our age by confrontation with other, different views of the world. This need not mean regressing to a paradoxical embrace of discredited myths or dead gods but rather under-

---

34. Lao Tzu, *Tao Te Ching: A New Translation*, trans. William Scott Wilson (Boston: Shambhala, 2010).

35. Ames and Hall, *Dao-de-Jing: Making This Life Significant*, 45–46.

standing why human existence, when experienced and thought most profoundly, has so often required such figures of transcendence to render—and to dynamically realize—its full and unlimited significance.

Robert Smid avows that Hall and Ames's "tendency toward dogmatism can be seen in their patent dismissiveness of those who disagree with them on the issue of transcendence."[36] Through their definition of "important" as "contributing significantly to the shaping of the cultural milieu" (*Anticipating China*, xv), Hall and Ames define their framework against admission of the notion of transcendence into the understanding of Chinese thought and enforce this position dogmatically against their critics, whom they even aggressively deride in the cases of Gregor Paul and Michael Martin.[37] They accuse these scholars of being narrow-minded and insufficiently educated in either their own philosophical traditions or those of others. Rather than taking the opportunity to clarify and extend their own conceptions through the way others interpret and react to them, Hall and Ames have reacted negatively to criticism: "When the question of transcendence in the Chinese tradition is raised by dissenting voices, they are suppressed to such an extent as should disquiet one committed to encouraging the diversity and plurality of perspectives."[38] Smid also notes, however, that in their responses to other critics Hall and Ames have shown themselves to be exemplary of scholarly fairness and respect. It seems to be something about this particular issue of transcendence that pushes philosophers to the limits of their ability to be dispassionately reasonable.

For Smid, the "methodological blindness" of Hall and Ames is a "weakness" balanced by the strength of tailoring the results of philosophy as answering to a task of self-critique and liberation from one's own endemic cultural prejudices. Smid's assessment is that Hall and Ames "arguably overstate the case concerning the lack of any notion of transcendence in classical Chinese philosophy in order to provide an effective counterweight to the mistaken assumptions of the broader population" (250). In order to combat supposedly reigning prejudices in favor of transcendence, Hall and Ames

---

36. Robert W. Smid, *Methodologies of Comparative Philosophy: The Pragmatist and Process Traditions* (Albany: State University of New York Press, 2009), 133.

37. In fairness, it must be noted that some inflammatory language had already been directed against them by Gregor Paul, "Against Wanton Distortion: A Rejoinder to David Hall and Roger Ames by Gregor Paul," *Journal of Chinese Philosophy* 19/1 (1992): 119–22, and Michael Martin, "A Rejoinder to Ames and Hall," *Journal of Chinese Philosophy* 18/4 (1991): 480–93.

38. Smid, 133. See, further, 128–32.

polemically deny its relevance in categorical terms. In Smid's words, "Hall and Ames' primary concern in suppressing consideration of the presence of transcendence in classical Chinese thought is to countermand the transcendental pretense that still pervades much of contemporary comparative philosophy" (124). Thus, for Smid, even at the price of a certain distortion, there may be a strategic justification for this emphasis based on a particular assessment of what is necessary in "our" present situation of relative ignorance of Eastern cultures. However, such an exclusion, then, should be understood not as philologically and philosophically necessary but rather as personally or collectively justifiable and as valid only in a particular historical context. Otherwise, such relative and strategically motivated expedients tend to take on airs of objectivity, as if they were strictly dictated by the realities in question.

It is not by excluding transcendence in favor of immanence, or by denying unity in favor of multiplicity, that the ungraspable, apophatic wholeness envisaged by Chinese wisdom can be discerned or attained. I grant that any term such as "transcendence" needs to be constantly subjected to critique in order to avoid becoming an instrument of unchecked power wielded by the irresponsible and unscrupulous. There are, naturally, reasons for the attack against transcendence that deserve to be understood. Indeed, no terms whatever can be finally adequate, and terms such as "transcendence," if they are lent the pretension of scientificity, are perhaps the most objectionable of all. It is hardly tolerable that, being just one form of representation, "transcendence" and the like terms should lay claim to transcend and thereby to have a right to regulate the others. But to take them this way is to remain uncritically at the level only of representations, taking them for the real thing. If such terms are taken, instead, as no more than forms of representation, they can be effective and even necessary in order to undermine precisely the pretensions to absoluteness on the part of the conceptual idols that are ineluctably created by human language.

Controlling things by any representation whatsoever is, after all, contrary to the spirit of classical Chinese thinking—but also of critical thinking in general and most acutely of the radical, infinitely self-critical thinking of apophasis. In fact, only the transcendence of all possible vocabularies is the real burden of "transcendence" as used in apophatic thinking. Limit words such as "transcendence" remind us of the limits of any language whatsoever, and they point us toward something beyond words and representations. Contributions to thinking through this predicament under the rubric of "transcendence" are not to be excluded but rather should be honored alongside other approaches. Other possible terms, too, deserve to be appreciated—and also critiqued in their turn. In fact, in their most lucid moments, Ames and Hall reject the language of both transcendence *and* immanence as inadequate to Chinese thought and as appropriating it in either case to Western notions.[39] This double and reciprocal critique is the crucial moment of apophatic insight (classically expressed as "neither . . . nor," "neither this nor that," "*neti . . . neti*"), in which one is propelled toward the beyond of language—which can, of course, also be understood as always in some way relating to language nevertheless.[40]

In opting for "the presumption of radical immanence," Hall and Ames admit that "our language here is somewhat misleading, since, in the strict sense, the contrast of transcendence and immanence is itself derived from our Anglo-European tradition" (*Thinking through Confucius*, 12). What is, however, perhaps even more difficult to realize is that the truly strict sense of transcendence is to have no sense, to be beyond any determinate sense. The strict sense of transcendence lies in the transcendence of sense. This is where Hall and Ames miss what is most important about transcendence and, in fact, are unable to accommodate it in its fundamental meaning and purport. In the sentence that immediately follows, they return to their one-sided polemic against the language of transcendence only: "It will become clear as we discuss Confucius' thinking in subsequent chapters that attempts to articulate his doctrines by recourse to transcendent beings or principles have caused significant interpretive distortions" (12–13). I would like to suggest, however, that the problem here is as much or more with "beings" and "principles" as with "transcendent." If even terms such as "heaven" and the "Way" are understood poetically, their content cannot be definitively fixed but, instead, always transcends any given definition. As poetic images, such terms invite always further exploration and enucleation that makes a dimension of "transcendence" highly relevant to their interpretation. Hall and Ames emphasize the paramount importance of *indetermination* in Chinese culture (*Thinking from the Han*, 130) but miss it in the West. Seeing its often covert centrality there, too, would diminish the sense of contrast with—not to mention of essential difference from—China. It would redefine this difference as one of modes of representation or of interpretive choices revolving around not necessarily incommensurable visions of reality.

---

39. See *Thinking from the Han*, 191–92; cf. 230.

40. Insistence on precisely this point is found, for example, in Dale S. Wright, "Rethinking Transcendence: The Role of Language in Zen Experience," *Philosophy East and West* 42/1 (1992): 113–38.

Hall and Ames understand themselves as "interpretive pluralists." They aim to "promote open-ended typologies, and they celebrate the multiplicity of interpretive perspectives to which philosophical thinking has given rise as pragmatically useful devices for handling intertheoretical and intercultural conversations" (*Anticipating China*, 160). And yet they are very sure and categorical that those others who refer to transcendence are getting it wrong. They seem to have lost touch with (or is it rather that they strategically choose to ignore?) the dynamism of transcendence as the formless within changing form, a notion that is deeply embedded in Western traditions, for example, in Eriugena's divinized *Natura* and its afterlife in the Middle Ages.[41] Their own pragmatist assumptions are perhaps an effective bridge to much that is characteristic in Chinese classical culture, but these postulates, too, need to be relinquished in the end. Typology may be necessary for creating understanding and for any idea of China at all—but only to the extent that it is then given up in order to allow for an untrammeled encounter with the Other in its own reality. A question that lingers for me is whether Hall and Ames's approach to intercultural philosophy is not perhaps in some ways still answering to the demands of scientificity that are typically made by Western universities upon their "researchers." There still seems to be a taxonomic ambition at work in Hall and Ames, just as in Jullien. Their description of Chinese culture asserts itself as more objectively accurate than traditional and competing ones.

In the end, Hall and Ames's target remains unrelentingly the "inappropriateness" of "transcendent interpretations." Jullien is similar in this regard: he most often attacks appeals to transcendence. However, at certain moments he backtracks and finds a way of accommodating transcendence, too, once it becomes clearly only a metaphorical mode of approaching the unnameable and unsayable. On the whole, the degree to which the French and the North American researchers' projects run parallel to each other—but with very little interaction or even mutual recognition—is what is most remarkable. They are saying many of the same things about China and about the West, and yet their own cultural differences by and large prevent them from seeing or acknowledging what they share in common. Both parties are positioned to be effective critics of the secular ethos of the West and its tendency to take on the authority of an unprejudiced, scientifically accurate approach to culture, for both are sympathetic expounders of a type of thinking that defies and refuses to be contained by just such a method and ethos. Yet they ground themselves in the anti-transcendence prejudice

---

41. The affinity here with Chinese Daoist thinking is elaborated by Joseph Grange, "An Irish Tao," *The Journal of Chinese Philosophy* 29/1 (2002): 21–34.

typical of this culture in order to gain traction and make their discourse persuasive to their predominantly secular-minded contemporary audiences.

Dialectically speaking, there is, admittedly, an important mission for objective reason in approaching even classical Chinese "thinking." As Hall and Ames observe, Daoism thinks objectively, but without objects: it is responsive to a kind of ungraspable absolute givenness of things (*Thinking from the Han*, 52). Rather than "construing" the world and its objects, Daoism takes a "deferential" attitude towards things. Hall and Ames characterize this attitude apophatically as non-knowing (*wu zhi*), non-asserting (*wu wei*), and non-desiring (*wu yu*), or as unprincipled knowing, non-assertive action, and deferential or objectless desiring (46, 57). Just such unknowing, unsaying, and renunciation of desire are the common motifs also of Western apophatic sources from ancient Neoplatonism and medieval and baroque mysticism through modern and postmodern thinkers and poets and sages.[42] Rather than seeing this apparatus as anti-transcendental, I suggest that it may best be taken as an apophatic interpretation of transcendence, of a transcendence that cannot be construed at all but must simply be acknowledged and deferred to, even though there is no objective "it"—indeed, precisely in *its* absence.

The very Heideggerian word "thinking" (*das Denken*), which in its French form (*la pensée*) is integral and very often titular to the project of Jullien (for instance, in *La pensée chinoise dans le miroir de la philosophie*; in *Pensée d'un dehors [La Chine]*; and in *Entrer dans une pensée*), just as is the English form "thinking" for Hall and Ames (it occurs in each volume of their trilogy: *Thinking through Confucius*; followed by *Thinking from the Han*; and finally *Anticipating China: Thinking through the Narratives of Chinese and Western Culture*), suggests that we are dealing with something that evades the ontology of objects and exceeds calculative or instrumental reason. Nevertheless, when a typically modern faith in secular reason without transcendence (visible in Jullien, but not in Hall and Ames) installs itself as the governing paradigm, a barrier is erected against what Chinese and Western sources of wisdom alike are attempting to communicate.

SECULAR SELF-CRITIQUE AND THEOLOGICAL TRANSCENDENCE

An interesting and correlative counterweight to the finally secularist trend of modern thinking from which Jullien, at least, is not quite free can be

---

42. See Franke, *On What Cannot Be Said: Apophatic Discourses in Philosophy, Religion, Literature, and the Arts*, vols. 1 and 2.

found in the work of Robert Cummings Neville. Neville is avowedly and determinedly a theological thinker of transcendence, one who takes up the challenge of comparative religions in extensive multivolume works based in part on collective research projects.[43] He is constructing a systematic philosophical theology.[44] He explicitly criticizes Hall and Ames's position that the idea of transcendence or of a transcendent source for the world and its values is in no wise applicable to Chinese classical thought and has been made to seem plausible only by faulty translations that project Western metaphysical assumptions onto Chinese texts inappropriately.[45] In this debate, the lack of any interest in transcendence has become for Hall and Ames the defining characteristic of classical Chinese thought in contrast to the dominant Western tradition.[46] They deny that classical Chinese thinkers conceive the idea that the world's values and principles are or even should be grounded in a transcendent source.

Smid evaluates whether Hall and Ames are right in "suppressing consideration of the presence of transcendence in classical Chinese thought" (Smid 124; cf. 121) and concludes that it depends on the goals pursued

---

43. Among the most relevant of Neville's many books are *God the Creator: On the Transcendence and Presence of God* (Chicago: University of Chicago Press, 1992) and *On the Scope and Truth of Theology: Theology as Symbolic Engagement* (New York: T&T Clark, 2006). The Comparative Religious Ideas Project (CRIP) produced three volumes (*The Human Condition*, *Ultimate Realities*, and *Religious Truth*) published in 2001 by the State University of New York Press. The same press earlier published Neville's *Axiology of Thinking* in three volumes: *Reconstruction of Thinking* (1981), *Recovery of the Measure* (1989), and *Normative Cultures* (1995).

44. Neville, *Ultimates. Philosophical Theology*, vol. 1 (Albany: State University of New York Press, 2013).

45. Neville, *Boston Confucianism*, 47–50, 147–66. Neville musters other comparatists including Tu Weiming, Wm. Theodore de Bary, and Joseph Grange into his camp as well. See Smid, 120. More about Neville's approach comes later, toward the end of this section.

46. They, too, are not alone. A similar position is taken notably by A.C. Graham, *Disputers of the Tao: Philosophic Argument in Ancient China* (La Salle, IL: Open Court, 1989). Ames claims to have as allies in this critique the most important and authoritative researchers at work today, including Graham, Nathan Sivin, Chad Hansen, and Norman J. Girardot. However, there is also much equally determined opposition. Robert Wardy, *Aristotle in China: Language, Categories and Translation* (Cambridge: Cambridge University Press, 2004) admires the remarkable achievement of the seventeenth-century Jesuit translations and mounts a massive attack specifically on Graham as mistaken in his fundamental assumptions, notwithstanding the impressive sophistication of his linguistic analyses.

and on how comparative philosophy of culture is to be defined. Simply presenting the purported facts of the matter is never decisive or definitive. Theses and counter-theses never articulate the complete truth: they must also allow for their own disarticulation, whether deliberately or not. What is accurate or not in describing another culture is culture-dependent, and Hall and Ames in the end claim validity for their interpretation only in our specific cultural context—presumably the modern, secular, Western world.

In such a context, Hall and Ames are convinced that transcendence is a distorting lens introduced by Western philosophy and imposed on non-Western thought, and that this must be resisted and dismantled. In their own words, "One of the principal barriers precluding the Westerner from understanding China on its own terms is the persistence in Western cultures of what Robert Solomon has so aptly termed the 'transcendental pretense'" (*Anticipating China*, xiv). There has indeed been a peculiarly intense development and theorization of transcendence in the West. In reality, this is much more than just *theorization*. Historically, concrete and often tragically suffered religious *experience* of a purportedly transcendent power and love, particularly in the stories recorded in Judeo-Christian sources, has been powerfully mediated by theological imagination and conveyed by metaphorical elaboration of concepts. The biblical stories of the Exodus from Egypt and the Exile in Babylon serve as heart-rending records of such experience. Of course, it is in reacting to their own cultural context of origin that Hall and Ames choose to see China as (relatively) free from transcendence in the sense that it has taken on in the West. This position can perhaps justify itself as self-critique and self-deconstruction but not simply as accurate description.

In fact, self-critique carried out without limit is exactly what characterizes apophatic thought: it is predicated on the denial of more direct, positive, descriptively accurate representation of the real in one's own, or indeed in any, culture. This self-disavowal of objective validity is required by the pragmatist principle as well, which Hall and Ames embrace. And yet, somewhat inconsistently, they seem still to allow the pretenses of scientificity and objective knowledge of an independent field of objects to operate covertly in the certitude with which they judge scholars who see a relation with transcendence operating in Chinese thought to be demonstrably wrong.

However, Western scholars are not the only ones who persist in making such a "mistake." Among distinguished "New Confucian" scholars writing in Chinese, Zongsan Mou and Minghui Li concertedly explore various notions of transcendence in Chinese classics. Hall and Ames themselves stress the irony that transcendence should be revived and advocated as crucial to classical Chinese culture even by Chinese scholars, whereas transcendence is in eclipse and virtually defunct in the West (*Thinking from the Han,* 222). China *seems* in this regard to be foolishly following a failed model. However, the situation may actually be just the reverse. We maybe need China more than ever today precisely in order to understand why transcendence has had such a crucial role in our own history. Being reminded of this may be necessary in order to save us in the West from misunderstanding the meaning and importance of transcendence along lines of interpretation such as those of Hall and Ames that reduce it to a mere form of representation. Their interpretation of Chinese community as a self-ordering harmony without coercive legal imposition from without, and as constituted rather by spontaneous deference to excellence in the form of accomplished human self-cultivation, helps to clarify how transcendent values work in society. Such values can never be legislated or imposed by fiat. Revered in living masters and ancestral models, their authority requires just the sort of spontaneous recognition that Hall and Ames discern in Chinese social norms based on creative religious rites rather than on static and abstract human rights (269–85). And yet Hall and Ames take their own provocative analyses and sensitive interpretations as counting unilaterally and unequivocally against recognition of transcendence in Chinese culture. How can they be so categorical?

Hall and Ames, after all, may still be unwittingly beholden to a Western scientific exigency and its pretense to describe essential phenomena, even in expressly distancing themselves from it. Attempting to be accurate observers of a foreign culture in its evident characteristics is not necessarily the right approach. Gang Zhang argues that the interpretive framework that Hall and Ames impose is, in fact, "totally wrong." Although appreciative of many important insights in their book (*Anticipating China*), Zhang rejects their most basic assumptions and whole approach as still blindly Western and as fundamentally uncomprehending of classical Chinese thought and culture: "There are many incisive insights in this book, like pearls strewn here and there. However, the basic views presented in the book are wrong, and the elements of Chinese culture, such as analogy and symbolism, taken by the authors of *Anticipating China* as essential properties, are only superficial phenomena."[47]

Gang Zhang explains that the most fundamental Chinese theories, those of yin-yang, the Five Elements, and the *Dao* and *Fo* (the latter, 佛,

---

47. Gang Zhang, "Form and Formless: A Discussion with the Authors of *Anticipating China,*" *Frontiers in Philosophy in China* 6/4 (2011): 585–608, citation 585–86.

being a term from Chinese Buddhism for Buddha-being or the imageless Void that is neither existence nor nonexistence) are types of "formless thinking" that work from the "top down" (602). All things are comprised in a "universal code." The Western system by contrast is built on particulars from the "bottom up." In the latter, "nominalist" perspective, particulars are assumed to be the ultimate, or at least the most evident, reality. By contrast, in the Chinese system, Zhang maintains, "a paramount law appears first." This law is "formless" (603). Thus, for Zhang, "Hall and Ames are quite right in saying, 'Chinese thinking does not presuppose the unity of Being behind beings, a One behind the many.' But they are totally wrong in saying, 'All you have in the Chinese world view is 'the ten thousand things' as an ad hoc summing up of beings and events" (603). Zhang is quoting Hall and Ames, *Anticipating China*, 140–41, who in turn are quoting Zhuangzi and Laozi. But Hall and Ames are quietly eliding reference to the *Dao* that flows through and works in all things and regulates them, as is marvelously conveyed, for example, by *Dao-de-Jing* 34. While Hall and Ames focus exclusively on correlations among things as the only ontological foundation, Zhang holds that such correlations are "only a matter of empirical experience and conventional interpretation" (603).

Most tellingly of all, Hall and Ames themselves qualify their statements reducing all to things and their correlations, schematically yin-yang, with the admission, quoted from *Yi Chou*, or the art of interpreting the *Yijing*, that "what yin-yang does not fathom is called inscrutable (*shen*, 神)" (*Thinking from the Han*, 71). This inscrutable factor is the apophatic. Indeed, *shén* 神 is also commonly translated as "god" or "divinity." It cannot be adequately expressed, but this very marking of its transcendence of all possible expressions entails a crucial qualification of everything that can be and is expressed.

There is a unified order and law to the Chinese cosmos that Hall and Ames are at risk of erasing in order to make such thinking of unity, with its transcendence of knowledge and expression, an imposture based only on Western importations. It seems that their presuppositions blind them to an aspect of what is most fundamental to Chinese thought and, I would add, likewise to Western thought, which (at least by apophatic lights) is aiming at a formless source of form and order, too. This unattainable, inconceivable "source" is what gives sense to metaphysical constructions. Once reduced to their own letter, metaphysical constructions are indeed arbitrary impositions. But in spite of their efforts and intention to achieve just the opposite, what is being imposed by Western scholars such as Hall and Ames today is basically a scientific and nominalist worldview characteristic of their own cultural horizon. What makes it even more problematic is that this view eliminates the most deeply self-critical aspects of their own culture. In a classical Chinese outlook, according to Zhang, on the other hand, the whole *does* come first: it transcends the parts, although it is never grasped in itself or as such. It does not even have any thinkable or sayable form. For Gang Zhang, there is in the Western world "no wholeness at all," since the whole is opposed to the parts and therefore no longer truly whole. Of course, he, too, ignores the unthought and unthinkable wholeness envisaged by Western apophatic thought. For him, consequently, only Chinese thinking grasps oneness: "Unlike the Western system, which sums up these 'ten thousand things' into a composite, Chinese philosophy makes all of them as one 'oneness' " (603).

What in the West is comparable to Chinese thought, I submit, is rather the apophatic thinking that has thought all along the anti-system concealed in every system. Hall and Ames apply Western logical analysis in order to discern, or more exactly to deduce, the difference of Chinese from Western culture, but they miss what is most fundamental because it has no form or definition or place within any ontology. The scientific worldview is itself an ontology, indeed a metaphysical one, if we listen to Heidegger. But what is expressed in apophatic thinking both East and West is what precedes worldviews and their accompanying, often covert ontologies. It is rather the undifferentiated and formless source of them all. Yin and yang (each only nominally and provisionally exclusive of its opposite) are a code for this formless source of thinking that operates unnoticed in all thinking. Other such codes are the transcendent One or God understood apophatically, as in radical Neoplatonism, Kabbalah, Sufism, etc., rather than dogmatically or analytically.

Hall and Ames are surely not wrong in writing that "an appropriate and adequate explication of the meaning of Confucius's thought requires a language of immanence grounded in the supposition that laws, rules, principles, or norms have their source in the human, social, contexts which they serve" (*Thinking through Confucius*, 14). But, still, they are altogether missing the very dimension in which transcendence is paramount. This occurs not at the level of particular laws, rules, principles or other determinate forms of representation. Consequently, Hall and Ames employ only a very superficial understanding of transcendence. For them, it entails "a radical separation between the transcendent and nondependent creative source, on the one hand, and the determinate and dependent object of its creation on the other" (18). But this separative transcendence is not transcendence that is thought profoundly. They write, further, "The creative source does not require reference to its creature for explanation" (18). Yet, on a more adequate understanding, there can be any explanation of the creative source of all *only* in terms of its creations. Thomas Aquinas, for one, is absolutely clear about the Creator's inexplicability per se or as such. God is "known" only in terms of "his" creatures as effects.[48] This limit of only indirect access is what makes God "transcendent." In itself or in its essence, the transcendent divinity cannot be known or explained at all. To the extent that they concern themselves with an expressed, determinate source or known principle, Hall and Ames operate at the level only of representations. They treat the transcendent source as still another instance on the same plane, as one individual among others, in effect *primus inter pares*. It is not treated as truly transcendent but rather as one among others, only the greatest. They are, in effect, thinking only of precedence and not of true theological transcendence. They deal only with *representations* of transcendence and not with what is more profoundly intended by such representations. Intended, above all, is what transcends representation. The not-being-dependent of the transcendent, with which Hall and Ames deal, is merely asserted and represented. It not realized: its realization is even precluded by their construal of transcendence as a representable, formalizable principle. Religions have often provided such images of transcendence, but taking those images simply at face value does not do justice to their deeper intention and lived meaning qua images of the unfathomable depth and richness of experience of human relatedness transcending all possibilities of conceptualization.

Hall and Ames find the concept of transcendence problematic and even disastrous because their own thinking is unwittingly circumscribed by it. Rather than using representations to think transcendence, they let the representations of transcendence impose themselves so as to prevent truly original, or even just adequate, thinking of transcendence. This is, in fact, what representations of "transcendence" have done over and over again throughout our history, and that is why Hall and Ames, along with many others, are anxious simply to be rid of them. But to react this way is to perpetuate misrecognition of the meaning of this vocabulary and its linguistic-pragmatic implications, specifically its operating so as to exceed and disrupt the application of concepts and images. To deny the possibility of transcendence of our own reality is simply to ignore the dimension of the authentically religious and, what is more, of the truly or irreducibly intercultural as well. What we need, instead, is to find other ways to relate

---

48. Aquinas, "De Deo Uno," *Summa Theologica*, pt. 1, question 12.

to this dimension that transcends conceptualization. If we ignore this dimension, we merely compare the different manifest phenomena of religions and cultures and misrecognize their meaning, their inexhaustible human and perhaps even trans-human or ultra-human significance. The relational logic of Hall and Ames, taken to its logical conclusion, requires placing human-centered religiousness into relation with what that very concept excludes: only in being exceeded and transcended can it deploy and develop its full potential for meaningfulness.

NEW DEBATES ON THE RELEVANCE OF TRANSCENDENCE TO CLASSICAL CHINESE THINKING

Smid finally and cogently attributes to Hall and Ames a methodological "blind spot" concerning transcendence. By virtue of the fact that they define it as not significant to the Chinese conception of the world, or as "not a defining priority," they are not able to take account of it at all and indeed exclude it in principle on the basis of their conviction that it is misleading and erroneous. However, for other researchers there is evidence that transcendence *is* significantly present in Chinese conceptions of the real. Smid, in principle, is disposed to grant that if transcendence is only marginally significant in Chinese culture, then Hall and Ames could be relatively justified in excluding it for the sake of gaining clarity in their presentation of the features of Chinese culture that count most or are "determining" (123). I would suggest, instead, that this is not a matter of degrees of presence but of the recognition and recognizability of transcendence *tout court*. "Transcendence" is not showing up for Hall and Ames not because of its scarcity and marginality but, on the contrary, because it is so pervasively and overwhelmingly significant everywhere in Chinese thought. It is not manifest as any particular phenomenon, not even as a kind of reality or unreality or surreality that Hall and Ames's ontological optics can register and perceive. Seen thus, the question of transcendence cannot be just a minor issue or one that can be marginalized: the whole basis of our approach to and understanding of the distinctive nature of Chinese thought hinges on it.

Not so surprisingly, then, there are numerous scholars today who are turning back to transcendence and zealously defending the centrality of a dimension of transcendence in Chinese philosophy. One such comparative philosopher is Eske Møllgaard.[49] Møllgaard's counterattack addresses itself

---

49. Eske Møllgaard, "Zhuangzi's Notion of Transcendental Life," *Asian Philosophy* 15/1 (2005): 1–18.

also to Jullien's denial of ontological difference in China—that is, of any categorically other, higher reality, noting that the *Zhuangzi* explicitly states that the Way is "beyond the dichotomies of 'full' (*ying*) and 'empty' (*xu*), 'root' (*ben*) and 'branch' (*wei*), 'to accumulate' (*ji*) and 'to disperse' (*san*). The Way is thus beyond the continuum that, according to Jullien, constitutes the totality of the ancient Chinese philosophy of process" (2). Møllgaard cites Chinese and Japanese scholars of Daoism who, unlike Western scholars, find that "in Laozi and Zhuangzi there are two distinct realms: the realm of 'things' (*wu*), which is under the constraint of time and space, and the realm of the 'Way' (*dao*), which transcends beings and forms in time and space" (3). Recognition of this ontological difference leads to clearly apophatic formulations of the Daoist project: "Therefore, according to Zhuangzi, the highest attainment of the ancients was to realize that there is 'a realm [or state] before there are things' (*weishi youwuzhe*). The realm before there are things is the 'Way' (*dao*), which 'things things' (*wuwu*) but is 'not a thing' (*feiwu*) itself, and so, is strictly speaking 'nothing' (*wu*)" (3). Møllgaard invokes Giorgio Agamben (*La communità che viene*, 1990) in order to elucidate the notion of transcendence as not a supreme entity above others but rather simply the taking-place of all things: the inarticulable fact *that* they are, which Wittgenstein, too, echoing a long apophatic tradition going back at least to Philo Judaeus, designated as "the mystical."[50]

In support of his revisionary thesis concerning the place of transcendence in classical Chinese thought, Møllgaard levels a likewise devastating critique against the abstraction that he finds in the American philosophical approaches of Hall and Ames and also of Chad Hansen.[51] He shows the reductiveness of arguing for an overarching theoretical model of linguistic logic to "make sense" of the ancient texts (Hansen) in terms of postmodern pragmatic philosophy as anticipated by ancient Chinese thought (Hall and Ames). For this purpose, Møllgaard annexes criticisms by Haun Saussy of the idea that postmodernism can render China legible as "a figure of its own future self."[52]

---

50. Hall and Ames turn out to be very receptive to the vocabulary of "mysticism" (*Thinking from the Han*, 203–12), since they consider it to be "immanentalist" and "nontranscendent" (204), although it is by transcending all such representations, as well as their contraries, that mystic discourse opens into the apophatic or indeterminate.

51. Møllgaard, "Eclipse of Reading: Or the 'Philosophical Turn' in American Sinology," *Dao* 4/2 (2005): 321–40.

52. Saussy, "No Time Like the Present: The Category of Contemporaneity in Chinese Studies," in *Great Walls of Discourse and Other Adventures in Cultural China* (Cambridge, MA: Harvard University Press, 2001). Cited by Møllgaard, "Eclipse of Reading," 330.

My apophatic interpretation, too, admittedly unfolds at the level of a general framework and theory rather than of a practice of reading specific texts. After all is said and done, we do need to reflect on our theoretical presuppositions. However, Møllgaard is arguing for "An Anti-Philosophical Reading of Chinese Thought" (332–38), as a section heading at the culmination of his last-cited article states. And I, too, fundamentally, am advocating apophatics as an *anti*-philosophy—or, more exactly, as philosophy's infinite self-critique, undermining all possible philosophical principles that we might advance in justification of ourselves and our thought. My approach is, to this extent, perfectly in line with what Møllgaard himself envisages.[53]

But perhaps the most influential voice of all today, at least in China, who is leading researchers to recognize (and helping them to understand) the relevance of transcendence to Chinese thought is that of Wolfgang Kubin. Kubin, incidentally, acknowledges Jullien as having enabled him to discover another way of *reading* ancient Chinese texts, not for their propositional content, famously pronounced by Hegel to consist in nothing but banalities, but rather for another kind of meaning that cannot be so directly delivered, one that has to be inferred instead from the master's art of conversation. Through his painstaking reading, Kubin discovers the centrality of religion to Confucius's texts, thus belying the commonplace that denies this content and makes Confucius a secular, agnostic humanist. He points out how Confucius is portrayed in the *Analects* as used by Heaven or by "God" like a "bell" for transmitting their "word" to humans (3. 24), since Heaven itself never says anything (17.19).[54] We find here once again the motivation for apophatic thinking in the negation of any direct access to transcendence. The transcendent must be indirectly experienced and discerned in the finite, particularly in the latter's defects and deficiencies: on this basis, transcendence can be conjectured, but only negatively.

The common misapprehension that Confucius has nothing to say about religion usually takes its point of departure from his statement in the *Analects* that the better part of wisdom consists in consecrating oneself to the service of humans and keeping at a safe distance from the gods (6.20). However, Kubin interprets this passage not as implying the irrelevance of the gods and of their supposed transcendence but, instead, the lack of any humanly commensurable means of approaching divinity.

---

53. See, further, Møllgaard's *Introduction to Daoist Thought: Action, Language and Ethics in Zhuangzi* (London: Routledge, 2011).

54. Kubin, "Niemand, der mich kennt: Konfuzius und der Himmel," *minima sinica* 2 (2009): 15–23.

The apophatic move is precisely to make this failing and difficulty not an excuse for ignoring the transcendent but rather a call for acknowledgment and perhaps even for concentration on our interface with what exceeds our comprehension. Chinese philosophy, after all, devotes acute attention to *un*knowing as the source of wisdom.[55] This is an apophatic attitude, and it induces Kubin to underscore a different posture vis-à-vis transcendence. For Kubin, instead of indifference, Confucius's statement expresses the highest respect for the gods and an urgent warning against humans making themselves equal to divinities, lest they lose their sense of awe and fear. This sense, for which Kubin refers us to Otto Friedrich Bollnow, "Die Ehrfurcht," is fundamental to the kind of teaching that Confucius, in agreement with other great religious founders, inculcates. He consistently reverences the gods and the ancestors. What Confucius exactly means by his references to the gods remains, admittedly, shrouded in vagueness and enigma, but that is in the nature of the case and exactly as it should be, once divinity is understood apophatically.

Kubin emphasizes the importance for Confucius of something higher than humanity standing over against it and limiting it. This is Heaven, but also "a divine being that cannot be grasped once and for all and unambiguously" ("ein göttliches Wesen, das sich nicht singulär und nicht eindeutig fassen läßt," 23). Confucius acknowledges and prays to this being (3.10–17). In a similar key, Kubin reads the poetry of Li Bai (701–62) as presenting the world of the *Dao* as a world distinctly other than that of humans.[56] Kubin reads the well-known ancient Chinese wisdom that all is in flux (*wanwu jie hua*) as implying also that something has to be "changeless" ("unwandelbar"), and this something he finds to be not inappropriately interpreted through Western concepts of essence and substance.[57] He is

---

55. Kubin, "Nichtwissen: Eine chinesische Perspektive," in *Was sich nicht sagen lässt. Das Nicht-Begriffliche in Wissenschaft, Kunst und Religion. Festschrift für Wolfram Hogrebe*, ed. Joachim Bromand and Guido Kreis (Berlin: Akademie Verlag, 2010), 623–31.

56. *Geschichte der chinesischen Literatur*, vol. 1 (Munich: Saur, 2002), 140–42.

57. Kubin, "Alles ist in uns selbst vorhanden: Zum Problem vom ich und selbst im Chinesischen Denken," *Dem Text ein Freund: Erkundungen des Chinesischen Altertums*, eds. Roland Altenburger, Martin Lehnert, Andrea Riemenschnitter (Bern: Peter Lang, 2009), 283–95. "Wir verstehen hier auch, daß um ewig fließen bzw. scheinen zu können, Fluß und Mond über mehr verfügen müssen als über ihr reines Ausströmen in der und in die Zeit. Deswegen muß es etwas geben, das ‚unwandelbar' ist. Dies möchte ich wie oben mit dem abendländischen Begriff des Wesens bzw. der Substanz bezeichnen" (286).

deliberately reversing the clichés that have excluded self and substance from Chinese wisdom in recent Western interpretations.

Given such testimonies, both expert and intuitive, transcendence, too, should be left open as a question rather than being shut down dogmatically. We do not know what transcendence means, after all, if it really transcends our understanding and concepts. Presumably, something akin to this insight has been behind Robert Neville's theology and comparative philosophy in the shape of "vagueness" all along. This vocabulary of vagueness, which is developed systematically by Neville, suggests another way of approaching what I am calling "the apophatic."

In some respects, Neville's approach to comparative philosophy builds on the same type of conviction as mine does, even without programmatically aligning itself with the apophatic. The fundamental difference is that he is interested above all in what *can* be said, even in a kind of systematic approach to philosophical theology, even while acknowledging the limits of the sayable vis-à-vis "ultimate reality." In the end—as Møllegaard suggests and as I also affirm—more than philosophical reading and translation, which takes place always in a circumscribed perspective, we need "antiphilosophical" (or, I would prefer to say, negative-philosophical) ways of approaching Chinese thought. It is from this exigency of relating also to the uncircumscribable that the apophatic, as philosophy's unlimited self-critique, finds its overpowering motivation.

Neville's fundamental point of reference is Charles Sanders Peirce's pragmatism and particularly Peirce's notion of a "vague" hypothesis. As opposed to a "general" sign that is specified the same way in every instance, Peirce theorizes vague signs whose objective content is open to being specified in different ways: "A sign that is objectively indeterminate in any respect is objectively *vague* in so far as it reserves further determination to be made in some other conceivable sign, or at least does not appoint the interpreter as its deputy in this office."[58] A vague hypothesis can always be further specified, even with contradictory determinations. And precisely this is the nature of God as source or "Creator": he is everywhere and nowhere, in all, yet contained by none, etc. Neville begins to name some specific determinations of what he treats in its metaphysical logic as a vague hypothesis in order to attempt to find common ground among religions without any set limits. "I hope to show that the main claims of the various religions are

---

58. Charles Sanders Peirce, *The Essential Peirce: Selected Philosophical Writings* (Indianapolis: Indiana University Press, 1998), vol. 2, 351.

special instances of the vague hypothesis; although the religions' claims may conflict with each other, they all illustrate the vague hypothesis. Maximally, I hope to show that the vague hypothesis illuminates the religious claims themselves, particularly, that it resolves conflicts between claims by showing that on a higher level they are either compatible or identical."[59] In his most recent work, such vague hypotheses as God are what Neville calls "ultimates."

Working thus from American pragmatist matrices, Neville articulates a sort of philosophy of transcendence that bears some affinities to what I have developed on the basis of apophatic thinkers. Tellingly, he also works from theology: the theological notion of creation ex nihilo, for example, is crucial for him in order to envision the radical dependency of all beings. This dependency of beings can also be expressed as their existing only in their mutual relations. For the transcendent Ground never appears as such—whereas Hall and Ames abstractly assume it to be the supreme Principle and postulate from which all observations and inferences are made. The radical contingency of all created beings was a basic teaching also of Nagarjuna and his Madhyamaka school of Mahayana Buddhism. The diversity of these starting points does not prevent such expressly different ways of thinking from having something potentially in common, however nominal. They can be made to work together in order to disclose what has been variously aimed at through terms such as "the real" or "the world" or "the absolute" in various different philosophies. Neville's efforts are worked out in dialogue with other recent approaches to comparative philosophy, notably those of David Dilworth, Keith Ward, and Walter Watson, who are all seeking to devise methods for encountering non-Western philosophies in a new global arena of interaction.[60]

It is highly instructive to take note of how the debate over the place (or the lack thereof) of transcendence in Chinese thought has evolved on

---

59. Neville, *The Tao and the Daimon: Segments of a Religious Inquiry* (Albany: State University of New York Press, 1982), 112–13. This quotation also occurs in earlier form in his essay "A Metaphysical Argument for Wholly Empirical Theology," in *God Knowable and Unknowable*, ed. Robert J. Roth (New York: Fordham University Press, 1973). The same insight is developed further in *Behind the Masks of God: An Essay toward Comparative Theology* (Albany: State University of New York Press, 1991).

60. David A. Dilworth, *Philosophy in World Perspective: A Comparative Hermeneutic of the Major Theories* (New Haven, CT: Yale University Press, 1989). Walter Watson, *The Architectonics of Meaning: Foundations of the New Pluralism* (Chicago: University of Chicago Press, 1996 [1993]). Keith Ward, *Religion and Revelation: A Theology of Revelation in the World's Religions* (Oxford: Oxford University Press, 1994).

the American continent, where religion has been accepted as an academic subject of high seriousness and does not labor under the same inherited burden of anticlericalism as is typical in the French context. The anticlericalism of Jullien is, in fact, deeply rooted in the French Enlightenment, in which there proved to be no possibility of mediation between the church and the *philosophe*. Even in neighboring Germany, by contrast, Enlightenment led to reform and to rethinking religion and, conversely, to understanding reason in its relation to—indeed in its historical filiation from—revelation. Momentously, both reason and revelation together began to be historicized by Johann Gottfried Herder and Moses Mendelssohn. Drawing from both of these epoch-making thinkers, Gotthold Ephraim Lessing's *The Education of the Human Race* (*Die Erziehung des Menschengeschlechts*, 1780) compellingly demonstrated the inextricability of the new self-affirmation of reason from the tradition of theological revelation out of which it developed.

There are, accordingly, multiple heritages whose influences are felt in comparative philosophy in the American academy today. Holding them together in tension, in their mutual negations, is the essentially apophatic way of taking them. Yet there is still in Anglo-American ambiances a deep-seated resistance to the unscientific aspect of the apophatic that reveals objective judgment to be impossible except within artificially created domains. The difficulty of relinquishing our ultimate power of self-determination in the face of something absolute shows up ever again as a formidable hurdle: it is a universal and perennial human challenge.

Negotiating this interface with the Uncontrollable has been the mission of religion ever since certain of its earliest forms, for example, in myths and rites. However, the scientific age has specific difficulties of its own in giving up the pretense of objectivity and in admitting the impotence of rational method and of finite reason vis-à-vis the ultimate concern that is addressed by religion and that, like death, threatens us with our own nullity. A blow is struck to human self-esteem that proves difficult to sustain. Yet, after the motto that where danger looms, there grows rescue, too (Hölderlin, "Patmos"), the wound inflicted by this realization is in fact the site of our only true and authentic universality, the site where we must seek for universality through understanding, as well as through ethically and courageously assuming our human condition. Our aesthetic experience of the world and our religious bond to the cosmos are bound up likewise with this relation to all in and through the open wound of the universal. A wound that unifies all inserts itself as a connecting tissue between those inclined to favor rupture and those, on the contrary, in search of possibilities of synthesis.

Neville looks for continuities between traditions, whereas Hall and Ames emphasize differences. The latter are interested in a more adequate academic and scientific characterization—avoiding confusion and contamination of typologies—while Neville is more intent on mutual understanding as an activity of forging syntheses. The aims of comparative philosophy vary accordingly, as Smid suggests. We could say that Hall and Ames are oriented to the *inter*cultural and Neville to the *trans*cultural, even though in both cases the one entails the other: the question is that of which one has priority. Neville is above all interested in creating a theory, albeit a nonreductive theory, of comparative religious ideas. Hall and Ames are mainly out to dismantle theories that they deem responsible for distortions in currently accepted descriptions of Chinese thought. The problem is particularly the introduction of notions of transcendence that Hall and Ames contend have no place there.

Fundamentally, this dispute hinges on a matter of whether the goal of comparative philosophy is to accurately describe an object or rather to engage in an exchange in which objects are not perceived as such but only in their appropriations by the subjects involved. Curiously, Neville is the one, in this discussion, with a realist outlook derived from Peirce and Duns Scotus, whereas Hall and Ames are Rortian nonobjectivists. And yet these philosophical commitments are belied and reversed in their implications once the opposed parties proceed to the actual application of their respective comparative methods. Hall and Ames treat Chinese culture as an object that can be demonstrably *mis*described, even if it is never possible definitively to "get it right," and Neville aims not to isolate an objective reality but to approach it interactively through non-reductive theorizing and synthesis.

Whereas Hall and Ames begin from a fundamental duality between "first and second philosophical problematic" thinking, which they find already within both Chinese and Western cultures, for Neville there is no such fundamental fault line that prevents gathering and thinking the unity of culture. All cultures for Neville are attempting to deal with the same reality ultimately, and so all have some kind of common measure. Hall and Ames, like Jullien, are likely to be skeptical of the idea of "philosophy in general" in order to respect the differences of different cultures as more radical than any theory or system designed for synthetically uniting them into a common understanding. For Hall and Ames, Chinese culture can be understood only "on its own terms," and thus in a manner preserving its distinctiveness and integrity. Unfortunately, this position can become dogmatic, creating the fiction of terms that are properly one's own. What terms can ever be simply and purely "one's own"? All have their remote as well as proximate provenances and are never purely autochthonous. Moreover, the qualities in question cannot be apprehended absolutely and in themselves but only in and through relation and interaction with other cultures. Cultures are revealed in their distinctive characteristics only through mutual contrast and resistance. The aim of respecting differences is laudable and necessary in order to make comparative philosophy viable, and yet it is also impossible strictly to achieve.

Hall and Ames's critical intervention remains focused on questioning every pretense to universality. Neville, by contrast, is seeking what all philosophical traditions share in common: his comparative project is turned toward the universal. The fact that Jullien embraces a type of philosophical universality *together* with his critique of transcendentalism as the nemesis of Western approaches to China (in which he is fully aligned with Hall and Ames) suggests that he maybe encompasses what is strongest in *both* of these contrasting currents within Anglo-American comparative philosophy.

Smid finds the common ground for a comparative philosophy that aims to engage both Western and Chinese traditions chiefly in pragmatism and process thought. What I am suggesting is that there is another model of thinking that spans and embraces both, a model that belongs properly to neither tradition nor to any specific school within them but that is positioned instead in between all such cultural-historical crystallizations. It is a pervasive subterranean current that has never as such been constituted as a school in the West: it rather refuses to be incorporated by any definable paradigm. It remains always on the outside.

This "outside" is the common ground, or rather groundlessness, in which the different philosophical approaches in question can truly meet. The fact of its theological heritage and genealogy is the principal stumbling block, the *scandalon*, that prevents apophasis from taking up this role without contestation. For many in the post-Heideggerian age of philosophy, "theology" is a code word for everything that philosophy needs to overcome: hence "onto-theology" serves as alias for metaphysics, which philosophers, especially since Nietzsche and Heidegger, have striven in every way to overcome. The irony, again, as Hölderlin writes, is that where danger lies, there grows what also redeems or saves ("wo aber Gefahr ist, wächst das Rettende auch," "Patmos"). My hope and expectation is that recent innovations in the study of religion, ones which I am characterizing as apophatic, will help us to see these source traditions in terms other than just as oppressors opposing freedom. They consist in and convey also enabling practices leading us beyond the reductiveness of our consciously and culturally defined and divided humanity, with its otherwise perhaps insuperable invidiousness.

REALITY THAT REPRESENTATION FAILS TO REPRESENT

Transcendence, as Hall and Ames understand it, creates the famous dualisms between intelligible and sensible, appearance and reality, etc., unlike the correlative poles of yin and yang that govern the Chinese cosmology and defy the law of non-contradiction. However, transcendence, apophatically understood, is precisely what resolves, or rather dissolves and dismantles, such intractable dualisms. Their mutual exclusion on the plain of manifest phenomena is relativized by reference to another formless "space" in which the exclusive and conflictual realities are more deeply embedded and subsumed. Such transcendence, despite knee-jerk associations of monotheism with monarchy and rigid social hierarchy, also permits radical ontological equality among all worldly beings, since it undermines all merely human, finite distinctions and hierarchies. Radical transcendence does not as such ex-ist; it does not "stand out" as one among others, yet it levels all existents. All superiority in power or prestige is leveled vis-à-vis the absolute and the infinite disproportion of everything finite in relation to the transcendent.[61] Judeo-Christian monotheism is not just by accident associated with the democratization of society in the West and thenceforth in the wider world: it is a crucial enabling condition of the whole historical movement of modernity.[62] The complete erasure of such transcendence risks preserving human hierarchies, beginning with natural filial relations, as absolute and beyond the possibility of being challenged.

For Hall and Ames, the lack of such a notion of transcendence, as it comes originally from Greek philosophy and is integrated into Christian tradition, counts as the decisive difference at the foundation of the classical Chinese worldview in its radical distinction from the Western worldview. Ames writes,

> Indeed, our best interpreters of classical Chinese philosophy are explicit in rejecting the idea that Chinese cosmology begins from and is informed by some independent, transcendent principle, and as such, entails Plato and Aristotle's reality/appearance distinction and the plethora of dualistic categories that arise in

---

61. This logic of monotheism is elucidated provocatively by Jan Assmann, *Of God and Gods: Egypt, Israel, and the Rise of Monotheism* (Madison: University of Wisconsin Press, 2008).

62. Seminal for this outlook is Marcel Gauchet, *Le désenchantement du monde: Une histoire politique de la religion* (Paris: Gallimard, 1985).

the wake of such a worldview: God/world, good/evil, objective/subjective, mind/body, self/other, reason/emotion, and so on.[63]

However, Ames is dealing always only with representations of transcendence rather than with transcendence in its radical meaning, which first and foremost means to transcend representation itself. Ames is taking the "transcendent principle" as a determinable representation on the level of other representations that it somehow grounds and/or norms. Yet a true transcendence cannot be defined or placed into a common frame with phenomena: it is altogether different. Ames quotes the *Zhongyong* on the way of the world as being summed up in a single phrase: "Proliferation is unfathomable" ("Paronomasia," 42). His point is that "the totality is not dominated by any one thing" (42). But the *Dao* or God is precisely not a *thing*, which is always to be one thing among many. There is indeed no real thing standing as the "assumed 'One-behind-the-many,'" no one thing, and yet even this type of representation is no less valid than its denial for capturing certain aspects of the widely experienced fact (for which no discrete representation can be adequate) that everything does relate, at least potentially, to everything else.

To define the world as a "pluriverse" and unequivocally affirm that it is a "no single-ordered world" is to state what the world is. Such an affirmation limits our receptivity and imaginative response to the manifestation of unity and oneness that the world does also exhibit in myriad and amazing ways. It does so often by producing unexpected, unaccountable harmony and organic wholeness. In any case, the issue is not what the right description is so much as the relinquishment of the authority of description itself. Granted, "There is no 'God' in this 'pluriverse'" (42) because these ultimate definitions cannot be adequate to the totalities and ultimate ground (or *un*ground, *ungrunt*, to speak with Jakob Böhme) that they intend: all expressions for the truly transcendent can be uttered only under erasure.

Ames conceives of "paronomasia—defining a world by associated living" (46) as antithetical to transcendence, but this entails construing transcendence as another thing alongside and in addition to the relations that are constitutive of interacting persons. Although transcendence is sometimes clumsily represented as a thing above other things, for example, God

---

63. Roger T. Ames, "Paronomasia: A Confucian Way of Making Meaning," in *Confucius Now: Contemporary Encounters with the Analects*, ed. David Jones (La Salle, IL: Open Court, 1992), 41.

as one individual among many, this is not the meaning of transcendence in the incalculably subtle apophatic thinking that has constituted Western metaphysical, religious, and philosophical traditions—very often dialectically reversing their most overt and obvious sense.[64] From the apophatic perspective, indeed, the magic thread tying things together is not graspable or conceivable—but neither is it reducible to particulars or individuals that *can* be grasped. In practice, the transcendent can never be grasped as such but only in the mutual relations of things and in the totality of their relations. Since this ensemble is per se unsoundable, speaking of it as transcending our finite grasp and language is poetically and semiotically appropriate. Arts and religions across very diverse cultures have created innumerable semiotically innovative approaches for endeavoring to figure transcendence often by metasemiotic representations that signify the failure and impossibility of representation, as when the god is shown eating the eyes of the spectators of cult statues or is shown in an act of "hiding, making opaque or covering of the transcendent object."[65]

This type of semiotically based capacity for transcendence can be understood in an anthropological perspective that goes back at least to Giambattista Vico as founded on the human threshold ability to make signs. Matthias Jung underscores in the context of the Axial Age a new "semiotic transcendence" as consisting in recognition of symbolicity or, in other words, in the realization that symbolic representation reflexively and

---

64. Ingolf Dalferth effectively brings out the fathomless theological subtlety and complexity of "The Idea of Transcendence" in an essay so entitled in Robert N. Bellah and Hans Joas, eds., *The Axial Age and Its Consequences*, 146–90.

65. Massimo Leone and Richard J. Parmentier, "Representing Transcendence: The Semiosis of Real Presence," *Signs and Society* 2, Supplement 1 (2014): S1–22, citation, S5. This introductory piece usefully inventories some of the semiotically innovative means that art and religions across diverse cultures have invented in the self-subverting endeavor to represent transcendence. Significant works from the very rich, crosscultural bibliography on this topic include Valerio Valeri, *Kingship and Sacrifice: Ritual and Society in Ancient Hawaii*, trans. Paula Wissing (Chicago: University of Chicago Press, 1985); Neal H. Walls, ed., *Cult Image and Divine Representation in the Ancient Near East* (Boston: American School of Oriental Research, 2005); Kimberley Christine Patton, *Religion of the Gods: Ritual, Paradox, and Reflexivity* (Oxford: Oxford University Press, 2009); Herbert L. Kessler, *Spiritual Seeing: Picturing God's Invisibility in Medieval Art* (Philadelphia: University of Pennsylvania Press, 2000); and Giselle de Nie, Karl Frederick Morrison, and Marco Mostert, eds., *Seeing the Invisible in Late Antiquity and the Early Middle Ages* (Turnhout: Brepols, 2005).

infinitely transcends the world of empirically given objects.[66] Transcendence, moreover, cannot be construed as concretized in any existing principle but manifests rather as a dimension of sense. No symbolic object can fully saturate the potential of sense, which thus opens to the infinite. Sense depends on innumerable possible contexts or "fields of sense" (*Sinnfelder*).[67]

Hall and Ames are very lucid in arguing that the Chinese "world as such" is without any objective truth. There is no decontextualized knowledge of it from outside: "The viewer is always embedded in it" in such a manner that description entails prescription and thinking is automatically a doing (*Thinking from the Han*, 247). This insight into world as such is, in fact, achieved by apophatic negation of the very concept of cosmos in favor of a world that cannot as such be conceived (249). But, then, to attribute these advantages to the Chinese *representation* of the world as a categorically different representation from Western models, which are based instead on transcendence, is to mistake the subtlety and agility of such thinking as it is realized, for example, in the apophatic performances of the *Zhuangzi*. The *Zhuangzi* has no need for static formulas and fixed principles that would define the world. Its linguistic-textual performances are basically negative or deconstructive in import and, as such, representations only of what *cannot* be represented. The insinuation that they are a more accurate representation of the world that could be opposed to typical Western representations comes rather from the (professional) necessity of an academic discourse to assert itself as a correct and authoritative account of Chinese thinking. But such an assertion is in reality contrary to the spirit of that thinking. By freezing the characteristic modes of Chinese thinking into an alternative world-picture (one without transcendence), Hall and Ames betray, or at least compromise, their own insight into the impossibility of an adequate world-picture from the Chinese point of view, for which the world is "unique and boundless." Such an impossibility of representing the world, furthermore, is not exclusively Chinese but rather is common to apophatic approaches East and West. The impossibility of a world-picture does not exclude transcendence but, instead, requires transcending all representations. Transcendence is what cannot be represented, whereas representations are what make up the world as it is pictured and conceived.

In fact, what Hall and Ames rail against is always only a hypostatized or represented transcendence. This is "separative transcendence" in the

---

66. Matthias Jung, "Embodiment, Transcendence, and Contingency: Anthropological Features of the Axial Age," in *The Axial Age and Its Consequences*, 77–101.
67. Cf. Markus Gabriel, *Warum es die Welt nicht gibt* (Berlin: Ullstein, 2013).

vocabulary of Catherine Keller, as I have previously suggested in discussion of Jullien's bias against the language of transcendence. Hall and Ames's rejection of transcendence wholesale (rather than specifying that their "strict transcendence" is really only the *representation* of transcendence) amounts to ignoring all the nuances that transcendence has in Western traditions and blending out the dialectic of reflection on this topic among many of the most original Western thinkers. The strategic gain is to separate Chinese from Western traditions by a supposedly unmistakable *difference*: in Chinese thinking, no transcendence. Of course, that is a gross oversimplification. And this is what Jullien has turned against sharply, correcting his own work in some of its earlier formulations (at least as it was understood by interpreters such as Robinet and Møllgaard and many others), with his critique of *difference* as dependent on *identity* and his opting rather for a vocabulary of "gaps" or "intervals" ("écarts"). Bringing Jullien into relation with his Anglo-Saxon counterparts in this way shows his importance for leading out of the cul-de-sac of a comparative philosophy based on the premise of insuperable difference, a predicament that would forever frustrate the aspiration to universality. Jullien, by this account, finds the way toward genuinely dialogical thought opening access to Chinese wisdom along an (as yet largely unacknowledged) apophatic path.

Chapter 4

UNIVERSALISM, OR THE NOTHING THAT IS ALL

FROM THE GLOBALISM OF NATURE TO THE UNIVERSALITY OF THOUGHT

In *On the Universal: The Uniform, the Common and Dialogue between Cultures*, Jullien develops a theory of how Greece forged its distinctive brand of universal, logical thinking precisely by abandoning *nature* as its object of concern.[1] Greek philosophical thought constructed the tool of the concept that cuts thought off from its natural relation to and within the world of things—of things as they are without the artificial boundaries that are erected by thought. With the advent of logical thinking, which for Jullien can be dated precisely from Socrates, thought defines and delimits its own field of operation. Pre-conceptual thought does not set up any hard-and-fast division between itself and what is other than it, between thought and what is not thought, between word and thing, between language and the world. It has not yet separated itself from the world of things in and among which it moves and dwells. Conceptual thought *does* enact exactly this separation and thenceforth relates immediately only to what is of its own making and thus of its own kind and consistency. That is to say, conceptual thought relates directly only to conceptual creatures produced by thought—except to the extent that conceptual thought can still negate *itself* so as to be open to what is other than it.

---

1. *De l'universel, de l'uniforme, du commun et du dialogue entre les cultures* (Paris: Fayard, 2008). Failing other indications, this is the book to which page references are keyed throughout this chapter. The work is also available in an English translation by Michael Richardson and Krzysztof Fijalkowski as *On the Universal: The Uniform, the Common and Dialogue between Cultures* (London: Polity Press, 2014).

For all the empowerment that this momentous introduction of analytical, logical methods of conceptual thought brings with it, particularly in its full deployment in the technological development of modern civilization, with its awe-inspiring capabilities and staggering technical sophistication, such a conceptual metamorphosis of thought also entails a severance of the umbilical cord with nature as the mother of all. The artificial construction of the concept thenceforth intervenes and mediates thought's relation to everything, including its own natural source and grounds.

Jullien describes the birth of logical thinking in Greece as coming about in Socrates's shift away from the pre-Socratics' attempt to think nature or things as a whole concretely by means of analogy. With Socrates, begins the move to thinking rather in a formal mode "according to the whole," *kata holon* (κατά ὅλον). Jullien contrasts the conceptual thinking invented by Socrates with certain pre-Socratic philosophers' way of thinking things as a whole, particularly with the metaphorical mode of the so-called physiologists (φυσιολόγοι), for whom All was water or fire or air, etc. The whole of nature, *things* as a whole, could not be conceived except through such sensory images extended poetically to embrace all things. But just this whole of actually perceptible things, as intended by such metaphors for All, was erased, as wholeness became rather a *form of thought*. Thought's object or intent was thenceforth defined by criteria internal to thought itself and was severed from the infinite, from relation with the All of nature: *that* All, the All of nature, was simply abandoned as not worth thinking about, since it could not be logically grasped through a concept. Thinking a concept of the whole or of all substitutes for and supplants the forms of thought employed for relating imaginatively to the All that is always beyond thought but that nevertheless encompasses and comprehends thought wholly. As Jullien explains,

> Socrates is no longer concerned with the "all" of nature, as were his predecessors, the *phusiologoi*, who are named "pre-socratics" precisely on account of this rupture; but rather, investigating "according to the whole" (*kat-holou*), he makes the "whole" from now on a formal (or logical) exigency: to philosophize is no longer to inquire concerning the all of the world, taken as object, nor after the principle of this all, but to think "conformably to the whole," in the mode of the whole. That is to say, in the mode of universality, i.e. conceptually.
>
> Socrate ne se préoccupe plus du "tout" de la nature, comme l'ont fait ses prédécesseurs, les *phusiologoi,* qu'on appellera

précisément en fonction de cette rupture les "pre-socratiques"; mais, cherchant "selon le tout" (*kat-holou*), il fait du "tout" une exigence désormais formelle (ou logique): philosopher ne sera plus enquêter *sur* le tout du monde, pris comme objet, ni même sur le principe de ce tout, mais penser "conformément au tout," sur le mode du tout. C'est-à-dire sur le mode de l'universalité, i.e. conceptuellement. (68)

Thinking according to the whole rather than thinking the All entails a subtle but momentous shift from the All of nature to the all of thought itself. Thought takes this step because the latter alone is within its reach and can be defined rigorously in terms of thought and nothing else. But thought thereby also renounces the poetic saying, such as one found it in the pre-Socratics, of the All in a metaphorical word reaching beyond thought towards the unthinkable whole of reality that exceeds thought. Thought thus rigorously limits itself to itself—that is, to what it can encompass with its concepts, and thought thenceforth forgets the open, uncircumscribable mystery of All that it had previously endeavored to sound by a poetic word, a word for All. Words such as "water," "air," and "fire," as used by Thales, Anaximenes, and Heraclitus respectively, were made through titanic metaphorical stretching to span the entire spectrum of beings and to fathom the whole unencompassable element of circumambient nature. Precisely this is what Socrates's logical-conceptual interrogation puts an end to, at least as far as philosophy is concerned. According to Jullien, "In learning to think 'according to the all,' or universally, Socrates makes us forget the dream of saying with a word the total truth, and he forms—or forces—thought to conform to the hard path of its rigor" ("Ce faisant, apprenant à penser 'selon le tout,' ou universellement, Socrate fait oublier le rêve de dire d'un mot la vérité totale et forme (force) la pensée au dur chemin de sa rigueur," 69).

Of course, Plato is still struggling with the paradoxes generated by the unthinkability of the all (τὸ πᾶν) and the unanalyzability of the whole (τὸ ὅλον), for example, in the *Sophist* (starting from 236e, see particularly 242e and 244e), where the problem of how to say or think that falsehood really exists (ὅπως γὰρ εἰπόντα χρὴ ψευδῆ λέγειν ἢ δοξάζειν ὄντως εἶναι), without falling into contradiction, proves logically insoluble. Plato is forced to resort to myth in order to adumbrate the nonbeing (τὸ μὴ ὄν) of the false that in some sense does exist and so cannot be excluded from the whole of the all but is nonetheless inconceivable, inexpressible, unspeakable, and irrational (ἀδιανόητόν τε καὶ ἄρρητον καὶ ἄφθεγκτον καὶ ἄλογον, 238c). Aristotle rejects this solution of making recourse to myth. For him, moreover, there can be no science of all things (*Metaphysics* 992b30), since there is no genus of all genera, but only the principle of non-contradiction, which alone embraces all knowledge, without enabling the all as such to be thought (1062a2). In his dismissal of those who deny the principle of non-contradiction, he effectively excludes anything that is unthinkable from the whole as self-contradictory and therefore as simply nothing (*Metaphysics* Γ 6). He no longer admits in any way, shape, or form the unthinkable non-being that is part of and that haunts being as its "other" in Plato. Plato still in his *Parmenides* (142b1ff.) was wrestling with the aporiae of discourse about the whole and about the negations that are in some sense integral to it. And these aporiae can still be found today at work in the paradoxes of modern set theory, as it revolves around the set of all sets that are not members of themselves and the question of whether *this* set is, or cannot be, or *must* be a member of itself (cf. Russell's paradox).[2]

The All as such remains unthinkable from this point on, with Socrates, at the origin of self-consciously conceptual thinking in philosophy, since any object requires some kind of delimitation or closure in order to be thought, and such closure cannot but be artificial in the case of the All. There is always more to the All than what can be known or thought or gathered into a concept. But with the advent of formal logic or conceptual thinking, thought renounces, or in any case turns away from, its impulse to imagine the All from within an infinite, uncircumscribable relation to All. Conceptual thought turns, rather, to the task of mastering a delimited field of thinkable, formal objects that it has defined for itself in a frame it stands outside of and can thus control. The awesome powers of technology, with their terrific—and sometimes terrifying—effects and outcomes, are the remote result and consequence of this type of logical thinking and its sequestering of a field of objects. By such means, a humanly regulated domain that can be surveyed and controlled is set off from the All of nature that abides always beyond thought's control and yet remains the enabling ground and context of any and every human endeavor. Such a humanly cordoned-off realm is the result of what Martin Heidegger calls "framing" (*Gestell*) as the characteristic mode of technology. In "The Question Concerning Technology," Heidegger writes that "man exalts himself to

---

2. Bertrand Russell, "Letter to Frege" (1902), in Jean van Heijenoort, ed., *From Frege to Gödel* (Cambridge: Harvard University Press, 1967), 124–25.

the posture of the lord of the earth" and then "it seems as though man everywhere and always encounters only himself."[3]

By turning away from the All, humanity turns away also from all that constitutes the human being in its relationship to and within the overall order of things. Considered logically, thinking becomes universal by elimination of whatever belongs to the unique, concrete relation of some particular individual to and within the All—that is, by suppressing all that is one's own in order to think only what is identical or the same for all thinking individuals. This makes for the rigor of logical thinking such as it was forged in Greek philosophy. It requires a rupture of one's own personal relation to what is thought: nothing subjective or circumstantial can be allowed to enter into the purely logical content of thought. One's own thought thereby becomes equivalent to what can be thought by anyone else under any circumstances and in any relations whatever within the world. Such is the ideal still in modern times of rational and experimental science.

Such abstraction from the particular seems to mark an advance towards universality. However, there is another kind of universality of thinking, one that remains undefined and yet connected with nature, one which is lost in and through this "advance" to conceptual thinking. This other universality is what traditional Chinese models of wisdom can help us to recollect and recover. They can do so, however, not by substituting another paradigm, say, that of immanence for that of transcendence, but only dialectically, through sharpening our critical awareness of the liabilities of Western logical thinking, specifically of what is lost through the type of universality that logical thinking has invented and has "successfully" imposed on modern thought and civilization. This "success" is measured chiefly in terms of the power of intervening upon our natural environment and massively transforming it. This "power" of abstract logical thinking has enabled the Western model of civilization to impose itself, brooking no opposition, from one end of the globe to the other.

---

3. Martin Heidegger, "Die Frage nach der Technik," in *Vorträge und Aufsätze* (Pfulingen: Neske, 1954), trans. William Lovitt as "The Question Concerning Technology," in *The Question Concerning Technology and Other Essays* (New York: Harper, 1977), 27. This passage from Heidegger is quoted by Thomas Carlson, who pursues the question of nature and its transcendence of human technology especially in John Scott Eriugena and his tradition of apophatic theology, in "Theophany and the Chiaroscura of Nature: Eriugena and the Question of Technology," in *Eriugena and Creation*, eds. Willemien Otten and Michael Allen (Brussels: Brepols, 2014).

Aristotle describes how this type of generally or universally valid knowledge is to be constructed or attained. He theorizes the passage from unique, individual sensation through experience, in which abstraction is made from a series of cases and their diversities, in order to isolate what they share in common. On that basis, we are able to reach universal knowledge and, more specifically, knowledge of causes (*Metaphysics* A.1–2). This is the method of attaining knowledge through abstraction from the particularity of experience that becomes canonical in Western philosophy and science. Such knowledge by abstraction, however, has become an object of intensive critique in recent continental philosophy, given the latter's multifaceted and pluri-vocal, yet widespread and concerted, rejection of metaphysics in its traditional, pre-Heideggerean or pre-Nietzschean forms.

François Jullien has mounted a kindred critique from a specifically intercultural perspective. He suggests, moreover, that without such a perspective affording an external vantage point, philosophical critiques of abstraction are not able effectively to escape from the closures of Western metaphysics that they are attempting to bring to self-conscious reflection and thereby overcome. According to Jullien, classical Chinese philosophy, being typically naturalistic, is far more apt than Western philosophy to avoid abstraction as the artificial segmenting of reality into thinkable and manipulable objects. Nature provides a kind of normativity in Chinese philosophy and, more generally, in pantheistic or immantentist religions. In such forms of thinking, nature answers to the demands of the universal and supplies a universally and necessarily valid standard and an all-embracing ambit for all that is. It is, to this extent, an absolute.

Nature has very often been summarily dismissed in critical forms of Western philosophical rationality. Only by exiting from natural contingency, it seems, do people become the masters of their world and establish necessary norms and laws. But if nature is understood more apophatically, as is typically the case in the East, or even more in line with *natura naturans* than with *natura naturata* (in the terms Spinoza recycles in the West), then it can perhaps provide the kind of normativity that has been tortuously sought along the paths of abstraction to the universal in the West. In other words, perhaps the great but ungraspable All, as fathomed exemplarily by nature-oriented Chinese thought, is indispensable; perhaps it can serve us best in order to make good on the claims of universality that are still widely felt to be necessary, even if so very problematic, in Western philosophies. Claims to universality show up as transparently arbitrary, particularly in those philosophies that have resorted to constructive systems, which become merely formal and forced impositions. In contrast, there is something vital without limit in any thinking that remains still ensconced within the natural world. This is something that even sophisticated philosophical thinking needs to reconnect with in order not to suffocate in its own self-generated, self-enclosed sphere of autonomous, supposedly "free" activity. Apophatics aims to foster insight into, or at least reverent respect for, the nature of this nature that is beyond thought and speech and yet is more essentially natural than any manifest natural phenomenon could possibly be: such a nature is more universal than any universal concept that can be concocted.

Nature in Chinese thought is an all-encompassing reality and in this capacity provides a kind of universal standard of validity. The quest for universality in the West can benefit from being evaluated in comparison with certain modes of practice common in the East, particularly in classical forms of Chinese thought, which aim at corresponding to nature: the issues concerning universality map on to those concerning nature, notably that of its transcendence or immanence. Nature, in classical Chinese thinking, imaged particularly as "heaven" (*Tiān*, 天), is in crucial respects transcendent and yet also immanent to the world. Heaven as *Tiān* is constant or absolute and above all, yet it is also a principle of harmonization internal to the cosmos rather than a principle or will imposed on it from without, as if by a Creator.

The absolute or the All is conceived in classical Chinese wisdom, according to Jullien, on the model of a regulated natural process ("*processus régulé*"). In *Dialogue sur la morale*, Jullien, traces the evolution of "heaven" (*Tiān*) in Chinese thought from being a transcendent notion to being a factor of absoluteness in cosmic regularity that is then supposed to be embodied in right human conduct.[4] Mencius, in particular, reflects on humanity's relation to this process. Instead of proposing a speculative system of the universe, Mencius, like Socrates, regulates humanity's role in ignorance of any general truths of the universe as such—or apophatically, we might say. It is rather through a self-critical application day by day of the principle of cosmic regularity (which cannot be known in itself but only as invented and projected by human conceptualities) to one's own conduct that one discovers the virtue of humanity (*rén* 仁, also pronounced and translitterated *jén*). And this discovery grants humans, after all, a kind of "access to transcendence" through raising consciousness of the "process of things" along "the great Way of Regulation" ("ils pourront avoir accès à la transcendance et prendre conscience de la marche des choses [la grande 'Voie' de la Régulation]").[5]

---

4. Jullien, *Dialogue sur la morale*, 142–49.

5. Jullien, *Dialogue sur la morale*, 52–53.

We are accustomed to thinking that an urgent question concerning nature is that of whether a source and norm for our life and action are given in the nature of things, or whether they must be sought instead from somewhere else outside, beyond or above, nature. However, in consideration of a classical Chinese notion of nature, which envisages nature before it is reduced to a formal concept, we are led to ask whether this standard for conduct might be elicited in some way that breaks down the seeming exclusiveness of these alternatives. Perhaps in the end such a natural norm can be addressed adequately only by an *inter*culturally oriented philosophy, since the answer must avoid remaining enclosed within any one cultural-conceptual framework or, indeed, in any culturally given construction of thought whatsoever. In order to approach or envisage Nature as an absolute, supracultural standard or source of value, intercultural critique is necessary, for only by such means is it possible to ferret out and expose any given culture's inevitable blind spots. No culture's formulation of this natural absolute can be transparent to it, without biases and distortions or, in any case, arbitrary delimitations. The supracultural can never be positively present as such. It can only be elicited by the negation of its finite formulations in the limited vocabularies of any and every specific cultural code. It is only in the gap between cultures—what Jullien terms their "*écart*—that the truly universal, or any absolute type of natural norm, can emerge.

HISTORICAL PERMUTATIONS OF THE NON-NATURAL UNIVERSALITY FORGED BY THOUGHT

The question of all, or of the universal, is treated thus by Jullien in an intercultural dimension and context moving between China and the West, and it demands, accordingly, application of an intercultural method. In *De l'universel,* Jullien describes how China provides the methodological exteriority with respect to Western culture that is necessary to enable us to investigate the latter's claim to universality and to ask whether there are any truly universal notions—such as time, or being, or truth.[6] Although China and the West developed for millennia in complete independence from one another and in virtual ignorance of each other's cultures, they are neverthe-

---

6. The question of time is pursued by Jullien specifically in *Du "Temps," Éléments d'une philosophie du vivre* (Paris: Le Livre de Poche, 2012).

less symmetrical in representing fully developed and self-reflective forms of civilization, each in its own genre. "China is a world of thought that is as developed and textualized, as explicit and commented upon, as is ours in Europe: the two can thus be placed in relation as equal and symmetrical" ("la Chine est un monde de pensée aussi développé, textualisé, explicité, et commenté que le nôtre en Europe: la mise en rapport pourra donc être égale et symétrique," *De l'universel,* 129). The comparison that Jullien proposes as a philosopher is, accordingly, different from the kind of comparative undertaking typical of anthropology. Anthropologists' work is based not on parity but rather on the "dissymmetry" of the primordial cultures and peoples they study with respect to their own civilization.

But by focusing on the question of universality, Jullien discovers a very high degree of parallelism between China and Europe, particularly between classical imperial China and the Europe of the Roman Empire: both were for a long time fully engaged upon civilizing missions and did not even need to raise the question of the universality of their values. Both empires were implacable engines of ideological integration and cultural centering and, to a degree, homogenization. Their superiority as purveyors of civilization and humanity, where it had not yet been attained among those still living savagely or barbarically (by "civilized" standards), was typically taken to be self-evident. Neither for the Chinese Empire nor for the Roman Empire did the question of its universal validity as the most evolved and humanly desirable form of life even arise—not, at least, for the imperialists. They simply took their own superiority for granted.[7]

This leads Jullien to the hypothesis that reflection on universality is spurred specifically by crises of ideological unity in a culture: only such crises create the need for focusing on an ideal and justifying its universality. Such reflection occurs in earnest first in modern rather than in medieval Europe. The Middle Ages in Europe were characterized by the cohesion afforded by a nearly universal creed, the Christian faith. This faith convoyed also a *historical* mission and destiny, such as are alien to the Chinese experi-

---

7. This scenario could well be nuanced by an ironic reading even of Virgil as the reluctant and regretful poet singing the glory of the Empire and the praises of Augustus Caesar in a public voice while at the same time lamenting its costs in human sacrifice in a private voice of complaint that whines through the official rhetoric. I develop such a reading in chapter 3 of *The Revelation of Imagination: From the Bible and Homer through Virgil and Augustine to Dante* (Evanston, IL: Northwestern University Press, 2015).

ence. In this regard, China is closer to traditional Indian and even Islamic civilizations in their relative closure to history and the world outside the order that they themselves establish and transmit (117). The question of universality in such cases arises only technically and on a logical level rather than as fundamentally questioning the leading values of the triumphant civilization. It is when Europe finds itself in want of ideological cohesion ("en manque d'intégration idéologique") that the issue of its universalism becomes conscious and acute. Jullien sees this lack not as a state of self-doubt to be avoided or overcome as quickly as possible but rather as a peculiarly productive or "fecund negativity" ("une négativité féconde," 119).

The idea of universality in the West has evolved historically, and the historical nature of universal values in the West owes very much to biblical religion and especially to Christianity, with its missionary spirit. Unlike the cosmic universalism embraced by the Stoics as something natural and necessary, Saint Paul's universalism is a sheer historical event. He proclaims an act of God on the world-historical scene and urges all to recognize that this divine event demands in response action on the part of human beings everywhere—namely, an act of conversion, an act that will inaugurate for each individual a new personal history and destiny.[8] Such an event rises up against the givens of time and place, tribe and family, country and culture, affirming a new belonging that transcends all such natural communities and their contextually given circumstances. It constitutes a radical break with all natural givens in the name of a unique historical event, one that is supposed to become a personal experience of salvation.

With Christianity, the figure of the universal becomes individual, personal, and incarnate (95). The universal opening of the Christian subject to participation in the event of Christ empties the subject of all that is merely proper or its own and of all determinations that may be deemed natural ("Il en découle un complet *évidement* du sujet chrétien ne possédant plus rien en propre, par sa nature," 94). By virtue of this self-emptying or "kenosis," Jullien remarks, the Christian subject comes to possess nothing that is its own by nature: instead, it is made radically open to the universal ("ce sujet libéré de toute détermination spécifiante, l'affectant en lui-même, est le plus radicalement ouvert à l'universalité," 94). It is in this sense, I would add,

---

8. Paul has galvanized contemporary philosophical discussion of universality thanks especially to Alain Badiou, *Saint Paul: La fondation de l'universalisme* (Paris: Presses Universitaires de France, 1997), trans. Ray Brassier as *Saint Paul: The Foundation of Universalism* (Stanford, CA: Stanford University Press, 2003).

that Paul can say, "I am crucified with Christ; nevertheless I live; yet not I, but Christ lives in me" (Galatians 2:20).[9]

This Christian subject constitutes a reversal of the ancient Roman subject, with its rights rooted in natural determinations of birth, family, class, and citizenship. The ancient Roman citizen was a subject constituted by plenitude. But Paul's new universality reaches to what is unique in each person called to the faith as a single individual summoned out of all previous ties of belonging. Instead of superimposing itself on regional identities and customs, as was the case with Roman law and institutions in their extension all around the Mediterranean basin and beyond, Christian universality (in Jullien's reading) abolishes all such particularities (83). In tandem with this eradication and replacement of indigenous cultures, Europe develops the idea of its own exceptionalism, of its having a unique right to rule and a mission to educate and to civilize all peoples. These pretensions and self-understanding are hardly unprecedented and unparalleled in other civilizations. Nevertheless, they underwrite the notion of the West's own values being extendable to other cultures elsewhere—indeed as by rights trumping those cultures' own native values. Such beliefs were implemented, in all their far-reaching and often dire consequences, in the historical colonization of the globe by Western powers in modern times, especially since the discovery of the "New World."

For Jullien, Paul's new Christianity entails a loss of our rootedness in nature rather than the radical rediscovery of an enriched, authentic nature and therewith of a new vocation to universalism. Here, however, Jullien perhaps underestimates the extent to which Christian universalism propagates not just an abstract philosophical truth, the same for all, but a lived event that becomes incarnate differently in the cultural-historical particularity of individuals who offer their own unique bodily *witness*. This *testimony* of the individual is all their own, and no other person can authentically experience or share in it except through an experience

---

9. For Paul's provocation in the rediscovery of universality among contemporary philosophers, see further *St. Paul Among the Philosophers*, eds. John D. Caputo and Linda Martín Alcoff (Bloomington: Indiana University Press, 2009) and John Milbank and Slavoj Žižek, *Paul's New Moment: Continental Philosophy and the Future of Christian Theology*, ed. Creston Davis, (Grand Rapids, MI: Brazos Press, 2010). I treat this topic more extensively in "Saint Paul Among the Theorists: A Genealogy of the New Universalism," in *The Routledge Companion to Literature and Religion*, ed. Mark Knight (New York: Routledge, 2016), 146–55.

appropriating it to *their own* particular background and to the unique determining coordinates of their own lives. Such witness must be expressed bodily, since all members of the church are constitutive of the body of Christ. Jullien wishes to see Christianity as extending the erasure of a self-generating nature, an erasure that has been operative in Western metaphysics since its inception. But he seems here to ignore the radical reversal of intellectual abstraction that is effected by the biblical revelation of an incarnate universality—of God as incarnate logos. This is a universality that can and must be assimilated existentially and even corporeally. Elsewhere, in the context of other arguments, Jullien does, after all, appreciate Christianity's radical contradiction of the (Greek) *logos* by the "folly" of the word of the cross, in the historically resonant and shattering terms of I Corinthians 1.[10]

One pertinent question raised, in any case, by Jullien's analyses is that of whether the *un*natural universality of Christianity, in distancing itself from the tribe or clan does not—by an irresistible logic and energy—incur difficulties, paradoxes, and contradictions and thereby eventually induce to its own demise. Nietzsche's backlash against Christianity in defense of instinct, race, breeding, and the like, develops just this kind of reaction. Yet Nietzsche typically targets chiefly the philosophical appropriations and reformulations of Christianity. The Christianity against which he inveighs is heavily alloyed and amalgamated with Platonism. According to Nietzsche, the supposed disinterestedness of universalism brings with it the destruction of our life instincts and of our natural base of motivation. It produces, as a fatal consequence, the Kantian ideal of disinterestedness, in which the narrowly universalizing penchant of philosophy peaks. To counter this, we require—and Nietzsche presumably would recommend—a critical movement that turns against disinterest and particularly against the claim to disinterested universality. In order not to sap our own vitality, we need to be able to return to and connect with the drives of particular, *interested* individuals striving against one another in their inevitably conflictual situations. Our inextricable involvement in particular historical situations is recognized, for example, even by Hegel in his constant endeavor, pushing apparently beyond Kant, to elicit the *concrete* universal. Hegel turns attention to the collective, historically determinate, cultural morality of *Sittlichkeit* as necessarily undergirding any purportedly categorical imperatives issued for isolated wills of agents. This mediation is, for Hegel, still very

---

10. See especially the final chapter of *Si parler va sans dire*, 173–74.

Christian in its inspiration. And yet, for Hegel, it is all still a construction of thought, all still the work of the concept. In this regard, Hegel conducts the Aristotelian heritage of universal, thinkable, conceptual essences to its apogee and indeed to a sort of apotheosis.

Especially as informed by a consideration of Chinese approaches to universality, in particular that of Mencius, a certain apophatic wisdom is called for here that can serve to put us on guard against any universality that can be thought. Universality is not what it is *thought* to be by means of any of the universals that we can think. The naïve faith of the Enlightenment in thought and education, moreover, as per se emancipatory is belied by history (*De l'universel*, 64). Nazi Germany sprang up from the midst of a rich and explosively creative period of cultural ferment and flourishing in the effervescent civilization of the Weimar Republic (1918–33). Already to Hegel himself, in the wake of the French Revolution, it was all too evident that history manifested no natural necessity to realize the ideals that it nonetheless projected as possibilities and as regulatory principles.[11] The universal remains an ideal rather than a manifest fact in the course of history. It cannot be approached except always by making allowance for a margin of the negative. The reality of history, in its specifics and in the human sacrifices it exacts, indeed tends to be profoundly anti-universalist and anti-utopian. Rather than speaking glibly along with Enlightenment-style idealists about emancipation, we need to consider the real and pragmatic conditions of freedom. The ideal of universality—of a universal order of justice and peace—has proven itself to be a chimera more often than not in the course of world history, with its empires and alliances and *Reich*s and global economic orders: at present, in effect, capitalism without limits. The conditions of freedom and equality for all in real historical contexts are very often the opposite of what we would expect on the basis of principles alone. The principles tend to be contradicted by their applications and to require creative adaptations reversing their immediate, first-order effects in order to reinstate their original sense and intention. Universality that is defined and thereby circumscribed by thought quickly becomes dystopian.

An exemplary case is human rights as they emerge from a specific, contingent history and yet are oriented and take their aim by reaching toward something unconditioned. If they are defined and spelled out, they

---

11. Thoughtful reflection on this head is proposed by Mario Wenning, "Hegel, Utopia, and the Philosophy of History," in *Hegel and History*, ed. Will Dudley (New York: State University of New York Press, 2009).

inevitably reflect a certain cultural code and its attendant biases. Their universal application cannot be expressly justified except through appeal to merely conditional motives.¹² There is, then, no pre-established universal principle that could validate them. Such validation can only be a matter of persuading others to adhere to such principles through a kind of common sense that can be proposed and that must then be recognized as binding by any single individual—and potentially by all. But its terms of expression need still to remain open for negotiation with others arriving with their own different convictions concerning the unconditioned. All see something that is unconditioned from the situated ground of their own specific cultural history, with its different narrative models and social contexts and motivations in terms of values accepted among them as normative.

BEYOND CULTURAL RELATIVITY AND THE CONSTRUCTION OF UNIVERSALITY

Jullien cites Kant's theory of aesthetic judgment as depending on a universal rule that cannot be explicitly given ("ein Beispiel einer allgemeinen Regel, die man nicht angeben kann," *Kritik der Urteilskraft*, § 18). It cannot be given as binding by purely logical reasons but rather only by appeal to a common sensibility (*Gemeinsinn*). Jullien does not wish to posit some innate common sense that is the same for all everywhere independently of cultural difference. Nevertheless, there is something that can be called a common sense, which is "refracted raw in all experience," however variously, just as it "never ceases to speak in all language" ("ce sens commun est bien ce qui transparaît à vif dans toute experience, de même qu'il ne cesse de nous parler dans tout langage," *De l'universel*, 158). But the common sense of the human is rather a possibility and an ideal, not a ready-made psychological faculty

---

12. In "Agamben's Logic of Exception and its Apophatic Roots and Offshoots," *Concentric: Literary and Cultural Studies* 41/2 (2015): 95–120, I carry this specific critique of human rights further through reference to Giorgio Agamben's *Homo sacer: Il potere soverano e la vita nuda* (Turin: Einaudi, 1995), vol. 1. For some dilemmas and imperatives of applying human rights to China, see, further, Anthony C. Yu, "China and the Problem of Human Rights: Ancient Verities a Modern Realities," in *Comparative Journeys: Essays in Literature and Religion East and West* (New York: Columbia University Press, 2009), 351–90, and Wm. Theodore de Bary, "Confucianism and Human Rights," "China and the Limits of Liberalism," in *The Great Conversation: Education for a World Community*, 277–325.

or a given biological endowment. To explain it, Jullien evokes Kant's idea of a "universal communicability" (*allgemeine Mitteilbarkeit*, 159).

Jullien notes that when Europeans endeavor to extend their values universally, for example, under the aegis of the "rights of man," they are overlooking the way in which their judgments are culturally conditioned, for instance, by their (supposedly) characteristic striving after autonomy and abstraction. As part and parcel of such tendencies, in his view, European values are beholden in particular to theology, as well as to the West's own specific history of battles for emancipation from theology. Jullien admits that there is in all European thinking an inveterate "feudal" dependence on "the theological" that cannot perhaps be completely overcome ("inféodation invétérée—à quel point dénouable?—au théologique," 156). Just as for Derrida and for other thinkers of the French left, theology tends to be targeted also by Jullien as the deeply embedded, unreflected and yet fettering ball and chain from which Western thinkers today must strive to free themselves.

However, this purge against theology and "God" as typically Western hang-ups that have kept the West from achieving genuine wisdom does not do justice to the deeper logic of Jullien's intercultural critique. Jullien and I strongly agree, in any case, that one must be able critically to negate whatever is one's own. Self-negation, in the form of unlimited self-critique, is the only formula—actually a subversion of all formulas—for progressive and potentially unlimited growth and emancipation and for avoiding the constrictive confinement of the concept. Yet this critical stance vis-à-vis theology has been built into theology itself, I maintain, all along in the form of negative theology, alias apophasis.[13]

Jullien himself proposes what is, in effect, a perfectly apophatic approach to the universal that proves still to be inescapable, even after the shipwreck of Europe's attempt to impose its particular brand of universality on the rest of the world through colonization. Contemporary philosophical and intercultural discussion concerning the universal may have reduced it to next to nothing: nothing seems to be able to stand up as truly universal, once the singularity of diverse cultures is duly respected. And yet this does not necessarily mean that the universal is dead and powerless. Instead, "It is

---

13. I bring to focus this specific point in "Le commencement et la fin de la philosophie dans la mystique apophatique: De Platon au postmodernisme," in *Philosophie et mystique chez Stanislas Breton: Colloque de Cerisy-la-Salle (août 2011)*, eds. Jean Greisch, Jérôme de Gramont, and Marie-Odile Métral (Paris: Éditions le Cerf, 2015), 129–43.

this void itself, which no signification can fill in or satisfy, that renders the universal still operative" ("c'est ce *vide* même, qu'aucun signifié ne comble ni ne satisfait, qui fait qu'il opère encore," 144). Jullien, guided by classical Chinese wisdom, explains that the universal is nothing positive or possessing a distinct content, but just the opposite: in other words (which Jullien does not as such employ), the universal is the apophatic. Jullien speaks of the "operativity" of the universal, but this in the end is exactly the opposite of anything positively manifest and verifiable or directly observable and identifiable.

> It [operativity] does not consist in a positive given, whatever it may be (and it is always suspect), of the order of values, but in this negative function: that, precisely, of *emptying* every formation-or-institution of its assurance, born of its self-sufficing totalization, and reopening a breach in the comfort of closure.
>
> Elle [l'opérativité] ne consiste effectivement pas dans un donné positif, quel qu'il soit et toujours suspect, de l'ordre des valeurs, mais dans cette fonction négative: celle, précisément, de *vider* toute formation-institution de son assurance, née de la totalisation dont elle se suffit, et de rouvrir une brèche dans ce confort de la clôture. (144)

Jullien completes this description of the new form in which universality is still operative today by stressing that it is intrinsic and immanent. And yet such universality is not a given or common ground but rather a vector of motion and *pro*motion pointing in the direction of a "passing beyond" ("dépassement," 145), beyond any given culture's achieved formulations. To this extent, one could say that it is also a form of transcendence. It is at least a form of self-transcendence along a horizontal axis. To the extent, moreover, that self-deconstruction is carried out without limit or reserve, it opens theoretically to all others and thus even to others imagined along a vertical axis, which means, of course, also to the God imagined by theology. An impermeable categorical distinction between human others and transhuman or suprahuman alterities cannot be maintained without some fixed sense of what is human, but exactly such sense is abandoned by negative theology, which necessarily entails also a negative anthropology.[14]

---

14. Thomas Carlson, *Indiscretion: Finitude and the Naming of God* (Chicago, IL: University of Chicago Press, 1999) effectively brings together these two domains of logos in their inextricable, reciprocal coimplication.

While Jullien sees Christianity as extending imperialistically the non-natural universality of the concept to some of its most lethal consequences, I bring out instead a kenotic side of Christianity, which breaks the concept open to the inconceivable and finds there the true universality that can unite without the divisiveness which is inevitable in the concept. In this apophatic perspective, there is a kind of intrinsic self-deconstructive propulsion at work in any conceptually *stated* form of universalism. Its definition *of itself* will be undermined and pass into the more truly universal instance that it does not and cannot grasp or say—except indirectly, figuratively, projectively, and poetically. Universalism, so construed, instead of being the imposition of one's own paradigm, to the exclusion of others, becomes practically the opposite: it becomes an opening to others and to their paradigms as prerequisite to having any sense of one's own. What is at stake in intercultural philosophy and religion is negating one's own cultural frame, with its inevitable background assumptions, and thereby relativizing culture per se so as to open to the dimension of the absolute or religious. What is interesting to me about intercultural philosophy and religion is that it opens a space between cultures and even *beyond* culture—what may be clumsily called the absolute or the religious—a realm that no culture can adequately conceptualize.

The exploration of another culture is a privileged opportunity to (re)discover one's own. Curiously, what François Jullien discovers in China, as the counterculture to Europe, is the lack of need for anything theological: all transpires on a plane of immanence. This is in essence the view that has been taken since Voltaire and other philosophers of the European Enlightenment, most significantly Christian Wolff (1679–1754), who, thanks to the reports of Jesuit missionaries, discovered with wonder and amazement China's incomparably ancient, rationally administered, and hierarchically ordered civilization. What struck Wolff most was that this organizational structure seemed capable of bringing an enormous empire under the unified rule of a single authority without any appeal to God.[15] The considerable archive of such accounts, inaugurated by the explorations of Saint Francis Xavier and Matteo Ricci in the sixteenth century and extended into subsequent centuries, made a great impression on Europe, particularly in the eighteenth century, the century of Enlightenment ("siècle des lumières"), as demonstrating that universal order in human affairs could be perfectly well

---

15. See especially Wolff's *Rede von der Sittenlehre der Sineser* (1740) and the *Lettres édifiantes et curieuses de Chine par des missionnaires jésuites 1702–1776*, eds. Isabelle et Jean-Louis Vissière (Paris: Garnier-Flammarion, 1979).

achieved without recourse to a monotheistic deity.[16] There was, however, also the countervailing theological view, represented eminently by Gottfried Wilhelm Leibniz (1646–1716), that ancient Chinese wisdom embodied a natural theology compatible with Christianity and disclosing in its own way the universal rational principles of understanding and peace among humans.

Leibniz was reacting against Nicolas Malbranche's *Conversation Between a Christian Philosopher and a Chinese Philosopher on the Existence and the Nature of God*, which was itself informed by Niccolò Longobardi's *Traité sur quelques points de la religion des Chinois* (1701). Longobardi (1559–1654) had succeeded Matteo Ricci (1552–1610) in directing the Jesuit mission in China and had set about, with determination, to reverse his great predecessor's work of cultural mediation. He believed that translating the Bible into terms understandable on the basis of Confucian philosophy could lead only to total misunderstanding. While the Chinese converts talked about the Lord on High (上帝, *Shàngdì*) or the Lord of Heaven (天主, *Tiānzhǔ*) and "spirit" (神, *shén*) in their own language, they only aped the Christian discourse without understanding what it meant. What they really understood by these terms was informed instead by a pagan and pantheistic worldview: "While they *seem* to speak of our God and his angels, they are mere apes of the truth."[17]

In effect, Longobardi denies the very possibility of translation, implying that the Chinese mind and language, being mired in the material, are incapable of comprehending the sublimely spiritual conceptions of the Christian religion. Against this onslaught, Leibniz defends Ricci's project of cross-cultural translation and communication as formulated chiefly in his *Tianzhu shiyi* (*The True Meaning of the Lord of Heaven*), written and published in Chinese in 1604. Of course, Leibniz is aware that understanding undergoes shifts in the translative process, but that is the nature of understanding per se. How could we presuppose one identical meaning for terms even in "our own" language, and which language is that? Hebrew *Elohim*,

---

16. For detailed discussion of these complex relations, see *Discovering China: European Interpretations in the Enlightenment*, eds. Julia Ching and Willard Oxtoby (Rochester, NY: University of Rochester Press, 1992).

17. Longobardi's treatise was informed in turn by Antonio Caballero (Antoine de Sainte-Maire), *Traité sur quelques points importants de la mission de la Chine*. The citation is from this Franciscan father's work as cited by Jacques Gernet, *Chine et christianisme: action et réation* (Paris: Gallimard, 1982), 50.

Greek *Theos*, Latin *Deus*, not to mention Jesus's own Aramaic vernacular, are already very different in their conceptual approaches to divinity.

Unlike Longobardi, for whom an accurate translation would have to be anchored to a true literal meaning, Leibniz concedes that no language has an objective or adequate grasp of divinity. The problem, then, is not just one of translating between languages (which presumes the perfect adequacy of the Western source language) but one of translating in the first instance *into language* something that infinitely transcends it and exceeds human capacities. Leibniz, in effect, makes a kind of negative-theological argument. He argues that we can know divinity not as it is in itself but only as it is experienced or felt by human beings, "anthropopathically" ("ἀνθρωποπαθῶς, à la manière humaine").[18] The most telling passage is in section 17 of his letter to Monsieur de Rémond:

> Moreover, I respond that if the classic Chinese authors refuse life, knowledge, and authority to the first principle *Li*, they certainly mean this ἀνθρωποπαθῶς, in the human manner, and as these things are present in creatures. By life, they will understand the animation of organs; by knowing, the knowledge acquired through experience; and by authority they will understand power such as that of a prince or magistrate, who only govern their subjects by fear or by hope. But giving *Li* all the greatest perfections, they accord it something more sublime than all that, something of which the life, knowledge, and authority of creatures are but the shadows and feeble imitations. This resembles the way certain mystics, among them particularly Denys the Pseudo-Areopagite, denied that God was a Being, *Ens*, ὠν, but at the same time said that he was more than being, *super-Ens*, ὑπερουσία. This is how I understand the Chinese who say . . . that *Li* is the law that directs and the intelligence that governs things: that it is not itself intelligent, but that by a natural force it has operations that are so well ordered and sure that you would say that it was. This is to be more than intelligent, taking the term in

---

18. Gottfried Wilhelm Leibniz, *Lettre sur la philosophie chinoise à M. de Rémond* (Geneva: Fratres de Tournes, 1748), available online at www.chineancienne.fr, ed. Pierre Palpant, May, 2013.

our sense, for whom it is necessary to make an effort and to deliberate in order to do well, whereas the first principle is infallible by its very nature.

We can see here that negative theology enters early on into the controversy that plays itself out as the famous "rites controversy" of the seventeenth and early eighteenth centuries. Should Catholic rites in China eagerly assimilate—or rather scrupulously avoid—adopting the terms of Confucian philosophy? Longobardi insisted on avoiding any associations with Confucian ideas, since they were based on a different worldview, one that he held to be materialist and without the conceptions of spirit, soul, or true divinity. Leibniz carefully examined these assumptions and came to the opposite conclusion. His decisive point is that the Chinese texts that deny intelligence and consciousness to the supreme principle ordering the universe, *li*, can be read as intending to deny such attributes *only* as they are humanly understood, not absolutely. *Li* (理, lǐ), reason or the logos, might have a higher kind of consciousness or intelligence than any that we are acquainted with in our human experience. Leibniz adapts from Patristic authors the negative theological argument attributing an *eminent* sense (*sensus eminentior*) to words for properties or perfections as predicated of God. This is a sense transcending all that can be understood in human terms, so that it would be more accurate to say *not* that *li* is *un*intelligent but that it is incomparably *more* intelligent than what we are even capable of understanding as intelligence. These are the traditional arguments of negative theology, and Leibniz himself makes explicit reference to Dionysius the Areopagite, the founding figure of Christian negative theology.

Haun Saussy, in commenting on the rites controversy, recasts this negative-theological insight in rhetorical terms. He argues that the dispute over allegory or its impossibility in Chinese literature today is a repeat of these same theological issues, but now understood fundamentally in a rhetorical register. He outlines a parallel between contemporary literary critics' treating "Chinese allegory" as an "impossibility" and the rites controversy, in which purist missionaries after Matteo Ricci rejected his approach and considered it impossible to translate Christian scriptures into terms intelligible on the basis of Chinese classics. Saussy suggests how the controversy pivots fundamentally on the tension between transcendence and immanence as lying at the bottom of the two opposed approaches to translation. "Reading Chinese texts in an immanentist way, Longobardi detects their immanentism; reading them as if their rhetoric had to transcend their grammar, Leibniz sees evidence of transcendence—a hyper-transcendence in fact, one that differs from the standard version of theological transcendence by just as far as allegory differs from metaphor" (*The Problem of a Chinese Aesthetic*, 42).

In Leibniz's negative theology, all our language for God is metaphorical or figurative, as Thomas Aquinas himself demonstrated in *Summa Theologica*, pt. I, Question 13. There is no literal language adequate to God. The transcendent and absolute can be intimated linguistically only in culturally relative terms by comparison and images. So translation is inevitable and legitimate but also always inadequate, and this places all languages and cultures on an equal footing vis-à-vis transcendent divinity.

TRANSCENDENT UNIVERSALITY AND THE NEGATIVE WAY: RECLAIMING THE ENLIGHTENMENT FOR RELIGION

With this insight into the inescapable rhetoricity of language about God, and without taking sides for or against theism, one can discover through intercultural experience how transcendence, even and especially in a theological sense, need not be opposed to immanence and its unfolding in unlimited variations of form and expression. In this sense, classical Chinese thought does not exclude heaven or the transcendent and divine but rather lives and thinks such dimensions in and through the sphere of what Jullien and Gilles Deleuze call "immanence." Such immanence is a "sphere," however, which, more deeply considered, cannot be called properly by any name at all. This is what Western theology, which must be understood more radically as negative theology, has signified all along, even though much of the rhetoric of theology, particularly in its more exoteric, prescriptive, and dogmatic forms, typically has seemed to intend the opposite. More profoundly considered, theology is an especially intensive form of language that fails to attain any proper object or definable reference but rather opens language to its indeterminate potential for referentiality.

Chinese culture, too, since ancient times is actually no stranger to this implicitly theological dimension, which is, more exactly, negative-theological or apophatic. David Keightley lays great emphasis on the metaphysical and divinatory aspects of ancestor worship as it has been disclosed through decipherment of the oracle bones of the Shang. Piecing together an implicit metaphysics from the archeological record, he interprets the oracle bones in terms of a Late Shang dynasty (ca. 1200–1045 BC) ancestral "theology." These records, he writes, "should not, of course, be considered in terms of a purely secular historiography. The oracle-bone inscriptions record a series of ritual acts, and the theology of those acts affected the nature of the records kept."[19] Such theology may, admittedly, be very positive and even crudely idolatrous, but it nevertheless lays the ground for apophatic negations that raise theology to the level of a critical insight indicating something beyond all merely finite determinations.

Starting right from its foundational Ur-text, the *Yijing* (the *Book of Changes*), Chinese culture displays its reverence for the endless play of changes, for what remains always other than what has already been formulated, while at the same time keeping in play the metamorphosis of forms of expression that never completely capture what they intend (see first section of chapter 3). Chinese culture awakens us to this always evasive, unspecifiable universality as the more subtle meaning also of our own traditions. This meaning is manifest not in any set of unchanging ideas and dogmas but in their ever renewed and newly revealing incarnations in evolving, shifting cultural contexts.

Critical or apophatic negation as opening to the infinite and universal (and in this sense as negatively theological) is perhaps most manifest and biting in the evasive ironies of the *Zhuangzi*. At the end of chapter 17, when Huizi asks Zhuangzi how he can know the happiness of the fish that they have observed, since he is not himself a fish, Zhuangzi replies in a way that underscores their situatedness "above the river Hao." He refuses, moreover, to divide and hierarchize the presumably absolute first-person knowledge of direct experience and the more empathic and intuitive ways of knowing something only vicariously. He retorts: How can you know that I don't know the fish's happiness, since you are not me? This is a sort of reduction ad absurdum of Huizi's assumption that he can know absolutely the human, or even just his own, experience. Knowing is always situated and perhaps also projective and conjectural. Zhuangzi, by contrast, takes knowing or feeling happiness as prior to knowing even oneself. There can be a kind of awareness of happiness before reflection about whose it is and thus prior to self-reflection that divides self from other or even species from species. Huizi, even in order to contest Zhuangzi's statement, must have some idea of what it means—and thus of what it means for fish to be happy. This vague, undifferentiated sort of knowing is what is first and immediate, and it is universal. It is not a deduction or construction based on separate units

---

19. David N. Keightley, "Theology and the Writings of History: Truth and the Ancestors in the Wu Ding Divination Records," in *These Bones Shall Rise Again: Selected Writings on Early China* (Albany: State University of New York Press, 2014), 218.

of knowledge verified by and for self-conscious individuals. Universality, for Zhuangzi, is grounded in the radical equality of all things as nothing in and for themselves. All share in a common instability as evacuated into nothing but their unlimited relationality. Their universality consists in what they are not—through which each flows into what all share in common.

The very idea of universality in recent decades has undergone radical transformation, and yet the notion has proven to be resilient and has become ever more indispensable in a world of vertiginous complexity that is spinning ever further out of control so that it can no longer be comprehended by any static formulas. A wide variety of current philosophical initiatives testifies to this continuing and intensified indispensability of the universal. Jullien notes the way that the critique of universalism inevitably turns against those who deploy it as a weapon for whatever interested ideological cause. The apparent challenges to universalism in the name of particular ethnicities, gender identities, or social classes turn out finally to confirm its claims and aspirations. The protest or fight on behalf of excluded minorities (Chicanos or blacks or gays or women or the disabled) remains dependent on the universality that it contests—not as such but rather as not being universal enough because not yet including *them* among the recognized. The "recognized" means almost inevitably also the privileged, given the virtual impossibility of not creating vast shadowy areas of anonymous neglect through focused recognition of defined categories of individuals. The exigency of recognizing every *other* excluded group as equally entitled to the status in question, in effect, dissolves the particularism of the claim that is being asserted. The universal claim to rights cannot be fulfilled except in being emptied of all specific content and of all differential identity. Therefore, not a full-filling but rather a self-emptying is the *telos* of universalism. According to Jullien, the universal is:

> the *effect of lack,* which reveals every identity to itself and constitutes its vocation; and which, never filled, spurs it to transform itself at the same time as it transforms its other, and therefore to not satisfy itself with its own identity either; to not close itself and stop there, at the risk of otherwise finishing in a form of exclusion which, in its triumph, would be equally abusive—and in need of being overthrown.
>
> cet *effet de manque* qui la révèle à elle-même et fait sa vocation; et qui, jamais comblé, la porte à se transformer elle-même, en même temps qu'elle transforme son autre, et donc à ne pas se

satisfaire non plus de sa propre identité; à ne pas s'y clore et s'y arrêter, au risque, sinon, d'aboutir elle aussi à une forme d'exclusion qui, dans son triomphe, serait également abusive—à renverser. (146–47)

For Jullien, the universal is not purely residual, not just a reaction against particularist claims, or their necessary opposite. Universality has more presence and power than that, even if only through and as negation. As lacking plenitude or fullness, as continually defective (*continuel défectif,* 148), it exerts the continual and indefectible power of the negative. From the inside, the universal is turned toward its own overflowing. The universal keeps up a constant pressure of self-surpassing on all forms of achieved identity: it undermines the self-satisfaction or sufficiency of any institutional form or structure. As such, it is the unconditioned that moves in history, reversing and overstepping all exclusions in its path. It keeps the common run of history and politics on the march and constantly in search of itself throughout all its metamorphoses, which are never final. The universal prevents the common from declining into mere communitarianism, with its inevitably sectarian tendencies.[20] The universal keeps humanity in quest of itself—guided by an ideal of always-greater unity. Even though no culture can ever step outside of its own singularity, so as to be universally valid as such, since there is no *position* (or stable ground to stand on) outside all cultures and their respective languages, still a transcendental Unconditioned nevertheless motivates such universalistic aspirations. In Kant's terms, which Jullien evokes, the universal is effective as a "transcendental ideal" ("transzendentales Ideal").

The Kantian aesthetic judgment is a model of a singularity that paradoxically lays claim to a form of universality, even though it is not of the same categorical nature as logical judgments, since it depends on some commonality of sensibility that might be inborn but might also need to be constructed or sought out and produced. Jullien endeavors "to integrate the absolute into the singular perspective proper to diverse cultures" ("intégrer l'absolu dans la perspective singulière propre aux diverses cultures," 155). The key, for him, to doing this is recognizing that we are "cultural subjects" rather than merely epistemological or purely transcendental subjects. He thereby seeks to circumnavigate the Scylla of a "facile universalism" ("l'universalisme facile") that uncritically projects its own vision of the world

---

20. Compare Jean-Luc Nancy, "La communauté désœuvrée," *Aléa* 4 (1983): 11–49.

onto others, ignoring their cultural difference, as well as the Charybdis of "lazy relativism" ("relativisme paresseux"). The latter uncritically leaves each culture, with its own specific values and identity, in mutual isolation, as if these specificities could never be called into question or be challenged and contested from without. By steering such a course, Jullien endeavors to extend the Kantian project of critical Enlightenment in a specifically intercultural direction. This entails, however, some highly significant differences with respect to similar undertakings conceived in terms of Western logos philosophies. Jullien critiques in particular Jürgen Habermas's extension of the same project in the direction of a universal logic of rational argument and an ethics of dialogue.[21] Some of the specific differences here will be brought out in the next-to-last sub-section of this chapter. But my reading and argument continue to insist on the importance of (negative) theology and religion to the project of the Enlightenment and its critique—indeed on the fundamental importance of negative theology to understanding enlightenment *as* critique, particularly as *unlimited* critique.

Theology and religion were most often conceived of as the main enemies of the Enlightenment and of the universalism to which it aspired. Something of this attitude can still be found in François Jullien, as in many of his contemporaries: it is plausibly traced to eighteenth-century French anticlericalism. What I endeavor to show, in contrast, is that theology, particularly negative theology, can be the agent effecting an opening of cultures to a religiously tolerant and spiritually attuned universalism that can fulfill the Enlightenment's aspirations much more satisfactorily than can any exclusionary cult of universal reason. The self-deconstruction of reason carried out to the end without limits, in fact, opens upon the unrestricted openness that ideally characterizes religious revelation—contrary to the more common, rigidly dogmatic understandings of revelation.[22]

Accordingly, I take myself to be basically aligned with Jullien's analysis of the universality of culture, even while reversing the vector of his narrative concerning theology. In my view, theology and its claim to absolute transcendence are no longer the obstacles to untrammeled communication

---

21. Habermas, "Diskursethik—Notizen zu einem Begründungsprogramm," in *Moralbewußtsein und kommunikatives Handeln* (Frankfurt a. M.: Suhrkamp, 1983), trans. Christian Lenhardt and Shierry Weber Nicholsen as *Moral Consciousness and Communicative Action* (Cambridge: MIT Press, 1990).

22. I develop this as a "Critical Negative Theology of Poetic Language" in part 1 of my *Poetry and Apocalypse*.

between cultures that they were in a certain scenario of the Enlightenment descending from the French *philosophes*, in which religion was supposed to be in the process of being overcome historically. On the contrary, theology, particularly in its negative form, tenders essential keys to precisely the type of insight necessary to make possible and to promote cross-pollination and mutual illumination between and among cultures. Obviously, Jullien and I understand different things by "theology." My argument aims to persuade that theology should be viewed in terms not of static historical dogmas enforced by authority through ecclesiastical power hierarchies but rather in terms of its dynamic revolutionary potential to undermine all fixed conceptualities whatsoever in the face of "God" as the inconceivable par excellence. Drawing inspiration also from other apophatic thinkers such as Jean-Luc Nancy, I argue, particularly in the final section of this chapter, that theology is most originally negative theology and that as *negative* theology it is the original iconoclastic reflection of human reason turned ultimately (in the postmodern age) against itself in a self-critical apotheosis.[23]

UNIVERSALITY IN THE (APOPHATIC) GAP BETWEEN CHINA AND THE WEST

We saw how Jullien, in *Le Détour et l'accès,* undertakes to differentiate between Chinese and Western ways of thinking. His premise is that these two civilizations have developed virtually without contact over millennia and consequently represent independent forms of mind or culture. He discusses the classical treatises on the art of war (notably Sunzi or Sun Wu's fourth-century BC "The Art of War," the *Sunzi bingfa*) and the *Book of Odes* (*Shi Jing*), as well as political discourse in modern China's official newspapers. He treats all as embodying the techniques of indirection that characterize Chinese culture's very different approach to communicating information as well as to reflecting on knowledge and values. As a caveat, nonetheless, one has to bear in mind that what is foreign to us is more likely to seem indirect. And conversely, customs of our own, including ones that seem perfectly natural and direct to us, might strike people of other backgrounds, with a different understanding of their aims and priorities, as curiously and perhaps even absurdly indirect ways of going about what they believe they achieve through much more direct and obvious means.

---

23. I offer an extended reading of Nancy in this frame in chapter 4 of *A Philosophy of the Unsayable* (Notre Dame, IN: University of Notre Dame Press, 2014).

Such differences register even in the most banal details of daily life. Putting the appellative "Miss" or "Ms." before personal proper names seems natural for Westerners, whereas (according to native informants) it is inadmissibly awkward for the Chinese. The personal name has to precede the title—arguably because it identifies and recognizes the person being addressed before qualifying his or her status. Or again, in writing postal addresses, the Chinese begin from the country and region and city in order to narrow the focus progressively to the neighborhood, street, building, and unit number, whereas for Westerners the "natural" order is the reverse, moving from the local habitation *toward* the greater space of the world at large. Or, to take an example perhaps more deeply embedded in the visceral and unconscious that reaches beyond what may seem to be only conventional codes: the color white tends in traditional Chinese culture to be perceived as negative, as tantamount to death. Clothing and decoration for traditional weddings cannot be in white, whereas white has generally been preferred as the color of purity for such ceremonies in the West.

There certainly do seem to be fundamental differences between cultures and their respective ways of thinking. But how can they be described? There is no neutral language for doing so. One can doubt all claims appealing to deep "essences" as being mere metaphysical illusions and figments. And yet, deep differences between cultures certainly are felt and experienced. They can be characterized at least negatively. Yet the condition for doing so is still some common ground of understanding, however empty it must be of specific and explicit cultural contents. That just such a common ground could be nothing but a hidden one is the basis also for rendering possible a dialogue between Chinese and European thought in the perspective of comparative philosophical thinking (see Burik, 3).

It is above all at their apophatic frontiers or margins, where they both border on "nothing," nothing determinate or specifiable, that Chinese and Western (apophatic) viewpoints meet and communicate. Both cultures emphasize the key role of negativity in producing the forms of cultural identification and differentiation necessary for any discourse. There is perhaps more theoretical reflection on this in Western traditions and more directly experiential witness to it in Chinese traditions—as illustrated, for example, by the riddling narratives and teasing paradoxes of the *Zhuangzi*. Still, this could also be simply the impression made by what is most commonly known of each tradition. On both sides, apophatic reflection operates with a logic of double negation, or of negation of the negation. Such a logic is enshrined equally in Hegel's *negatio negationis* and in Zhuangzi's *Wúwú* (無無). In either case, this anti-logic is the apophatic moment in which each culture's respective metaphysics of transcendence subverts itself. Such self-subverting moves are wrought to a refined art by Chinese classical sources. This has been appreciated especially in the analyses of comparative philosophers and researchers on religion who can place them in cross-cultural and historical perspective. Metaphysics can be seen to become, in effect, negative metaphysics or, even more subtly, *trans*metaphysics already in Zhuangzi: "If, say, regular metaphysicians were guilty of clinging to 'Being' and Laozi was guilty of attaching to 'Non–being' [wu], Zhuangzi could be seen as the first transmetaphysician who surpassed the duality of Being and Non-being by his notion of *wuwu* or No-nonbeing."[24]

Jullien finds in China the cultural Other he needs in order to be able to think otherwise so as to keep the recursive self-negating aspect of discourse alive and active in his own philosophy. I attempt to do this by drawing from the apophatic currents underlying and inherent in Western philosophical reflection in its most radically critical, and especially self-critical, manifestations. This is an internal other—often figured as divine Other—that can serve some of the same purposes as does Jullien's exterior cultural Other. Even the exterior alterity to which Jullien turns can never be apprehended as simply and absolutely exterior. It is only by an inevitable translation into our own terms that we are able to talk about it at all—and so also to confront the limits of all such talk. Conversely, the internal other is neither so completely internal nor so wholly other as it is what we cannot say, what remains as the unsayable in relation to which all that we *can* say promises to make a sense that is not merely reductive. Not any identifiable, delimited paradigm or cultural archetype but the shadowy underside—or invisible inward fold—of our own thinking is the deepest otherness with which we are always confronted from the moment we begin to think. Just this is the ineluctable stumbling block for all attempts to discursively understand and expound whatever culture by means of differentiation through definable identifying types and characteristics.

Paradoxically, by speaking of China and the West as radically different and separate civilizations and models of knowledge and culture, Jullien seems to situate his work within a radical binarism. He often *appears* to advocate recognition of this ineffaceable difference between two historically autonomous worlds as a necessary starting point for a critical philosophy of culture pursued by a consciously intercultural subject. However, Jullien's

---

24. Charles W. Fu, "Laozi, Zhuangzi, Guo Xiang, and Zen—A Hermeneutic Exploration," in *From Western Philosophy to Zen Buddhism* (Taipei: Dongda Press, 1986), 408–15, quoted by Lingshang Ge, *Liberation as Affirmation: The Religiosity of Zhuangzi and Nietzsche* (Albany: State University of New York Press, 2006), 16.

purpose is not finally to absolutize the separateness and incommunicability between cultures but rather to make them communicate. In the end, Jullien is a powerful and passionate advocate of a certain kind of cross-cultural or intercultural universalism.

And yet, Jullien has often enough seemed, at least to some among his most qualified peers in the study of China, to argue for recognizing insuperable cultural difference and so to idealize the Mandarin fixity of Chinese culture and thereby to militate against the inherent dynamism of history. Indeed, Jullien has been severely criticized for simply perpetuating the myth of China as quintessential "other" that began with the exotic, orientalizing accounts of the Jesuits in the seventeenth century. We need to understand why this is so.

The distinguished Swiss sinologist Jean François Billeter has published a polemical argument *contra* Jullien on just such grounds as these.[25] Jullien has, in turn, been defended by some of the leading luminaries of the French academy today, including Alain Badiou, Bruno Latour, J.-M. Schaeffer, and Paul Ricoeur, in a riposte *pro* Jullien.[26] Jullien, furthermore, defends himself and his approach in a book whose title *Chemin faisant* significantly echoes Heidegger's *Holzwege* in its French translation (*Chemins qui ne mènent nulle part*), thereby situating his work in relation to some central "ways" or "paths" running through Western philosophy, paths that could best be recognized as apophatic.[27] Jullien's *Pont des singes* (2010), moreover, is a scathing rejection of just the sort of exoticism of which he has been persistently accused: he lucidly portrays the historical consequences and poignantly displays the deathly implications for our present and future of such orientalizing handling of traditional cultures.

Paradoxically, Jullien finds himself attacked both for isolating China in a unique exeptionalism and for amalgamating it into a general paradigm of alterity. In either case, Jullien's being defended by the Parisian philosophical establishment against the Swiss sinologist who contests him and the kind of philosophical culture he represents appears to be a sort of atavism repeating in suggestive respects the battle between the rebellious Genevan Jean-Jacques Rousseau and the authoritative Parisian intelligentsia of his day. It was a day

---

25. Jean François Billeter, *Contre François Jullien* (Paris: Allia, 2006).

26. A. Badiou, B. Latour, J.-M. Schaeffer, P. Ricoeur, *Oser construire. Pour François Jullien* (Paris: Seuil, 2007).

27. Jullien, *Chemin faisant: Connaître la Chine, relancer la philosophie, Réplique à**** (Paris: Seuil, 2007). For Heidegger as apophatic, see chapter 11 of my *On What Cannot Be Said*, vol. 2.

of crisis in the history of the Enlightenment, which found itself confronted with the revolutionary new impulses of a nascent Romanticism. The possibility of resistance on the part of a particular individual in the name of personal liberty against the power and morality of an authoritative system of culture (the Parisian in the eighteenth century and, analogously, the Mandarin in the classical period in China) becomes an issue again today in this exchange, just as it was in the eighteenth century. The archetypal scenario is that of the apostles of Enlightenment from Paris battling down errant obscurantists who purportedly erect barriers to their universal principles through appeal to irreducibly personal and emotional elements recalcitrant to reason.[28]

Billeter recalls, significantly, in the postmodern philosophical context, that Chinese culture has its own unique individuality and historical character and is not just generically "other." In reality, however, in spite of his philosophically universalizing approach, Jullien, too, is concerned to emphasize China's uniqueness and incommensurability: he is very wary of the reductions to common denominators characteristically wrought by the "comparative" method. His universalizing project does not efface historical difference but actually sets it into relief—so much so that he is sometimes in danger of reifying and immobilizing cultural differences into contrasting typologies. For there are inevitable difficulties and impasses inhering in any attempt to deal in words and descriptions with a dynamically evolving historical reality.

This, I suspect, is the underlying reason for yet another polemically oppositional, yet in the end highly illuminating, critique of Jullien's project that is developed in painstaking detail by Fabian Heubel. Heubel's stance pivots especially on consideration of modernization as an "a priori" connecting Europe and China and thus belying all comparatism based on the thesis of their mutual exteriority.[29] He accuses Jullien of becoming blind to the realities of hybridization in modernity, realities that leave no specifiable essence of classical Chinese thought and culture intact. This is a critique that enters more penetratingly into some of the most significant and pressing issues facing Western approaches to China and its classical tradition today.

Heubel argues lucidly and relentlessly that Jullien's theoretical remonstrances against comparatism, with his appeals to "working the gaps" (*tra-*

---

28. Frédéric Keck, "Une querelle sinologique et ses implications. À propos du *Contre François Jullien* de Jean-François Billeter," *Esprit*, février (2009/2): 61–81, richly reviews the debate in this historical perspective.

29. Heubel, "Kritik der konformistischen Immanenz: Wider das Klischee vom chinesischen Denken bei François Jullien." I work from the German manuscript sent to me by the author.

vailler les écarts), instead of defining the differences, not to mention the similarities, between cultures, in effect remain at the level of cultural clichés because of Jullien's refusal to engage with the mediation of classical Chinese culture by contemporary Chinese intellectual history and social reality. Such engagement would require dealing with the traumatizing facts of modernization, which irrevocably affect and irreparably dislocate any purported Chinese classical tradition or character of the past.

According to Heubel, Jullien rightly affirms the fecundity (*Fruchtbarkeit*) of working in the intervals between cultures when he rejects in principle the sterility of fixing their differences. Nevertheless, he refuses the actual fertilization (*Befruchtung*) of one culture by another *in the present* in which horizons fuse so that ancient and modern can no longer be neatly separated. In the name of creative "transcultural" transformation springing from within Chinese thought in such hybridizing encounters, Heubel effectively disputes the notion that cultures work on one another at a distance (as Jullien imagines, with his trope of the interval or *écart*) rather than in real and fruitful mutual appropriations.[30] Although Jullien constructs the subtle theoretical apparatus necessary to parry charges both of exoticism, on the one hand, and of assimilation or uniformization, on the other, in his treatment of Chinese alterity, he does nevertheless intend to philosophize in a broad, synthetic manner about classical Chinese thought from his avowedly European point of view. In doing so, he tends to take classical Chinese philosophy as an object of study isolated from its dynamic mediation by Chinese thought in the present, and this inevitably contributes to a certain type of mythologization creating the illusion of an eternal Chinese character.[31]

Whereas Heubel stresses the fertility of mixed or "hybrid" forms of thought and speech, Jullien works to maintain fundamental distinctions between Europe and China, ancient and modern. However, these distinctions are not given as such but always appear only in a present that transforms everything in both object fields and leaves no essence that can resist unchanged. Heubel's point is valid: and yet the distance is not only *between*

---

30. Heubel's "manifesto" bases itself at this point on Enrique Dussel's "Eurocentrism and Modernity (Introduction to the Frankfurt Lectures)," *boundary 2*, vol. 20, no. 3 (1993): 65–76, and "Europe, Modernity, and Eurocentrism," *Nepantla. Views from South*, 1/3 (2000): 465–78.

31. Another prominent critic who reproaches Jullien for a philosophical reduction of China by the myth of its alterity is Ann Cheng. See: "Introduction: Pour en finir avec le mythe de l'alterité," in *La pensée en Chine aujourd'hui* (Paris: Gallimard, 2007), 8–11, as well as her *La Chine pense-t-elle?* (Paris: Collège de France, 2009).

cultures. It exists also *within* them. It is an abyss in our midst—in the nothingness in which, beyond its determinate form, any word or cultural artifact consists. Such nothingness pertains to the *Dao*, which rises above and emerges beyond any concrete or delimited form, as the *Book of Dao* insists in so many striking and ingenious ways. For this reason, all the characterizations and typologies of a culture that one can infer and define will be belied by what these supposed cultural characteristics actually become in concrete applications and in interactions with other cultures. Ultimately, they shed their light only in being negated. That is the inescapable apophatic margin that must be factored into understanding realized in terms of whatever cultural code or context.

My own project of critically reading Jullien is completely in agreement with Heubel in refusing the idea that "traditional Chinese thought and culture" can be approached neutrally as an object of description in abstraction from our present problematics. The object "China," and especially the ancient or classical Chinese thought that we actually deal with, is inevitably produced, or at least shaped, by our own interests and perspectives. Heubel refers to Michel Foucault's self-critical, historical ontology ("Qu'est-ce que les Lumières?"), in effect to the premises for his "history of the present" ("l'histoire du present") and conjugates this with Walter Benjamin's thinking of history from the crisis of the present in the famous "Theses on the Philosophy of History" ("Über den Begriff der Geschichte"), according to which the significance of everything past is radically revised in each new revolutionary present. In similar fashion, my own approach to China is leveraged, in effect, from the apophatic revolution in postmodern thinking that has enabled the metaphysical and mystical pasts of Western culture to come back in new and challenging guises that can open the way toward new appreciations of China as well. This is also exactly what is happening, I maintain, in Jullien and in his American counterparts, even though in mostly under-acknowledged ways, since both are focused on vindicating their interpretations as objectively valid sinology. Yet this, in any case, is not where the main value of their work as philosophy really lies.

A historian of early Chinese thought of a more scientific temperament or at least conviction such as Edward Slingerland frequently complains that both Jullien's and Ames's interpretations of the texts are philologically indefensible. In "Body and Mind in Early China," Slingerland takes Jullien as a "habitually egregious example" of the unscientific style of orientalizing scholarship that he scathingly critiques.[32] My sympathies lie much more *with*

---

32. Slingerland, "Body and Mind in Early China: An Integrated Humanities Science Approach," *Journal of the American Academy of Religion* (2013): 1–50. Citation 23.

Jullien and Ames than with Slingerland's rejection of them. But his critical contestation nevertheless highlights for me the quite astonishing differences produced by looking at classical Chinese thought as a matter of facts proved by archeological evidence and approaching it as a living philosophical vision. Claiming to nakedly portray the true facts about China is a game that philosophers do best not to play but rather to critique and eschew.

I am also less uncompromisingly and aggressively critical of Jullien than Heubel in that I appreciate Jullien's approaching China—or at least plausible and widespread images of China—out of his engagement with contemporary philosophical problems regarding particularly the status of alterity in our Western cultural milieus. Hall and Ames, too, mediate their claim to know—or rather to "anticipate"—China by their effort to answer to the problems of Western thinking in our own postmodern moment. So, on my reading, there is a mutual impingement of the past on the present and vice versa for the American philosophical sinologists and for Jullien alike, even though for Heubel this does not go far enough, certainly not in Jullien's case. Heubel charges Jullien with ignoring the rupture of modernity and with completely sidelining contemporary Chinese thinking (inevitably a reaction to this cataclysm) as not relevant to his study and elucidation of the classical texts. And yet, there is a penetrating and insightful meditation on modernization and its tragic perils in the book that Jullien wrote about his visit to Viet Nam (*Le pont des singes*, 2010). Consequently, I do not see Jullien's work as totally lacking in engagement with modernity and with current social, political, and philosophical problems, in spite of the fact that his focus has been intensely trained on the classical texts of ancient China. Nevertheless, it is difficult to deny that the striking clarity of Jullien's characterizations of classical Chinese thought in many of his books has been purchased at the price of a certain schematization that fixes the Chinese past. Just such schematization is perhaps a liability endemic to philosophy as a genre and would constitute a motivation for its necessary metamorphosis along intercultural paths into anti-philosophy. In fact, I have advocated just such a natural transformation of philosophy into extra-philosophical or ultra-philosophical *wisdom* in previous chapters of this book.

In a typical example, in *Procès ou Création,* Jullien draws a stark contrast between two forms of thought and two approaches to being in the world.[33] He insists on the complementarity of poles in never-ending mutual relation and exchange (yin/yang, heaven/earth, landscape/emotion)

---

33. *Procès ou Création: Une introduction à la pensée des lettrés chinois (Essai de problématique interculturelle)* (Paris: Seuil, 1989).

as integral to Chinese thought at the same time as he separates categorically the Chinese processual, correlative mode of thinking from Western, metaphysical modes that give priority to being over relation. The irony is that his own *modus operandi*, consisting of categorical division, performs the typically Western gesture of separating cultures into different worlds that purportedly do not communicate with each other, even while throwing into relief the lamentable shortsightedness of such a procedure when viewed from the perspective of Chinese relational thinking.

Heubel very usefully suggests how the interaction between Chinese and European thought becomes fruitful by virtue of mixing "being" and the "between," giving ontological priority to the between, as Heidegger, Adorno, Foucault, and Derrida do in ways that turn out to be of a piece with contemporary Chinese philosophy. This means working with hybrid concepts rather than through dividing the two worlds, in Jullien's manner.[34] By avoiding the opposed general pictures of one culture and the other, many subtle insights open into thinking in the "between" that separates *but also joins* cultures. These are, in fact, just the types of insights that Jullien himself elucidates, yet the very success and coherence of his discourse in projecting satisfyingly whole images generates contradictions, ones that Heubel heavily underscores and exposes. My point is that, in the Chinese and especially the Daoist perspective, this contradictoriness should be seen as inherent to discourse as such. The ultimate issue and value of such discourse is not in the coherence that it fabricates but in the "beyond of discourse" that it can serve to indicate or intimate and even to pry open by the force of contradiction.

What I most wish to highlight in Heubel's critique is how he, too, proffers or at least approaches an essentially apophatic outlook in stressing that a crucial a priori for intercultural philosophy consists in the unthinkably traumatic experience of modernization. This is the shared condition from which different cultures and languages today communicate with one another in their inaccessible depths. While modernization does not necessarily exhaust the experience that can be shared in common across cultural divides, it is certainly among the most pertinent and pressing of factors in such exchanges. Nonetheless, we should still make room for recovering the classic modes of mystical and metaphysical awareness—among other types of experience—that can also be shared in common between and across cultures. Such cross-cultural recourses are bearers of an unprogrammable

---

34. Sec. IV, "Das Zwischen öffnet Spaltung und Verschmelzung," of Heubel's essay.

adaptive capacity to change in response to changing conditions. They can set the dislocations of modernization themselves into a dimension of transcendence of any specific form that they may take on in one culture or another. This relativizes such phenomena and delimits their implacable, seemingly irresistible omnipotence.

Against the twin dangers of effacing difference and reifying it, the strength and deeper strategy of Jullien's project, I maintain, lies in its bringing into relief the universality of *what is not*, of what therefore in some manner always arises from, but at the same time also escapes from and evades, the particular historical actualizations that he discovers and exalts in classic Chinese wisdom. Jullien's shifting to a discourse of distances or gaps (*écarts*) rather than of differences (*différences*) between cultures is an apophatic or kenotic move emptying definable contents into the dynamism of their evolving forms. The emptiness between different cultural typologies says something more fundamental about them than what can be encoded and stated in any of their overt, specifiable characteristics, and this space between is the apophatic dimension.

THE COMMON BROKEN(OPEN)NESS OF CULTURES

As indispensable to the central vision of his book and to his whole philosophical project, Jullien advocates an ideal of universality. He aims to avoid closing each culture into its own separate historical universe without access to one another and, as such, cut off from the universalist strivings that, in fact, all share in common and bear witness to—each, naturally, in its own very different way. Jullien's China and his Occident are, of course, his own figments. They are produced by his discourse, even before they are realities independent of it. Every binary is, in some sense, a product of language and conceptualization. Never just natural objects, binaries are always actually produced in being defined. The historical realities of China and the West, and the abyss of difference between them, are not to be denied, but then neither can they be affirmed in any adequate or even neutral terms without some specific cultural bias and distortion. What Jullien endeavors to get at, as the guiding inspiration of Chinese thought in its otherness, is what by nature escapes any formulation in language. That does not mean, however, that it might not be approached best or even uniquely through language—or at least through the experience of failure at the limits of language.

In attempting to defend himself against the charge of "binarism," Jullien admits that as soon as he translates, he is inevitably within a binary ("dès que je traduis, je suis dans la binarité," *De l'universel,* 249). That much is inherent simply to the process of translation as such: it is integral to the relation between the languages from which and into which he translates. Jullien denies that there is any third or meta-language that would give him a position transcending the languages that he places into mutual communication, and this must be granted. However, it is the communication itself, in which each language is transformed, that reveals the reality in which both participate more fully than either one could possibly do alone. Neither language can be taken as an entity sufficient unto itself. Viewed interculturally, each needs the other in order to come to a fuller grasp and more abundant experience of itself and its own linguistic potential, and this exigency activates a dimension transcending both.

Jullien is strongest and most illuminating, I believe, in his critique of Western philosophy, which should be understood fundamentally as a *self-critique* and thus as "immanent critique." It is inspired by the Chinese currents of wisdom in both the Confucian and Daoist traditions. However, what Jullien draws from these sources is not perhaps so completely external, finally, to philosophical thought in the West as he maintains from the outset in outlining his project and its premises. It is, after all, decisively shaped and steered by Jullien's critical engagement with contemporary Western philosophers.

Jullien effectively critiques, for example, Habermas's and Apel's appeal to a universal rule of communicative reason as binding for all. He invokes Daoist implicit understanding—which might find its counterpart in "tacit knowing" as expounded by Michael Polanyi in *The Tacit Dimension* (1967)—and Confucian communitarianism as not submitting to any such rule. The sage remains free and unpredictably responsive to all that happens or takes effect; he is eminently open and disposed or available ("éminemment *disponible*") to all rather than being subject to any formal rule.[35] How could any formal rule of logos, such as Habermas and Apel envisage with their pragmatic-transcendental project ("Universalpragmatik"), be binding a priori for all?

The attitude of availability ("disponibilité") that Jullien describes is, in the end, frankly opportunist. The Daoist does *not* deny the requirements of communicative reason. He does not put himself outside the pale of humanity, which is the unacceptable price that Habermas sees as exacted by such non-adherence to the universal rules of communicative reason. Still, the Daoist considers such rules as merely opportune. He may accept and employ them; however, not as necessary or required for truth, which would be to subscribe to a sort of cognitivism. The sage escapes the logic of

---

35. Jullien treats this theme most exhaustively in *Un Sage est sans idée, ou l'autre de la philosophie* (Paris: Seuil, 1998), 127–32.

exclusion. At least, he does not allow himself to be trapped and constrained by it. And yet he does not deprive himself of its resources either: he does indeed make pragmatic distinctions and exclusions—and acts accordingly.

A question that at first seems tangential arises ineluctably at this point: how can society be constituted by such free and spontaneous spirits without any external constraints? In other words, the Daoist seems to be in need of a theory of social responsibility. As with religious people of all sorts, this entails responsibility first and foremost to a source and authority transcending society, the *Dao*. But that *social* responsibility *is* entailed by the *Dao* is clear from the affirmation of respect and love of one's fellows in society, as well as of reverence for all creatures or beings in the universe. Near the origins of Christian tradition, Saint Paul grapples with the same dilemma and tension between transcendent authority and social responsibility. Even in declaring that Christians are no longer under the law—certainly not under any law made by men—he makes it clear that the secular authorities are still to be respected and given their due: "Let every soul be subject to the higher powers" (Romans 31:1). And here Paul is apparently in line with Christ's own directive to "give unto Caesar what is Caesar's" (Mark 12:17).

Freedom and spontaneity are exalted as the basis of Christian and Daoist ethics respectively. These different watchwords register nuances of an underlying attitude that is in certain crucial respects similar. Prima facie, critical theory would seem to demand other, more explicit bases for an ethics of social responsibility than those provided by purely free and natural spontaneity. However, at its self-critical limit, critical theory, too, cannot but embrace a kind of negative theological faith.[36] Not any explicit code of ethics or argument, but an irreducible and therefore indeterminate openness to all others, is the precondition for any claim to universality without exclusions. This entails a step back from the pretensions of objective judgment—a turning instead to the negative openness towards what is not (at least not yet). One form of this move is found in the recognition that an ethics of responsibility can be only a theory of *prospective* responsibility aimed at forming action in the future rather than at judging past acts as responsible or not. Such a conception of responsibility was famously expounded by Hans Jonas.[37] It is now being

---

36. I argue this in "The Coincidence of Reason and Revelation in Communicative Openness: A Critical Negative Theology of Dialogue," *Journal of Religion* 88/3 (2008): 365–92.

37. Hans Jonas, *The Imperative of Responsibility. In Search of an Ethics for the Technological Age* (Chicago: University of Chicago Press, 1984). Thomas Buchheim's paper "Two Concepts of Human Responsibility and their Common Prerequisites" at the Humboldt Foundation-sponsored conference on "Nature, Time, Responsibility" held at the University of Macao in April 2013 focused this topic.

further developed into a theory of the compatibility between Critical Theory and Daoism and even of their common aim and purpose.[38]

For Habermas, unconstrained rational discussion is necessary to determine truth, and it even issues in an "ethics of discourse" (*Diskursethik*). But Confucius adroitly dodges and escapes from all explicit rules and from fully expressed forms of argumentation. His discussions (*Entretiens*) refuse this "corset" and its attachment to words. Considered also from the point of view of the "word without word" (*yán wú yán*, 言 無 言) of the Daoists, discourse is not binding.[39] There is, instead, an implicit understanding without speech in a silence that is itself eloquent, and this tacit understanding is placed above all discursive exigencies and before all attempts at convincing the other by rhetorical persuasion to subscribe to whichever communicative rules or protocols. Jullien sees such tacit understanding as circumventing Habermas's ethics of discussion with its rules (*Diskursregeln*) and its claim to be binding for all those who do not want to place themselves beyond the scope of common humanity.[40]

Such universal communicative requirements, from Aristotle to Habermas, serve as mechanisms of exclusion: those who do not conform are condemned as being outside humanity, indeed as no better than vegetables or suicides, in the recurrent rhetoric that can be traced from Aristotle's *Metaphysics* 4.4. Jullien's alternative to normative constraints of communication consists in communicative capacities that can be infinitely shared and specifically in a power of universal communicability (*communicabilité universelle*," *De l'universel*, 212) that can be indefinitely extended and participated in by others. Jullien finds a model for this in Kant, for whom aesthetic and teleological judgments, even without being logically binding, nevertheless are able to be communicated or shared universally ("müssen sich . . . allgemein mitteilen lassen"), as Kant argues in the "Analytic of the Beautiful," § 21 of the *Kritik der Urteilskraft*. This is a universality that is effective and productive even in the absence of any demonstrable conceptual necessity. It depends rather on felt sensibilities that converge and prove themselves to be shared potentially by all in the actual experience of

---

38. Mario Wenning, "Daoism as Critical Theory," *Comparative Philosophy* 2/2 (2011): 50–71.

39. Here one should consult further, Jullien's *Si parler va sans dire: Du Logos et d'autres ressources*, which develops in detail the Daoist *antilogos* as the antithesis to Greek logos thinking.

40. Jullien, *De l'universel*, 207–09. See Habermas, *Moralbewußtsein und kommunikatives Handeln* (Frankfurt a. M.: Suhrkamp 1983), 88.

the beautiful. Something similar can be said concerning the apprehension of the morally good. Researchers have outlined the convergences between Kant's philosophy, with its appeal to practical postulates (God, freedom, and the immortality of the soul) as regulative principles for conduct, on the one hand, and the Daoist translation of metaphysics into ethics, on the other.[41] In both cases, the common admission and assumption of the merely negative possibilities of knowledge for theoretical reason searching by its very nature, but in vain, for metaphysical grounds and foundations issue in a universality that is productive for practical action. This action is normative and yet is not under the strict necessity of the concept.

Such work of mediation between cultures, drawing on the resources of each, suggests that Jullien's texts often create something of a myth of a fully external Chinese model in order to develop notions of non-action, non-language, and non-logical wholeness. Such negative notions actually belong, in some form, to Occidental thought as well. Even if principally in countercurrents to the apparently dominant positions, nevertheless, at least in the margins, these apophatic notions are there: and often they are there even in the most canonical of philosophical thinkers such as Plato and Aquinas and Kant and Wittgenstein. Apophatic thinkers in the West, moreover, are fully worthy of their counterparts in Chinese tradition. Apophatic thinkers in both traditions alike represent a shift in perspective relative to certain ordinary assumptions and conventions, and juxtaposing the two can make more visible and bring into focus the potential they both possess for reaching beyond all that had been suspected previously in the mainstream. The common bond that is discovered by this cross-cultural comparison and exchange is not a foundation or bottom (*fond*) that appears when all differences between cultures have been removed but rather a common fund (*fonds*) that it is possible to exploit as inexhaustible and participable without limits or exclusions (*De l'universel*, 213). This inexhaustible common resource of the infinite and uncircumscribable leads to continual surpassing of every achieved understanding and every particular frontier of shareable intelligence. Only so can the common remain an open experiment always still to be further participated in so as to evade the closure of the concept. We must always still learn to better understand and appreciate whatever seems to be opposed to the presuppositions of the knowledge that we have so far acquired.

---

41. Mario Wenning, "Kant and Daoism on Nothingness," *Journal of Chinese Philosophy* 38/4 (2011): 556–68.

For Jullien, the common is not a condition—and much less a state, or anything acquired—but rather a quest. He seeks a commonality less of the contents of experience than of the intelligible per se, of communicability (Kant's *Mitteilbarkeit*) itself, even though he does find something immediately communicable in the naked human emotions conveyed by classical poetry in Greek and in Chinese alike. According to Jullien's programmatic affirmation and core confession, everything in a culture is potentially intelligible. Indeed, precisely this intelligibility counts as "the only transcendental" ("le seul transcendental," 217).

Jullien's meditation on universality as emerging from the effectiveness of the common pursued not as a natural given but as a mutually catalyzed construction and discovery of a common basis of understanding (*fond d'entente culturel*, 228) leads him in the concluding discussions of his book *De l'universel* (chapters 12 and 13) to a theory of the gap (*écart*) between cultures as the greatest resource and the one most necessary for thinking philosophically: it is the catalyst for liberating human self-reflection in the world today and for the future. Only bringing cultures face-to-face across this reciprocal gap can render them intelligible to one another. This is necessary in order to avoid either obliterating their unique specificity by an imperialistic, homogenizing universality, or else leaving each in the inarticulate idiocy of its supposedly separate and incompatible essence. Culture is intrinsically homogenizing: it proposes models that are adhered to and imitated and disseminated. But, at the same time, culture is also inherently differentiating: its spread across widely extended geographical areas, over time, and across diverse social strata ineluctably produces variants and even divisive alternatives. These alternatives are sometimes set in rivalrous opposition to one another in such cases as Catholic versus Protestant, Shia versus Sunni, Tutsi versus Hutu, to mention only a few macroscopic and particularly catastrophic examples.

The differential character of identity builds a propensity to foster subcultures and counter-cultures and parallel, sometimes parodic, potentially conflictual cultures into the natural life and evolution of culture. Every large-scale cultural phenomenon proves prone to producing, within its overall scope and range, multiple versions of itself differentiated into more specific group and regional identities. Hence Jullien's theses that culture is intrinsically plural and in continual process of self-transformation. He gives priority to the *cultural* subject, since we are always already culturally determined before we can reflect epistemologically or morally, or in any other manner of awareness that renders our subjectivity self-conscious. The questions we pose, however fundamental and philosophical they may be, are always already folded into the cultural ("toujours *pliées* dans du culturel")—into the historical and linguistic and symbolic heritage that makes us up. This cultural a priori needs always to be brought into the light of critical reflection.

Jullien adopts an exterior point of view in showing how Chinese thinkers counterpunctually illuminate the Greeks in their implicit decisions determining the development of philosophy and, more broadly, the European ethos. His method turns on exposing, through cross-cultural comparison, what is conveyed by a certain aspect or facet of culture, like philosophy, without being expressly thought or interrogated as such. This type of reflection affords the basis of a possible understanding beyond the bounds of any given culture with its own presuppositions and unconscious habits of mind. Jullien explains how, before he began to read Plato and Aristotle from outside (*du dehors*) and from the point of view of Chinese philosophers, he focused on what they said and meant, but not on what was carried along unthought in their discourse as self-evident and as not needing to be interrogated. After encountering Chinese thought, he realized that precisely this latter, unarticulated and unreflective component is what reveals the deepest mechanisms and intrinsic character of any given cultural specificity (*De l'universel*, 225).

This implicit basis of understanding functions as a transcendental condition of the possibility of a culture and is more important for actual understanding than any of a culture's known features and schematized traits. It is the precondition for automatic connivance and instinctive complicity among the participants in any given culture, although they may be only half-aware of the grounds for their own mutual understanding. Since this unspoken understanding is not explicitly formulated in any specific cultural terms, it remains below the threshold of cultural differentiation and constitutes a stratum—some might call it a "cultural unconscious"—with the potential, paradoxically, for generating cross-cultural universality. In fact, the common turns out to be the universal: it has no definable content but simply orients understanding to the other. This lack of specific, differentiating content is the key to unlimited extension and application across cultures. All that is inscribed a priori in cultures on this view is a broken openness to ineluctable relationality in the definition of any particular culture. But that broken-openness of all human discourse to what it cannot comprehend is precisely what theology in its fundamentally negative orientation and purport interprets through its own uncannily symbolic language of the imagination.

THE SELF-NEGATION OF CULTURE
BY (NEGATIVE) THEOLOGY

Cultures are related to one another, according to Jullien, not just by their mutual similarities but, more importantly, by the gap (*écart*) that makes them heterogeneous and prevents any third term from subsuming them in a synthesis. Under this condition, their interaction is not guided or controlled by any superior kind of normativity but is rather endlessly open to adventure. They cannot as such even be properly "compared" (*De l'universel*, 239), as if a neutral frame and criteria for doing so could be given independently. Instead, they must be allowed simply to interact with, and so to mutually transform, one another. They are not only different but, more importantly, *distant* from each other, and they can effectively operate transformatively upon one another because of that distance.

Nonetheless, Jullien's exposition of Chinese thought proceeds, in effect, by defining and discussing differences. What else can students of culture, of whatever kind, do? Many Westerners have observed, for example, that the Chinese language and culture excels in its aptitude to express continuous transition and interaction, whereas European languages are capable of envisaging transcendence (of substance, substrate, or subject) with a sublimity of construction unattainable for the Chinese (*De l'universel*, 240). The Chinese language, as it has been described by Western philosophers from Wilhelm von Humboldt to Jullien, is characterized by its lack of morphological structure—that is, of grammatical inflection or of a "systematic scheme of variations."[42] Its relatively isolated, monosyllabic characters strike the mind with force as individual images or impressions whose meaning is less qualified and contoured by syntactical connection with other characters. The Chinese character, therefore, is more dependent on extra-linguistic context, or the situation of enunciation, for determination of its exact meaning in a sentence.[43]

But what has been presupposed already simply in observing this difference? Heubel argues cogently that the a priori condition for making such observations—namely, the mediation of modernity—has been elided and

---

42. Christian Wenzel, "Isolation and Involvement: Wilhelm von Humboldt, François Jullien, and More," *Philosophy East & West* 60/4 (2010): 458–75.

43. For a sophisticated, nuanced account taking an "interactive" view of the "grammar controversy" and showing "How the Chinese Language Lost its Grammar" and then got it back again in another sense, see Haun Saussy, *Great Walls of Discourse and Other Adventures in Cultural China*, chapter 4, 75–90.

occulted by Jullien's focus because Jullien isolates classical Chinese thought from its historical mediation through the present. I wish in this final movement on universalism to begin to expose how Jullien's thought is, after all, reacting, even if in mostly silent dialogue, to present philosophical thought (in which the East-West divide is increasingly contaminated and difficult to discern) and in particular to some of its most difficult dilemmas and debates—namely, those over immanence and transcendence.

The lack of a transcendent position outside of the two interacting, mutually transforming cultures turns into a cardinal principle of Jullien's intercultural method. It turns out to serve as a hobbyhorse for expression of a certain anti-theological polemic that consistently animates Jullien's work, just as it drives the agendas of numerous Parisian philosophers along with those of other secular-minded philosophers as well. Jullien is anxious to assert—against certain typical and still widespread representations of naïve theism—that there is no God controlling things from outside (such as the Jesuit missionaries presumably imagined and may have projected onto Chinese cosmology) but only an immanent development and interaction from within the encounter among distinct cultures. Interpreting immanence this way as *closed* to theological transcendence, so as to assert human and secular autonomy and self-sufficiency, repeats the Enlightenment impulse par excellence. It risks slipping into reenactment of the quintessential gesture of human self-empowerment through denial of any higher powers. A similar gesture apparently of human self-confidence surprises us also in Jullien's very Hegelian embrace of the idea of the total intelligibility of culture. However, this is where I suspect that Jullien is no longer thinking in consonance with the Chinese classics. For their vision *does* remain open to a dimension of transcendence that reaches beyond what is humanly and culturally intelligible. It is a dimension that cannot be grasped conceptually, and yet it lends itself to being variously figured as sacred and divine. It is acknowledged in a spirit that can sometimes be impudent, as when it lashes out in certain withering paradoxes of the *Zhuangzi*. It can also don highly reverent styles as diverse as those of Laozi and Confucius, each in their own ways deferentially honoring heaven (*Tiān*) or the ancients.

Jullien frequently makes the point that in Chinese tradition all theistic conceptions of "heaven" as a personal agent disappear from early on, from about a millennium before Christ during the Zhou dynasty. They are replaced—so this story goes—by images of natural transformation in accordance with the binary yīn (陰) and yáng (陽). However, likewise at the heart of Christian theism and of monotheism generally, all images of God are placed under erasure within the negative theological currents that constantly counterpoint positive, kataphatic, dogmatic theology and subject all such images to an uncompromising critique of representation as idolatrous. The exigency of relinquishing all claims to an adequate representation or intellectual conception of divinity, and of starting rather from the embodied experience of God incarnate in Christ, hews very near to the underlying inspiration of Christian revelation. For all the profound differences between Chinese and Western culture, surely neither one is wholly deprived of all relation to the transcendent and absolute, or the infinite and unsayable, however different the negotiation of the impossible task of grasping and articulating it may be in one cultural universe or the other. Jullien's own work clearly demonstrates this—*malgré lui*.

The greater wisdom lies not in opposing transcendence to immanence, nor in simply rejecting the theological—and thereby entering into an oppositional logic. As Jullien himself acutely shows, a culture *consists* in polarities rather than just in unilateral character traits. Europe is constituted historically by its Christian heritage *and* by atheism as an essential expression of its widespread and deeply rooted secular humanism. Only through such interpenetrating and reciprocal poles do cultures become intelligible: only so do their implicit bases of understanding (Jullien's *fonds d'entente*) emerge. The *dia* of dia-logue stresses the need for the antithetical, whereas the *logos* stands for "the fact that all cultures hold in common among themselves a communicability in principle" ("le fait que toutes les cultures entretiennent entre elles une communicabilité de principe," *De l'universel,* 247). Jullien pushes this latter conviction further to the point of claiming that "all that is cultural is *intelligible* without loss or residue" ("tout, du culturel, est *intélligible,* sans perte et sans résidue").

It should be emphasized that the residue of unintelligibility is properly located *between* cultures rather than within them, but the idea that it could be wholly eliminated seems in any case to be exaggerated and unrealistic. This is the place where the limit of Jullien's apophaticism declares itself and where he becomes perhaps something of an uncritical believer in the Enlightenment ideals that have been so influential throughout European, and more generally modern, history, especially as they emanate in certain essentials from eighteenth-century, revolutionary France. Jullien's belief in the total intelligibility of culture induces him to exclude the idea of anything in culture remaining definitively beyond verbal reach—namely, "the idea of an ineffable of culture" ("l'idée d'un ineffable de la culture").

In *Le pont des singes: De la diversité à venir,* a follow-up book to *De l'universel,* Jullien continues his attack on the notion of the ineffable specifically in relation to culture: "There is no cultural ineffable" ("il n'y a pas d'ineffable culturel," 11).⁴⁴ He repeats this thesis verbatim in his "manifesto" *L'écart et l'entre*, 46–47. This formulation is correct to the extent that what is ineffable is precisely not cultural. Nevertheless, this does not mean that an ineffable instance and even insistence cannot condition culture throughout its whole extent and that, therefore, the ineffable can be dismissed from a philosophy of culture. There are, in fact, important incidences of limits of such intelligibility that have been designated as "cultural untranslatability" and have been extensively analyzed as such.⁴⁵

Jullien's objection is that with such an idea as its untranslatability, "the cultural *exits from then on from the intelligible*" ("le culturel *sort dès lors de l'intelligible*"); this is to say that in embracing the ineffable, a cultural discourse "no longer holds itself to be participable by a common intelligence. The work of dialogue is abandoned" ("c'est-à-dire qu'il ne se tient plus pour partageable par une commune intelligence. Le travail du dialogue est abandonné," 256). This renunciation seems to Jullien to be tantamount to a giving up of responsibility, for once dialogue is renounced or transcended, one is no longer answerable to others, no longer accountable to make oneself intelligible to them. At this point, one appeals to some higher instance, such as divinity, that justifies one in terms beyond those that can be explained to one's human fellows in common language and dialogue.

However, it would be more accurate to say not that the work of dialogue is abandoned by turning toward transcendence in recognition of certain limits of intelligibility but rather that this work remains always and necessarily incomplete. Jullien himself, after all, champions an activity of translation without limits. Translation, he declares, is the operativity proper to dialogue and the only possible global ethic (248). Translation is constitutive of European culture—unlike the Chinese, which (so Jullien) was not seriously confronted with any other language of culture besides its own until the nineteenth century and massive, forced colonialism. Yet translation, precisely because it is infinite and without any intrinsic limit, relates inevitably to the ineffable: this limit of what cannot be said is what truly bonds all cultures in their orientation to a never exhaustible plenitude. This

---

44. *Le pont des singes: De la diversité à venir* (Paris: Galilée, 2010), 11.

45. *The Translatability of Cultures: Figurations of the Space Between*, eds. Sanford Budick and Wolfgang Iser (Stanford, CA: Stanford University Press, 1996). See especially Budick's introductory essay "Crises of Alterity: Cultural Untranslatability and the Experience of Secondary Otherness," 1–24, and Jan Assmann's "Translating Gods: Religion as a Factor of Cultural (Un) Translatability," 25–56.

is what unites them beyond any specific traits that they may share in common. In affirming the *infinity* of translation, Jullien himself touches upon the dimension that I call "theological": the in-finite, as the ultimate concern of (negative) theology, can be analogously indicated, imitated, and embodied by the endless striving of human works towards their unrealizable ideals.

Jullien is undoubtedly correct that a certain ideal of translatability is indeed necessary in order to keep the work of giving account of our reasons on the move, but this can be and in fact always *is* a work only of approximation. Total intelligibility of the real, of anything more than a formal, abstract model, is not attainable or hardly even conceivable—except as an ideal. I heartily agree with Jullien's resistance to the premature closing down of ongoing cultural mediation in exchange for myths of untranslatable essences of national character and identity. But that does not automatically eliminate all penumbra of indetermination or overdetermination at the limits of sense. Quite the contrary. Translation may well lead to the threshold of untranslatable "pure language" ("die reine Sprache"), as in Walter Benjamin's definition of the task of the translator ("Die Aufgabe des Übersetzers"): precisely what cannot be translated is what becomes mystically manifest in the *process* of translation itself. Translation of a literary classic can promote it to a higher life, an afterlife ("Nachleben"), through its being made to exist in another language besides the original one in which it is created and born. This potential for growth stands for the fact that translation is not simply a closed circle of immanence: there can be even more (in certain respects) in the translation than in the original.

In spite of this fact, a mostly tacit thesis that there is nothing that is not culture runs through Jullien's thought and works. It is an equivalent or a corollary of his taking an anti-theological stance: God or a divine absolute would presumably be an instance outside of and beyond culture and would thus delimit and relativize cultural discourse. Such a superhuman instance would seem to disempower humans in a way that Hegel was unwilling to accept—and Jullien no more than he. Yet ancient Chinese wisdom does pivot on this relatability of everything human to what is above humanity and its grasp. This higher instance might be called "nature" or at least nature's ground, *Dào* or *Tiān* or *Fó*, but it might just as well be called God, indeed *Deus sive natura*. The name is not really important, not ultimately anyway, since this unsayable, inconceivable "whatever" cannot in principle be named, even though it is fundamental in and to all that is human. "The Dao that can be named is not the universal *Dao*" ("*Dào kě dào, fēi cháng Dào*," 道可道, 非常道, *Dào-dé-Jīng* 1.1).

Jullien's positioning of himself in opposition to theological transcendence is, to my mind, complicit with the history of Western atheism and is not truly informed by classic Chinese wisdom. Its closest kinship and more organically related analogues might rather be found in the insistence on immanence, for example, by Gilles Deleuze. Indeed, Deleuze absolutizes immanence to the point where it becomes itself transcendent of every possible frame and figure of thought.[46] Classic Chinese wisdom, too, champions a total openness even to what transcends thought and therewith every frame for thinking. And that is exactly where I locate the indispensable movement of (negative) theology. Jullien presents the most fundamental Chinese text of all, the *Yijing*, the *Book of Changes*, as a manifesto of immanence in *Figures of Immanence: For a Philosophical Reading of the Yijing*, as we saw in chapter 3. But the all-inclusiveness of immanence must not be allowed to exclude transcendence, once the latter is understood apophatically as the unthinkable, and as having no fixed form of representation.

Jullien does, in a Heideggerian spirit, make space for the unthought ("l'impensé") and perhaps even for the unthinkable, but he resists according it any kind of substantial existence. That would be an unwarranted hypostatization. And yet, in this, he is perfectly in agreement with a negative-theological handling of this issue, which is not to be confounded with positing an abstract metaphysics. Negative-theological thinking is much closer to thinking in terms of what Jullien calls "operativity" or "effectivity": God is not known except by means of and in terms of "divine" effects. Negative theology makes no claim to grasping transcendence through any formal vocabulary. It critiques, instead, as idolatrous all substantifications of divinity. As infinitely and concretely real, divinity is ungraspable and inconceivable. There is in negative theology no pretension to possession of a superior code for the ultimate secret of the universe. It is only the constantly shifting vocabularies of human cultures that can gesture toward this dimension beyond their grasp. Evidently, this unidentifiable factor that some (notably Jacques Lacan) call "the real" (*le réel*) can never be made exhaustively intelligible. It therefore does not belong to the sphere of culture in Jullien's view, if for him culture is totally intelligible. And yet to cleanly separate it from culture, relegating it to *pure* transcendence, or else denying its pertinence altogether, marks a limit to thinking holistically that need not be accepted—except perhaps inevitably in certain pragmatic contexts, but not in principle or as a matter of theory.

---

46. Such a positioning is summed up in Gilles Deleuze, "L'immanence: une vie . . . ," *Philosophie* 47 (1995): 3–7, published one year before the author's death, but it is already pronounced from at least the time of Deleuze's *Spinoza et le problème de l'expression* (Paris: Minuit, 1968).

I agree with Jullien completely in his advocacy of an open universal ("universel ouvert") that is maintained by the deployment of negation (*De l'universel*, 261) and also with the idea that this brings about the self-critical "self-reflection of the human" ("*l'auto-réfléchissement de l'humain*," 259). Just such reflection is urgently necessary in order to interrupt and resist the narcissistic auto-reflex that is characteristic of modernity and that is still gaining ground in producing ever greater uniformity everywhere on the planet today. Against cognitivisms and their supposedly given universals, which are really only artificially reproduced uniformities, the only valid method for Jullien is inquiry into the gap between cultures that guides human thought to genuine self-reflection. This position is a compelling critique. But in his enthusiasm for this Enlightenment ideal, Jullien tends to flatten out its *self*-critical edge. Human self-reflection is perhaps not itself without a certain vis-à-vis upon the *non*-human and the *supra*-cultural. Its self-negating spirit can acknowledge what is not only just another form of human culture but is also unimaginably not itself, not human at all, the Other of all others—that is, of all possible, humanly experienceable others. This might be another and even more extreme degree of that "*someplace else* of thought" ("*ailleurs* de la pensée") of which Jullien wistfully writes, in a reprise of his (and Foucault's) notion of a heterotopy.[47]

This Other transcending our thoughts and ways would be difficult for Jullien to acknowledge without releasing some inveterate prejudices against theology and its figures of transcendence, prejudices that are widespread and deeply rooted among the left-bank Parisian intelligentsia. Such an anticlerical consensus excludes God and refuses to acknowledge any inscrutable, *un*intelligible divineness at the source of all human experience and intelligibility. This is the place where Jullien seems to take his stand *with* Hegel and a totalizing rationality *against* Kierkegaard's recognition of absolute paradox and an Other beyond all possibility of mediation. His assertion of the total intelligibility of culture wishes not to acknowledge that there could be anything which is not cultural, or at least not culturally mediated, and yet he tends to forget or ignore on just this point the inherent negativity of the cultural itself—its disappearing, like everything human, towards what it is not. The assertion of the total intelligibility of culture effectively excludes a certain positive conception of the theological, but it is also at risk of failing to acknowledge the unknowing and unintelligibility (at least to us, here and now) at the heart of culture. This acknowledgment

---

47. *Conférence sur l'efficacité* (Paris: Presses Universitaires de France, 2005), 12.

is crucial pragmatically to opening us all radically to dialogue and so to genuinely seeking enlightenment from one another. Poets from Hölderlin to Celan show excruciatingly how our wounds ("Wunde") are the authentic openings permitting communication between human beings, who are themselves understood as a conversation heard from one another ("seit ein Gespräch wir sind und hören von einander," "Friedensfeier"). And in this respect a certain inescapable woundedness is witness to what I interpret as a theological dimension of humanity's being torn open to what it neither knows nor can possess.[48]

Acknowledging unknowing has become the overriding imperative particularly of certain forms of postmodern thinking.[49] I am inclined to think that it is not the infinite mystery of things as such but only human codifications of this mystery in institutions and ideologies exerting power over people and sometimes inciting to violence that arouses opposition in Jullien and in other thinkers who are adamantly anti-theological. What they are rejecting, in the end, however, are only the empty vessels and ritual paraphernalia of theology, not its deeper sense and apophatic purport as *negative* theology.

What Jullien offers is a philosophy of culture. This might be seen as an alternative to, and as spelling the demise of, metaphysical philosophy and its often undeclared crypto-theology. Rather than claiming to have a transcendental viewpoint from which to evaluate the truth of a culture's enunciations and expressions in its arts and sciences and discourses in general, a philosophy of culture abides within the immanence of these symbolic, systemic, and aesthetic expressions. It eschews claiming access to any superior plane of transcendent knowledge and truth. This sort of positioning of Jullien's philosophy seems to give it a clear point and message in terms of what it is not—through stubborn opposition to all theological forms of transcendence-oriented rationality. However, in reality, the polemic against theology serves as a crutch for propping up Jullien's discourse: his argument is made to stand up by virtue of what it opposes.

---

48. I pursue this thought in "Paul Celan and the Woundedness of Language as our Common Bond," *Compar(a)ison*, special issue on Celan, edited by Michael Jakob, forthcoming. A moving probe of the theological valence of the woundedness of knowing is Johann Baptist Metz, *Memoria passionis: Ein provozierendes Gedächtnis in pluralistischer Gesellschaft* (Frieburg: Herder, 2006).

49. I undertake to show this in "Acknowledging Unknowing: Stanley Cavell and the Philosophical Criticism of Literature," *Philosophy and Literature* 39/1 (2015): 248–58.

More deeply considered, theology must also be taken as itself just a form of human culture, perhaps even as the most essential and representative and self-revealing form of such culture. What distinguishes theology in its truest shape or manifestation is its sensibility for the negation of culture per se, as demanded by the spirit of uncompromising self-critique. A sort of self-critical denial of culture, inasmuch as it is just a human construction, is expressed in the recognition of divinity as transcending and creating, or as rendering possible, humanity and its world. This imagination of a divinity who is even more a subject than we, more conscious than any human consciousness or than any consciousness that is humanly conceivable, pursues the possibilities of the most radical self-negation beyond the logic of concepts into the unfathomable depths opened by human imagination brought face to face with its own abyss. Yet this claim can (and must) be understood also in purely immanent terms simply as negating the closure and supposed sufficiency unto itself of any identifiable, conceptualizable "immanent" sphere.

Theology's relevance consists, then, in its forcing every cultural paradigm, with its inevitable human limits, into a movement of self-surpassing. Theology—understood thus fundamentally as *negative* theology—does not impose another content coming from elsewhere but rather forces every finite cultural content to its limits, where it must give up its own achieved form and open into other forms that are as yet unachieved and are perhaps unprecedented. Theology is a form of culture and can itself become *eminently* a form of the philosophy of culture. It can do so because negative theology, by virtue of its unsparing critique of every form of representation, can force culture to embrace, or at least to confront, its own most absolute and inconceivable Other. It can thus become most radically other than itself, turning into (among other things) a (negative) theology of culture.[50]

This mutual implication of culture and theology, or more exactly of humanism and the heavenly, at the self-negating limits of either discourse, is provocatively expressed by the Daoist classic *Zhuangzi* in the most barebones and yet essential terms:

---

50. Paul Tillich, in his *Theology of Culture* (Oxford: Oxford University Press, 1964), already moves in this direction by denying religion any particular or positive place among the cognitive, moral, and aesthetic functions of the human spirit and recognizing religion rather as "the dimension of depth" that is operative in all of these functions (5–6). Tillich's relevance to the kind of critical negative theology that I am outlining here comes out especially in his treatment (in "The Two Types of Philosophy of Religion" in the same volume) of "the dialectic of estrangement" that necessarily belongs to our approach to divinity.

our understanding can be in the right only by virtue of a relation of dependence on something, and what it depends on is always peculiarly unfixed. So how could I know whether what I call Heavenly is not really the Human? How could I know whether what I call the Human is not really the Heavenly?[51]

The impossibility of "fixing" the absolute in our language makes any distinction in language between the absolute and the relative, the heavenly and the human, itself merely relative. The two cannot but operate inseparably in our thought and speech. Absoluteness is never conceived by us otherwise than as our idea, with the part of arbitrariness that this inevitably entails. To speak of the heavenly is unavoidably to speak, at least implicitly, also of—or in any case *from*—the human, with its constitutive limits.

The Confucian classic *The Doctrine of the Mean* (*Zhongyong*), particularly in chapters 12 and 26, bears a comparable message concerning the virtue of absolute genuineness or extreme honesty (*chéng* 誠) as permanent and perfect, as infinite and endless. Such human perfection is an endowment from heaven as the groundless ground (or the "fond sans fond," in Jullien's terms) of the world, the horizon that exceeds and surpasses all human experience in the direction of the "unconditioned" or absolute. Jullien consistently recognizes this, but then his emphasis is always on bringing the opening to transcendence and heaven back down to earth so as to ground it in immanence. He writes as if the latter were better known and completely free from mystification or obscurantism—and therefore were more securely possessed. Even if that were the case, still in the spirit of especially Daoist wisdom, it is only by releasing our hold on all supposedly known quantities of experience that we allow them to live and evolve—and ourselves with them.

Along these lines, Jullien himself maintains that in classical Chinese thought "experience surpasses itself," but he adds the caveat: "without consummating the rupture with its sensory manifestation and without completely parting company with the logic of processes" ("l'experience s'y dépasse-t-elle, mais sans consommer la rupture avec sa manifestation sensible et décoller carrément de la logique des processus").[52] Jullien thereby marks out some important guideposts that are highly relevant for the further development of apophatic thought today. In particular, the apophatic project

---

51. *Zhuangzi*, chapter 6, Ziporyn ed., 40.
52. Jullien, *Dialogue sur la morale* (Paris: Grasset, 1995), 142–43.

is being pursued today with a focus on the body and on incarnation in worldly, historical processes, which at the same time unsettles history and dismantles all its set teleologies.[53] For apophatic thinking, too, transcendence cannot be thought in itself, or "positively," but only relationally—that is, in relation to forms of immanence such as the body. Bodily, incarnate, sensory forms of transcendent life are crucial to apophatic thinking from the beginning of Christian tradition, receiving explicit theorization already with Tertullien's AD 206 treatise on Christ's flesh (*De carne Christi*).[54] Conversely, however, immanence cannot be thought without the acknowledgment of transcendence. Otherwise, the real is reduced to a mere husk of itself, since, as self-contained, it is lifeless and empty. Cut off from transcendence and thus from relation to its outside and other, far from being the inexhaustible resource that Jullien celebrates, immanence suffocates and stifles because it is self-enclosed and isolated from the infinite circulation and exchange of all with all. Jullien's understanding of immanence, like Deleuze's, actually presupposes transcendence and most obviously self-transcendence as the very life principle that keeps immanence alive and on the move.

Indeed, Jullien recognizes, after all, that "there is transcendence—the 'heaven,' beyond our horizon." Still, he is convinced that this transcendent beyond must not be represented as another world rather than as a resource in the regulated course of *this* world: "But to the degree that its regulated course does not constitute another world with relation to the human one, this transcendence of Heaven converts into a *fund of immanence*. As a resource without bottom (*sans fond*) of the regulation of things, such transcendence confounds itself finally with the natural" ("Il y a bien transcendance—le 'Ciel,' au-delà de notre horizon—mais dans la mesure où le cours régulé qui est le sien ne se constitue pas en autre monde par rapport au monde humain, cette transcendance du Ciel se convertit en un *fonds d'immanence*. Fonds sans fond de la régulation des choses, elle se confond finalement avec le naturel," *Dialogue sur la morale*, 143).

Thus it is not that transcendence need not be recognized as absolutely decisive but rather that it cannot be *grasped* and thereby represented as such. Neither, however, can immanence or nature be so grasped and represented, since they are without specifiable or delimited foundations in themselves. They are each gaping open to their other, which cannot but be

---

53. On this head, see Chris Boesel and Catherine Keller, eds. *Apophatic Bodies: Negative Theology, Incarnation, and Relationality.*

54. On this, see Emmanuel Falque, *Dieu, la chair et l'autre: d'Irénée à Duns Scot* (Paris: Presses Universitaires de France, 2008).

called "transcendent," even if only, admittedly, with an inevitable degree of impropriety, since strictly speaking this outside or beyond is not properly nameable at all.

Transcendence, so conceived, as Jullien himself accurately apprehends, is precisely the absolutization and totalization of immanence (ibid., 173). But in order to become absolute and total, immanence needs not to exclude anything, especially not transcendence, as its contrary or opposite. To become absolute and total, therefore, immanence must negate even its own finite determination as "immanence." By such self-negation, it becomes in-finite. This is "totalization" through self-negation and opening without limit to all, including its opposite. Such immanence consists in relations of self-transcendence through which it is internally related to absolutely everything else. In these terms, Chinese wisdom and Occidental theology in its negative form both attain to a similar recognition of the insufficiency and mutual dependence of all conceptualities, those of transcendence and of immanence alike.[55] This is the point at which transcendence beyond conceptuality itself opens up and springs into action.

As with everything else that is absolute, absolute immanence transcends our conceptual framework. Jullien, much like Deleuze, is using "immanence" to indicate thinking without concepts that frame and delimit thought from the outside—from a position of "transcendence." This procedure has something in common with the metaphorical, non-conceptual thinking of the pre-Socratics, from which this chapter began. In its actual, immanent realization, such analogical thinking evades the self-enclosure of thought within concepts that makes thought all a relation still only to itself, one that abides within the circuits of self-reflection. But just as "immanence" thought through radically has been used to disclose this dimension of the unconditioned by Spinoza and Deleuze and Jullien, so "transcendence" has been used by philosophers from Plotinus to Kierkegaard and Levinas for the same purpose. A cultural bias in favor of secularism often leads to the exclusion of the sacred: but surely the balance and interpenetration of the two is rather the Way that classical Chinese thinking teaches.[56] The truly

---

55. See also Giorgio Agamben, "L'immanenza assoluta," the last essay in his *La potenza del pensiero: Saggi e conferenze* (Vicenza: Neri Pozza, 2005), 377–406, translated as "Absolute Immanence" in *Potentialities* (Stanford, CA: Stanford University Press, 1996), 220–42, for a kindred reflection issuing from Western culture and its own negative (apophatic) reflection. See, further, M.J. De Nys, *Considering Transcendence: Elements of a Philosophical Theology* (Bloomington: Indiana University Press, 2009).

56. Fingarette, *Confucius: The Secular as Sacred* elegantly demonstrates this.

universal needs to straddle this disjunction—and all other disjunctions as well. But especially this one and especially in our divisive times at the beginning of the twenty-first century of deadly strife between cultures and civilizations in the name of religion or the end of religion.

In "L'immanence: une vie . . . ," his final testament, Gilles Deleuze thinks of life and pure consciousness as an absolute, "pure event" before the distinction into subject and object and in the suspense between this world and any other, between life and death. Deleuze acknowledges his indebtedness to Sartre's *La transcendance de l'Ego* for this notion of impersonal, absolute, immanent consciousness, or "the absolute of an immediate consciousness" ("l'absolu d'une conscience immediate").[57] As Deleuze puts it elsewhere, this is "pure contemplation without knowledge" ("pure contemplation sans connaissance").[58] The plane of immanence, which Deleuze recognizes as unthinkable, as "there" but as "unthought" ("il est là, non pensé") and "vertiginous" (ibid., 59), stands for a refusal to let anything precede or upstage the undifferentiated ground or background of all experience.

Deleuze, followed by Jullien, takes this undifferentiated background as pure immanence and thereby excludes its separation from our experience and consciousness, avoiding Cartesian dualisms and other epistemological gaps. However, the undifferentiated ground or "field" is nevertheless what consciousness cannot comprehend or objectively think, and in this respect, as unrepresentable, it can just as well be understood as the transcendent, or even as pure transcendence, because any representation of transcendence is differential and therefore inadequate to it. This choice of vocabulary for what is beyond or before (upstream from) all language is undecidable. The nuance of difference between the two terms determines whether we begin from the immanence of "a life," my life, or from the transcendence of "life" *simpliciter*. "A life" is singular, and indeed we experience always only a particular life, our own. However, to qualify it in this way and as exclusive of transcendent life is already an act of reflection—no longer just pure immanence, nor simply life itself.

The deeper acknowledgment of strangeness and alterity is in some respects to be gained through acknowledging life itself as transcendent in a sense that theology strives to illuminate. At least this cultural archive of theology is the place where many of the most philosophically penetrating and religiously profound probes of the non-conceptual or trans-conceptual

---

57. "L'immanence: une vie . . . ," in *Philosophie* 47 (1995): 5, 4n.

58. *Qu'est-ce que la philosophie?* (Paris: Minuit, 1991).

are to be found. They are found explicitly or implicitly in various forms of negative theology. And as a cultural phenomenon, such thinking is widespread in the arts and humanities and critical disciplines. It is even found practiced in untold ways and in all manner of activities, such as sports and martial arts, which stretch players and practitioners beyond the borders of their own mental control.

In "L'immanence: une vie . . . ," Deleuze employs a negative or privative method of defining the "transcendental field" ("champ transcendental") of pure, pre-reflexive consciousness as "a-subjective" ("a-subjectif"), a "pure current of a-subjective consciousness" ("pur courant de conscience a-subjective," 3). The transcendental field as pure consciousness refers to no object and belongs to no subject: it is "savage" ("sauvage"), an "absolute, pure, immediate consciousness" ("conscience immédiate absoluë," 4) consisting in the passage from sensation to sensation without reflection and without "revelation." Thus Deleuze defines the transcendental field as the "pure plane of immanence" ("le champ transcendental se définirait comme un pur plan d'immanence," 3–4) because it escapes from all transcendence, whether of a subject or an object.

It is crucial, nevertheless, to specify here that this instance called "pure immanence" escapes from all *representations* of transcendence because it is itself the pure and absolute instance of life and consciousness that all conscious manifestations flow from and yet fail to attain and encompass in any form of representation. Representations could only reduce it to their own finite measure and frame. Considered phenomenologically, negative theology has not been aiming at anything other than this.[59] This instance of life and mind is, as such, without reflection and without inflection in its simplicity. The beliefs and traditions used subsequently to reflect on it, by contrast, are uncontainably diverse: they illuminate from countless different, culturally specific directions its infinite potential.

Thus Deleuze uses both terms, "transcendence" and "immanence," in conjunction with "absolute," in order to indicate the undifferentiated as a "transcendental field" ("champ transcendentale") or as a "plane of immanence" ("plan d'immanence," *L'immanence: une vie*, 3). Both belong within

---

59. Meister Eckhart's negative theology is explicit in this regard. See especially *Predigt* 7 and *Predigt* 48 in his *Deutsche Predigten*, trans. Edmund Colledge, O.S.A., and Bernard McGinn as *German Sermons* in *Meister Eckhart: The Essential Sermons, Commentaries, Treatises, and Defense* (New York: Paulist Press, 1981). Eckhart's famous "the eye with which I see God is the same eye with which God sees me" is axised on this phenomenology hinging from infinity.

his descriptions of the undifferentiated or indeterminate: "The indefinite as such does not mark an empirical indetermination but a determination of immanence or a transcendental determinability" ("L'indéfini comme tel ne marque pas une indétermination empirique, mais une détermination d'immanence ou une déterminabilité transcendantale," 6). "Une vie" ("A life"), by virtue of the indetermination of the indefinite article, is open to all possibilities of life, and this constitutes its existing as a "transcendental field" open in every direction towards all virtual others. Yet, as "immanent life," it is absolutely determinate and indeed singular. Of course, finally, Deleuze's own bias, his way of looking at the world, like Jullien's, comes down in favor of immanence. For him, "transcendence is always a product of immanence" ("La transcendance est toujours un produit d'immanence," 5). But that is a declaration of personal preference or, we might even say, of faith—in the immanent.[60]

Jullien chooses to use China in order to think culture otherwise than according to the canonized metaphysical framework of Western thought since the Greeks. Especially the sharp exchanges with critics such as Heubel have played up, and surely will continue to make even more evident and explicit, that this geographical displacement is, above all, a specific figure for the project of thinking against one's own enabling framework of thought. But precisely such self-critique is a project that is embodied and enacted most originally in theology as negative theology. Theology as a form of thought is based on thinking the necessary encounter with otherness as philosophy's preeminent and overriding motive, indeed as the original charter for its existence as springing from marvel, as Plato and Aristotle both remarked. It epitomizes exactly what Jullien's philosophy constantly attempts through its taking up the exterior point of view represented by Chinese thought and culture. That is a particular way and strategy for achieving what theology by its self-negation (in relation to others and to an absolute Other, to whom it opens itself) in apophatic thought has all along achieved also in quite remarkable and diverse ways within the West, especially in its countercurrents, specifically in apophasis.

---

60. The "immediacy" of which Deleuze writes might just as well be taken to lead to a mystical faith, even in relation to Chinese wisdom. Rolf Trauzettel, "Mystik in chinesischen philosophischen Denken," *minima sinica* 2 (1997): 1–16 finds an "immediacy" circumventing ends-and-means structures and a form of enlightenment that evades representation and that cannot be spoken or mediated linguistically ("Das Unmittelbare ist das sprachlich Nichtmitteilbare," 8) to be characteristic of ancient Chinese wisdom in all its principal currents—Daoist, Confucian, and Buddhist. This qualifies such wisdom as a kind of "mysticism" in his view.

Jullien's method, like negative theology's, is one of self-criticism. He does not finally believe in an object that he can accurately describe. This certainly has something to do with why his method has sometimes offended or perplexed professional sinologists. From his first comprehensive, systematic book, Jullien aimed to create a sinology that would be "truly occidental" ("une sinologie qui soit vraiment *occidentale*").[61] He seems not to be aware or not to care—but most probably chooses rather to strategically ignore—that this project of pursuing unlimited self-criticism by relating one's own framework of thinking to an absolute other is precisely the practice at work in Western thought in its negatively theological countercurrents. As such, negative theology is the ineluctable nemesis of dogmatic metaphysics—it breaks metaphysics open to its own unacknowledged truth.

Verisimilarly, Jullien's reasoning is that, in order to be responsible to one another, we need to eliminate the transcendence of God, since that claim to another pretended—and purportedly absolute—responsibility threatens to undermine the real and concrete claims of unconditioned responsibility that we bear to one another. My view is that in order to do justice to this infinite responsibility to one another, we need to acknowledge an unknowing and unintelligibility (at least to us) at its heart. We need to learn from one another how to be responsible to each other, and this we can do only by opening to an unknown beyond what any of us can possibly know. This is so because our thinking is always finite and, as such, systemically insufficient and needs to be critiqued: it needs to be subjected, indeed, to infinite self-critique. Negative *theology* is the acknowledgment that this critique is answerable to an instance such as nature or divinity that I cannot fathom or comprehend, but in and from which I nevertheless arise and remain beholden to inescapably and unconditionally.

---

61. Jullien, *La valeur allusive. Des catégories originales de l'interprétation poétique dans la tradition Chinoise* (Paris: École Française d'Extrême Orient, 1985), 4.

Chapter 5

AN EXTRA WORD ON ORIGINALITY

Jullien's thinking in the gap between cultures is a way of acknowledging the inadequacy of any paradigm for comprehending the endlessly complex and nuanced phenomena that culture produces. We do, inevitably, think in terms of paradigms, but the question is the extent to which we think freely with and through them or rather remain bounded and boxed in by them. This is a question of "originality" (at least in one productive way of considering this notion). It is a question that has been implicitly connected all along with that of "nature." The original is, in one important sense, the natural, or, that from which all else originates, but again this is a nature that is most akin to "nothing." Thus I wish to approach originality, too, like the key notions treated in each of the other chapters, from the angle of nothing. Originality turns out to be nothing that can be made explicit or be given a general law. The genius for Kant, just like the consummate person (*zhì rén* 至人) in Daoist tradition, is one who can create spontaneously, without specifiable rules, merely out of the unfathomable richness of one's own nature.

In *L'écart et l'entre* (*The Gap and the Between*), Jullien suggests that originality is the cardinal virtue in his ethics. He maintains that the only fundamental ethical choice is that between an original and a banal life (74–75). Nothing else can determine or define his ethical principles: there is no further basis to which ethics can appeal. This appeal to originality as ultimate is thus a negative approach to ethics, yet a way nevertheless of accessing its inexhaustible resources, in particular those of its core notion of "character" (*ethos* in Greek). Jullien's thinking in the gap or the nothing between cultures—or in the emptiness surrounding self-enclosed cultural codes and systems—is, in effect, a negative or apophatic positioning of his thought.

I make this connection with Western apophatic currents explicit in order to help us see Jullien's originality. My aim is not to absorb his thinking into another paradigm foreign to his own explicit sources but rather to relate it to a tradition that has for millennia transmitted the same sorts of insights as he appropriates from elsewhere, specifically from China. The unique conceptuality that Jullien invents is inevitably a hybridization, since it is expressed in his native French. He imports ancient Chinese concepts, while at the same time contaminating them with the predispositions and propensities of his own modern European language and thought. By taking a wider view, one which is inclusive of the closest analogues in Western culture to the Chinese wisdom that Jullien ostensibly expounds, we will be in a position to see more clearly what he has truly been able to accomplish. This wider view needs to encompass especially the resources of the apophatic models of thinking that typically have been marginalized in the West. Only then will we be prepared to discern what Jullien has managed to extend and elaborate—or to undermine and contradict, in Western and Eastern traditions alike.

Originality, on the account I advocate, turns out to be an irreducibly individual way of access to something universal. And this is where culture has its differentiating role to play in relation to nature as ultimately unmasterable and inexpressible. What cultures aim at is itself beyond the words that are used to indicate the goals typical of research, as well as of other cultural practices. This includes words such as "efficaciousness" no less than "harmony" and "truth." But if an individual person or culture undergoes the experience of constructing an approach of their own, in their unique circumstances, to what has motivated the search for vision and comprehension of things that is common to all ages and peoples, this approach can and should be recognized as "original." There are degrees of originality, as of almost everything else, yet discovering and developing one's own particular response to any given matter of universal intelligibility—rather than only repeating borrowed formulas—is in any case the basis of originality in this experiential sense.

In order to illuminate from a distance the nature of originality in Jullien's own special brand of philosophical thinking, I propose a side-glance at an intriguing episode in the history of Western sinology in a philosophical vein. The case of Ernest Fenollosa raises fundamental questions as to what types of philosophical inferences and theories can be drawn from Chinese models of language and culture—and with what warrant and degree of originality. At stake here, finally, is not only our definition of the nature of originality, but also the originality of nature itself. In what sense is nature an origin of culture and how, accordingly, can and should the striving after some kind of natural basis or standard of meaning in language impinge on and direct the task of thinking?

At a momentous turning point in cultural history, Fenollosa's essay "The Chinese Written Character as a Medium for Poetry" (circa 1906) published in 1919 as "*An Ars Poetica* with a Forward and Notes by Ezra Pound" made a certain idea of the Chinese language and its poetry central to numerous Western modernists' attempts to bring about a radical renewal of the art of poetry. This reception seems in retrospect to have had more to do with the way that the essay answered to strivings on the part of modern, especially Anglo-American poets after originality than with its adhering to the actual modalities of (re)presentation and expression characteristic of the Chinese language. At least, Fenollosa's theses seem not to have held up well in terms of the specific technicalities of the Chinese language as defined by specialized linguistic science. However, something about the universal *nature* of language as envisioned by the essay, and as approached in various ways across cultures by languages in general, is illustrated in an outstanding manner by Chinese. I wish to suggest, furthermore, that in some regards the originality of Fenollosa's essay might serve as a foil to illuminate the peculiar kind of contested originality that also distinguishes Jullien's *oeuvre* and makes it so exceptionally interesting.

Fenollosa communicated the idea of poetry as a language of things and as emanating directly from the world itself, as flowing immediately from natural actions and processes rather than from the conscious intentions of speakers. This idea was taken up with enthusiasm by Western modernist poets in their quest to discover or invent a more radical and original poetic language. Haun Saussy recounts how, years after the author's decease in 1908, Fenollosa's essay, as edited and published first in 1919 by Ezra Pound, became a kind of aesthetic manifesto. It served as a charter for the new poetics practiced by poets of the early twentieth century subsequent to the eruptions of modernism around the time of the First World War. Thus the essay could be celebrated later by Donald Davie in *Articulate Energy* (1955) as an epoch-making tract ranking alongside Sir Philip Sidney's *Apologie for Poetrie*, Wordworth's Preface to *Lyrical Ballads*, and Shelley's *Defense of Poetry* for its revolutionary interpretation of the nature and purposes of poetic language.[1]

Fenollosa proposes an ideogrammic understanding of the Chinese language: he views its characters as deriving originally from pictograms.

---

1. Ernest Fenollosa, *The Chinese Written Character as a Medium for Poetry*, critical ed. Haun Saussy, Jonathan Stalling, and Lucas Klein (New York: Fordham University Press, 2008). Davie's comment is relayed by Saussy at the beginning of his introduction to his critical edition of the essay (1). This edition of the manuscripts is indispensable for recovering Fenollosa's own vision and expression from behind Pound's very purposeful editing.

This makes the relation of language to its object natural rather than only conventional. Establishing or eliciting such a natural relation of word and thing had indeed long been a leading aspiration of modern poets. Rainer Maria Rilke (1875–1926), for example, exalts Orpheus (*Sonette an Orpheus*, 1922) as the emblematic, semi-divine founder of such a poetic word because he communicates with the animals and with all natural creatures by the magical enchantment of his song. An even earlier inaugural figure, Stéphane Mallarmé (1842–98), staged a revival of a "second-order Cratylism," by which he meant a poetic remaking of language by art so as to induce it to return to an at least simulated naturalness. In the homonymous Platonic dialogue, "Cratylus" is the name of the character who maintains that language is not just conventional but rather imitates nature. These masterful poetic predecessors represent two salient landmarks in the field of resonance that was vibrating around the American modernist poets during the opening decades of the twentieth century. This field was made to resound by Fenollosa's contention that "in reading Chinese we do not seem to be juggling mental counters, but to be watching *things* work out their own fate" (45). Such was the principle embraced by Pound as key to the revolution in poetic language that modernist poets were to bring about in their effort to recuperate the characteristic qualities of classic Chinese poetry. As Fenollosa explains,

> Chinese notation is something much more than arbitrary symbols. It is based upon a vivid shorthand picture of the operation of nature. In the algebraic figure and in the spoken word there is no natural connection between thing and sign: all depends upon sheer convention. But the Chinese method follows natural suggestion. (51)

Of course, the spoken word of phonetic language could also have an imitative, onomatopoeic relation with the object it signifies. Plato's *Cratylus* abounds in just such examples drawn from the sounds of Greek as embodying imitatively the things they signify. The same principle works in English for words such as "pop" or "crash" or "snap" (and many others): they sound like the action or effect that they designate. However, the long course of linguistic evolution and abstract reflection on their historical development has worked to distance phonetic languages on the whole from any such putatively natural, imitative origins. The confrontation with purportedly pictographic, calligraphic writing, especially given its foreignness in the West, served effectively to raise consciousness of the continuity between language and the world and to reopen to investigation the natural ties between language and the things it names—or, more profoundly, with the natural processes that it reflects and mediates.

Particularly the transitive sentence was seen by Fenollosa as condensing a kind of direct participation in the open-ended process of nature. Things are constantly changed into one another by action that is imitated and directly reflected in the transitive verb. A transitive verb is specifically "a reflection of the temporal order in causation" (47). Natural process consists in continual transfers of power, and this is what a transitive sentence perfectly mirrors. For example, "The sun warms the earth" embodies and enacts this natural order of things. It moves from subject through verb to object. Like the transitive sentence, the Chinese character depicts not just a thing but an action. In fact, things are inseparable from actions, since nature is a continuous flow. Things, in their deeper natures, are nothing but acts in Fenollosa's understanding of them, and so language fundamentally, in its deep structure, conveys nothing but actions: "The form of the Chinese transitive sentence, and of the English (omitting particles), exactly corresponds to this universal form of action in nature. This brings language close to things, and in its strong reliance upon verbs it erects all speech into a kind of dramatic poetry" (48).

All verbs, in Fenollosa's view, are originally transitive, and they can lose this form only by their object's becoming merely implicit. This happens in intransitive verbs (verbs without a direct object) and in reflexive verbs (verbs referring back to the subject and so lacking an independent object) and in verbs that otherwise negate their original objects or efface their own action by casting it into the passive voice. In all these cases, such elision of the explicitly transitive character possessed by all verbs in their, by his reckoning, original form represents for Fenollosa a decline from the direct apprehension of nature: "There is no such thing as a naturally intransitive verb. The passive form is evidently a correlative sentence, which turns about and makes the object into a subject" (49). In tracing all language from action, Fenollosa suggests that "our very word *exist* means 'to stand forth,' to show oneself by a definite act." Other examples make the same point: " 'Is' comes from the Aryan root *as*, to breathe. 'Be' is from *bhu*, to grow" (49). "Not" can be related to the Sanskrit *na*, meaning being lost or perishing.

Apart from such suggestive specifics and some very vivid images, Fenollosa's essay in comparative linguistics is cast into a generalizing language that aims to articulate universal truths about language and its relation to reality. It argues that the nature of language is contrary to rational reflection and prior to cultural categories like grammar: "All nations have written their strongest and most vivid literature before they invented a grammar. . . . Nature herself has no grammar" (50). Nature is what structures and animates the Chinese language, and it does so without the mediation of the grammar that would sublate and reelaborate language on another plane, a plane of culture severed from its natural roots. The Chinese language depicts things in the act of their becoming, without obscuring their natural dynamism by static structures of ontology such as are embodied in grammar:

> One of the most interesting facts about the Chinese language is that in it we can see, not only the forms of sentences, but literally the parts of speech growing up, budding forth one from another. Like nature, the Chinese words are alive and plastic, because *thing* and *action* are not formally separated. The Chinese language naturally knows no grammar. (50–51)

Whereas the parts of speech are totally artificial, the sentence, as describing the action of an agent on an object, is an inevitable and natural unit of meaning.

Fenollosa explains this naturalness of the Chinese language in terms especially of the figure of metaphor. The metaphor contrasts precisely with the concept inasmuch as it does not abstract from the actions in which words originate: "The Chinese written language has not only absorbed the poetic substance of nature and built with it a second world of metaphor, but has, through its very pictorial visibility, been able to retain its original creative poetry with far more vigor and vividness than any phonetic tongue" (55). Unlike the phonetic word, which is filed down to just its conceptual content, "the narrowest edge of its meaning," the Chinese character preserves the body of its history. "Its etymology is constantly visible. It retains the creative impulse and process, visible and at work. After thousands of years the lines of metaphorical advance are still shown, and in many cases actually retained in the meaning" (55). The Chinese character grows richer through the accumulated variety of its uses rather than being reduced to just a common notional denominator. The Chinese language, accordingly, remains near to the "heart of nature in its metaphors" (55), which are the means of passing over from the seen to the unseen (53–54). The process of metaphor consists in "the use of material images to suggest immaterial relations" (54). The relations in which things truly consist (their inter*actions* with one another) are captured as likenesses expressed by metaphor.

Our Western words, in Fenollosa's estimation, are typically *un*metaphorical. "There is little or nothing in a phonetic word to exhibit the embryonic stages of its growth. It does not bear its metaphor on its face" (55). The Chinese character, in contrast, "retains the primitive sap" (55), which has been drained away by logic in Western languages. Fenollosa locates the "inveterate logic of classification" at the heart of Western tradition and stigmatizes it as "scholasticism" (57). This logic—"the discredited, or rather the useless, logic of the Middle Ages" (49)—was the dominant paradigm presumably from Aristotle to Aquinas, and it was finally overcome only by modern science and more specifically by the theory of evolution, in which things are no longer supposed to have fixed essences. In Fenollosa's telescoped overview of Western intellectual history, then, science is aligned with poetry (and not with logic or grammar): both show how things interact quite apart from extraneous, artificial, intellectual categories. Poetry probes and reveals nature through its "thousands of active words, each doing its utmost to show forth the motive and vital forces" at work in the ongoing processes of things (57). Science investigates and elucidates, by its own empirical methods, these same vital forces.

Fenollosa's views were not generally accepted. They were contested and even virulently denounced by a number of leading specialists in Chinese language and culture. For Yale linguist George A. Kennedy, Fenollosa's essay was a "mass of confusion" propagating a "complete misunderstanding" of Chinese language based on the "ideogrammic method."[2] The polemic against myths of Chinese writing as ideogrammic and pictographic continues down to our own time.[3] In these debates, to my mind, everything depends on how rigidly writing and reading are construed. Linguists often are talking about language or writing as a narrowly conceived, formal object that can be scientifically defined and is not to be confounded with "constructions of a poetic nature" ("constructions d'ordre poétique," ibid., 258), whereas the latter, poetic aspects may well belong to the nature of language as it lives and evolves broadly in the world beyond the borders of any precise object

---

2. "Fenollosa, Pound, and the Chinese Character," in *Selected Works of George A. Kennedy*, ed. Tien-yi Li (New Haven, CT: Yale University Press, 1964), 462. A more balanced account of the matter is James J.Y. Liu's *The Art of Chinese Poetry* (Chicago, IL: University of Chicago Press, 1966), 3ff.

3. For a review of the question claiming to give definitive answers bursting the age-old myths still purveyed by the likes of François Jullien (quoted on 242), see Viviane Alleton, "L'écriture chinoise: mise au point," in *La pensée in Chine aujourd'hui,* ed. Ann Cheng, 241–69. For an in-depth discussion of the essay and its place in the history of theorizing writing in China, see Haun Saussy's *Great Walls of Discourse and Other Adventures in Cultural China,* chapter 3, 31–74.

of study. The poetry of language can penetrate in essential ways into the common experience of language realized by people in speaking, as well as in reading and writing. There are innumerable personal and cultural choices and sensibilities that come into play at the level of determining what and how language in any of its modes, including writing, is able to become meaningful and make sense.

However, Fenollosa's essential contribution is, in any case, not to sinology. His portrait of the Chinese language is steered primarily by a philosophical vision of language. He takes hold of certain aspects and features that characterize Chinese—particularly its residual, relative closeness to pictographics and therefore its connectedness to a phenomenal universe—and he sees language in general through these lenses (and vice versa). These characteristics are manifest in Chinese in a peculiarly high degree, but they are present as iconic features and residues also in other languages, including Western ones: arguably, they are constitutive of language per se. Fenollosa uses Chinese language and characters to open a universal vision of language—replete with a general theory of its sources and capacities.

Fenollosa's argument is about the way the Chinese language remembers (or at least unconsciously retains) its origins—and thereby reflects on the origins of language per se—more than about how it functions in the minds of its users today. He offers a philosophical interpretation of the origins of the Chinese character rather than a scientific analysis of its actual linguistic functioning. His account might best be understood as an "archeology" of knowledge in the sense in which this term is employed by Michel Foucault and, following him, by Giorgio Agamben. Origins are projected from the present and revisit the cultural archive of the past in its light. At stake here is the originality of a philosophical vision that communicates vitally with classical Chinese thought and writing not by means of description of a stable and inert object but rather by a creative extension that engages urgent problems of thought in the present. In this sense, Foucault understood himself to be writing "the history of the present." Pertinently, then, Longxi Zhang places Fenollosa's theory in the context of the "American Renaissance" and specifically of Ralph Waldo Emerson's interpretation of Egyptian hieroglyphics as a prelapsarian, natural, pictorial language. These are the very terms that Fenollosa's argument adopts for a natural and pictorial relation between words and things in Chinese.[4]

---

4. Longxi Zhang, *Allegoresis,* 27–28, in a section of chapter 1 entitled "Nature, Writing, and Chinese Poetry."

Fenollosa's ideas, moreover, although spurned as dilettantish by many experts, are far from being arbitrary inventions or fantasies of his own. They are in reality very traditional ideas. They belong to the self-understanding of Chinese literate culture that goes back to Xu Shen (AD 30–124), the original founder of studies of Chinese characters (*wénzìxué,* 文字学) in the Han dynasty.[5] With his *Shuōwén jiě zì* (*Explanations of Simple and Compound Characters*), presented to the emperor in the year AD 100, Xu produced the first comprehensive dictionary of the Chinese language. His own methods entail interpreting the meaning of characters in terms of their ideogrammic elements and most often emphasizing their value as picture language as well. These ideas are debatable, but they assert themselves persistently in the efforts of the Chinese themselves to understand the nature and origins of their language. As intuitions that may be reversed by critical reflection and analysis, they nevertheless remain relevant to understanding what motivates and animates Chinese characters. From an apophatic standpoint, I cannot but suspect that the profoundest insight into the origin of language is more likely to be opened up not by a (purportedly) fully adequate analytic description but rather by an acknowledgment of failure and by showing up the limits of our ability to account for such origins in purely scientific terms.

The origin of writing in China is evidently bound up with the sacred, with divination. Writing is understood at first as conveying communication from the gods rather than from and among humans. Some of its earliest forms were produced by techniques of burning tortoise carapaces and reading the cracks that resulted. Imitation of these graphic figures has proven to be essential in the origination of the script of Chinese characters. Such an understanding of writing as sacred, as coming from a transcendent source, entails a universalizing vision of its purpose and origin.[6]

Language is the element of universality, and it is eminently the universality of nature that classical Chinese culture has aimed to preserve. Nature (rather than the concept) is the universal in at least several strains of Chinese thought, including the Daoist, just as even in Western languages natural metaphors are what give general truths and propositions their concrete content and pertinence to life and experience. But nature is per se mute. It

---

5. See Zong-qi Cai, *Configurations of Comparative Poetics: Three Perspectives on Western and Chinese Literary Criticism,* 175–77.

6. On the Chinese character as bearing an inherently sacred worldview, see Christine Barbier-Kontler, *Sagesse et religions en Chine: De Confucius à Deng-Xiaoping* (Paris: Bayard/Centurion, 1996), 29–47.

merely embodies the universal that it does not articulate and that cannot be subjected to the categorical logic of discourse. This natural embodiment of the universal transpires in the continuous contradiction of endless flux. Yet there is also something invisible at work in all these observable processes of nature, and Fenollosa exalts the Chinese language precisely as pointing to the *invisible*. Its use of metaphor acts as a "bridge whereby to cross from the minor truth of the seen to the major truth of the unseen" (54).

Fenollosa defines the "process" of metaphor as "the use of material images to suggest immaterial relations" (54). The Chinese language excels in this: "Yet the Chinese language with its peculiar materials has passed over from the seen to the unseen by exactly the same process which all ancient races employed. This process is metaphor" (54). How is the dimension of the unseen opened up by metaphor? Presumably, the analogies between different physical systems cannot just be accidental. They reveal something else than the visible physical systems themselves—some kind of invisible law or order. The analogies of structure between the things that metaphor mirrors are "clues" furnished by nature of some actual, ontological connection rather than merely subjective impressions of similarity. Metaphor, then, is a revelation of the real nature of things and not just the arbitrary work of fantasy or rhetorical ornament.

By its visibly adhering to invisible nature through its preservation of language's constitutive metaphors, Chinese language and the thought it embodies are naturally apophatic, naturally turned toward the invisible and unsayable, and indeed this is the "major" truth that registers in Fenollosa's vision. The Chinese language, as he construes it, directs our vision beyond language to things themselves, to the concreteness of natural processes and even to what lurks unseen in things, so that "the known interprets the obscure, nature is alive with myth" (54). Language is a revelation of an unseen order of things. Its myths translate the mysterious life of nature that cannot be otherwise expressed or apprehended logically. These potentially apophatic tendencies of Chinese language and culture are articulated even more fully and informatively by Jullien, as I have attempted to show throughout this essay. However, other distinguished researchers have also developed kindred insights.

François Cheng's work on Chinese poetic writing represents more soberly than Fenollosa's, and in terms approaching those of Jullien, some of the same emphases on the poeticality of Chinese language and writing.[7]

---

7. François Cheng, *L'écriture poétique chinoise suivi d'une anthologie des poèmes des Tang* (Paris: Seuil, 1996 [1977]).

Cheng tells a tale of "a language conceived no longer as a denotative system that 'describes' the world but rather as a representation that organizes links and provokes acts of signifying" ("un langage conçu non plus comme un système dénotatif qui 'décrit' le monde, mais comme une représentation qui organise les liens et provoque les actes de signifiance," 15). As such, language is itself a dynamic process actually producing rather than only referring to concrete realities. This goes some way towards explaining why the artist in China practices simultaneously the arts of poetry, painting, and writing. All the spiritual dimensions of his or her art are activated together in symbolic creation. Incantatory chant and visualized words work together with music and myth in creating something of a *Gesamtkunstwerk*.

Most significantly, from the point of view of apophatic rhetoric, Cheng's analysis of Chinese poetry emphasizes the power of the negative, of emptiness and absence. The characteristic procedure of poets is to introduce empty words into their compositions so as to vivify the whole. Empty words evacuate determinate meaning in order to open meaning to infinite possibilities and indeterminacy. Cheng's study focuses on how poets eliminate certain elements from ordinary language ("poètes enlèvent du langage ordinaire certains elements existants," 39). By means of such ellipses, they "restore to the ideograms their ambivalent and mobile nature, permitting expression of a subtle symbiosis of man and world" ("restituer aux idéogrammes leur nature ambivalente et mobile, permettant l'expression d'une subtile symbiose de l'homme et du monde," 39). The elements commonly elided include personal pronouns, prepositions, terms of comparison, and verbs, which are replaced by empty words.

Poetic language was defined by Roman Jakobson (building on Paul Valéry's insights) in terms of its "poetic function" based on self-reflexivity, or on language calling attention to itself as language. This is a dynamic definition, although it shows traces of the tendency to treat language objectively in terms of its descriptive properties and typology. Chinese poetics requires, instead, a pure pragmatics. It envisages no longer a subject representing an object but rather a participation in the creative process of the cosmos. Poetry is exactly that in the most speculative theories of it, such as Coleridge's (imagination as the repetition in the finite mind of the eternal, creative act of an infinite Mind), which go far beyond the typical literary-critical understanding of the properties of poetry. Poetry shows itself to be just such a total act of making at least as directly and expressly in the case of Chinese poetry and poetics. The allusive incitation, as expounded by Jullien, brings together the infra- and the supra-linguistic levels between which the poetic process moves (*Le Détour et l'accès*, 177).

These select examples help us to glimpse Jullien's works as fitting into a considerable history of integrating Chinese texts and traditions into philosophical reflection attuned to the problematics of Western culture.[8] Jullien's work is detailed and precise in its treatment of both traditions. Nevertheless, he has an original vision of his own derived certainly in good part from Western philosophical sources regarding the fundamental philosophical issues raised, and this can tend to set him at odds with a certain mainstream sinology.[9] Despite certain initial appearances, he is not playing their game, in which one is supposed to start simply from the texts, and the task is to describe them accurately and not to interrogate them philosophically in terms of one's own culture and its contemporary concerns. A philosopher, especially an original one, is not governed by the goal of presumably objective description in accordance with scientific method. Speculative thinking simply does not take the same approach, even when practiced in conjunction with sensitive hermeneutic work in interpreting the texts. It is because Jullien's approach is original in this sense, I submit, that it encounters difficulty in gaining the assent of specialists. It is primarily a matter of not speaking the same (disciplinary) language.

For as much as Jullien has himself become recognized institutionally, with research centers and proliferating conferences dedicated to examining his work, he has not always found the resonance that one might expect, not even among the explicitly and programmatically philosophical approaches to classical Chinese culture that have been fostered in the American academy in recent years. This might seem baffling. There are some signs of attempts at accommodation, but the climate of reception for Jullien's work has often been cool and inclement. Anglo-Saxon pragmatic philosophy is in certain ways at loggerheads with the continental tradition out of which Jullien works. Of course, the striving for originality is also a struggle for distinction and is subject to the competition for recognition. These aspects of the academic profession certainly take their toll here, too, as they do in

---

8. Other ground-breaking works in the genre that are likewise predicated on defining fundamental differences between Chinese and Western thought include Chad Hansen, *A Daoist Theory of Chinese Thought: A Philosophical Interpretation* (New York: Oxford University Press, 2000) and Philip J. Ivanhoe, *Confucian Moral Self-Cultivation* (New York: Hackett, 2000).

9. Another telling index of this resistance is the ironic treatment by Jean Levi, "Réponses à un questionnaire sur François Jullien pour un journal vietnamien," in *Réflexions chinoises. Lettrés, stratèges et excentriques de Chine* (Paris: Albin Michel, 2011), 197–218.

virtually all collective human affairs. Supposed differences of philosophical principle must sometimes be suspected of serving as camouflage to cover over rivalries by fabricating consciously avowed reasons for guarding distance or withholding assent or even recognition.

Jullien treats questions of fundamental philosophical significance and opens new avenues for thinking in our present predicament by informed comparison with classical Chinese modes. He deals with questions at a philosophical depth where determinations such as transcendence and immanence are not always decidable in objective, scientific terms. They remain open to determination because they are not just matters of correctly describing and classifying objects but rather open the ground of objectivity itself to rethinking. Philosophical thinking at this level of originality is bound to escape and sometimes even to violate the supposedly definitive determinations of sinology. This makes some degree of conflict and incomprehension inevitable. But what is most remarkable—and at the same time indicative of intrinsic limits of the academic discipline—is simply the lack of engagement with Jullien's texts by specialized scholarship and the surprisingly widespread refusal to acknowledge their relevance. Even from a position of disagreement on certain fundamental orientations, notably with regard to metaphysics and theology, I have aimed to bring out the pertinence and fecundity of these texts in broad terms on basic issues concerning the human search for understanding in our increasingly intercultural world. I do so in a personalized and condensed form—and as an epitome of my argument—in the Epilogue.

Epilogue

INTERCULTURAL DIA-LOGUE AND ITS APOPHATIC INTERSTICES[1]

In order to speak of François Jullien, but also by chance to speak *with* François Jullien, I find myself constrained first to present myself, very briefly, yet nonetheless in my globality, as a thinker of the negative and the unsayable. I am obligated from the beginning, and I beg your indulgence for it, to lay down certain markers with reference to my own works and projects in order to render intelligible the dialectic in which I engage with the texts of Jullien. I am going to speak as a representative of Western apophaticism, and I will attempt to set this mode of thinking into dialogue with the thought of Jullien. I aim to show the largely unacknowledged affinities of Jullien's thought with this tradition, and therewith also its affinities with Eastern and specifically with classical Chinese thought, which is the acknowledged object of, and to a considerable extent also the seminal inspiration for, Jullien's philosophical reflection.

You are familiar with the texts of François Jullien, but I have to give you some guidelines for understanding what I mean by "apophaticism." I constructed a theory and a history of the apophatic in two volumes (*On What Cannot Be Said*) that show the configuration and the extension that I accord to this textual corpus, this archive, this cultural *resource*.[2] My current

---

1. Elaborated from an exposition delivered, in its original French redaction, in the presence of François Jullien and addressed to scholars of his work at the colloquium "Des possible de la pensée: Autour des travaux de François Jullien" in Cerisy-la-Salle, France, September 15, 2013.

2. *On What Cannot Be Said: Apophatic Discourses in Philosophy, Religion, Literature, and the Arts*, edited with theoretical and critical essays by William Franke, 2 vols. (Notre Dame, IN: University of Notre Dame Press, 2007).

approach to the unsayable is crystallized in a book entitled *A Philosophy of the Unsayable,* which advocates apophaticism as a perennial and at the same time original philosophy, one addressed to our own age.[3] This book, published in 2014, builds on and extends the work inaugurated in the two preceding volumes, dating from 2007, on negative theology considered in the astonishing amplitude of its deployment throughout the history of culture in the West.

Jullien has expressed strong reservations on multiple occasions with regard to philosophies that appeal to the unsayable or, more exactly, "the ineffable" and to anything that has an odor of mysticism about it. I aspire to draw attention to other possibilities of thinking the unsayable, possibilities that he has perhaps not glimpsed or has not, in any case, seized upon, possibilities that nevertheless are comprehended under this word ("l'ineffable") and its synonyms or cognates. I wish, however, to underscore that, in pursuing a thinking of the unsayable such as I understand it, I find myself remarkably close to the thought of Jullien and in profound resonance with the overall motivating intentions of classical Chinese thinking in the perspective that he defends. My thinking resonates specifically with a thinking that opens itself to what precedes and exceeds the articulated and systematic thought of philosophy. Certainly, there are some disputes that would still separate Jullien, at least at first, from a philosophy of the unsayable such as I construe and advocate. These disputes concern particularly the status and function of "transcendence" and what each of us refers to as the "theological." For Jullien, it is a grave misunderstanding to want to find something theological in classical Chinese thought. His work undertakes to show the contrary, and it does so in detail and sometimes with passionate vehemence. Nevertheless, if one understands the theological by starting from negative theology, things are different, indeed radically different and even the opposite of what they otherwise appear to be. A certain apophaticism is in its essence a rigorous and sometimes an aggressive critique of every concept, especially of every theological concept. It is then not so surprising, after all, that apophatic theology should suggest important analogies with the fundamental tendencies of classical Chinese thought that Jullien has helped us to rediscover in some new and particularly provocative ways.

In fact, as an apophatic thinker, I am deeply indebted and grateful to Jullien for having opened to me a whole series of paths leading from Europe

---

3. *A Philosophy of the Unsayable* (Notre Dame, IN: University of Notre Dame Press, 2014).

to China. My apophatic project advocating the *universality* uniquely of *that which is not* relies on the work of Jullien as its indispensable path-breaker ("défricheur de chemin") in entering upon the territory of intercultural philosophy. Jullien's work has enabled me to individuate aspects of Chinese thought that I understand as aspiring likewise to a type of universality that must necessarily remain implicit and which can in principle be only a negative universality in any of its actual expressions.

I engage in this dialogue with Jullien, furthermore, on the basis of a program of research, or more exactly of thought, that pivots on theology, or more precisely on negative theology taken as a critical resource and finally as a means of infinite self-criticism of every possible philosophical formulation.[4] This program parallels that of Jullien, who utilizes Chinese culture as an astonishingly rich resource for a comprehensive and radical critique—in reality a self-critique—of Western philosophical thought starting from the exterior vantage point furnished by China. My critique is more internal in the sense that it issues from within Western tradition and even from its deepest and most buried roots, those that are perhaps least known and most misunderstood. I evoke the *interior* Other, that of Western apophaticism, which functions in good part in parallel with the *exterior* Other, that of China, which is insistently evoked by Jullien all along in his philosophical reflections as remaining exogenous to, and as having practically no contact with, European culture up to modern times.

In proposing a thinking that is turned always towards the other, the other to speech and reason, I consider myself to come close in my approach to the method of Jullien, as well as to be in line with a characteristic orientation within Chinese thought itself, one that he champions. And yet I entertain a relation to an other that reveals itself to be other than his. The genre of thought in question for both of us fights shy of *philosophy* in the strict sense, which is also surely a reductive sense—namely, that of the proposition rigorously demonstrated or of logically argued and systematically developed discourse. This other way of thinking is deployed rather in the margins and between the lines of strictly rational discourse. Thus, the point

---

4. We might recall that Jean Trouillard, in "Valeur critique de la mystique Plotinienne," *Revue philosophique de Louvain* 59 (1961), pertinently defined negative theology as "infinite critique" (440). He is followed by Hilary Armstrong, in "The Escape of the One: An Investigation of Some Possibilities of Apophatic Theology Imperfectly Realised in the West," in *Plotinian and Christian Studies*, 23, who defines negative theology as "limitless criticism" (87).

of such pronouncements is to be found, rather, in what they do not say, not directly, anyway. It is what they, nonetheless, allow to be understood that enables us to open up a breach and create points of entry for what Jullien designates as *wisdom* (*la sagesse*) in its distinction from philosophy. Jullien pursues this distinction programmatically in *Un sage est sans idée* (*A Sage Has No Ideas*).

The apophatic can be found in the West, even before the Greeks, in divination and in magic, and then in Greece, with its mysteries, notably the Eleusinian, and their rites executed in the form of pantomime. It features prominently as well in the cult of silence among the Pythagoreans and among diverse types of shamans and other sages and proto-philosophers up to Empedocles and Heraclitus. In such forms, the apophatic precedes and in a way anticipates the logos, even before accompanying it along the course of its historical journey. The apophatic, in effect, rewrites and redesigns the history of philosophy and even the prehistory of the logos. It does this in negative—not by arguing against philosophical logos but by undermining and subverting it from within and even from before its entry upon the scene. In forms barely discerned in negative by cultural anthropology, which sound out the night of time, furthermore, the vestiges of the apophatic perdure and indelibly mark a whole ensemble of traditions that are propounded in contestation of the logos and its hegemony across the entire trajectory of Western thought.

Neoplatonism begins with Plotinus to disconcert and confound the logical propositions of classical philosophy by an experience edging upon and moving beyond the sayable. It eventually brings about the total collapse of the logos in the extreme and unsurpassable aporetics of Damascius (AD 480–550) at a historical point of closure for ancient philosophy—emblematically, with the dissolution in 529 of the Academy at Athens, of which Damascius was the last *diadochos* or "successor" following in the lineage of Plato, its founder. Apophatic thought or wisdom is passed along from these thinkers to certain mystic philosophers of the Middle Ages, including Christian mystics such as Dionysius the Areopagite and John Scott Eriugena, as well as Sufis, such as Ibn al-ʿArabi, and kabbalists, such as Moses de León. It is formulated thereafter in a more critical-rationalist speculative vein by Meister Eckhart and by certain Scholastics, drawing on Maimonides, and by Nicolas Cusanus, but it also issues eventually in the experiential mode of the Carmelite mystics and Silesius Angelus in the baroque era. It can be traced up to Romanticism (particularly to the Jena Romanticism represented by F.W.J. Schelling and indebted to Jakob Böhme), notably to this history-making movement's revolts and excesses aiming at the infinite. And it emerges irrepressibly again in the calamitous erosion of confidence in rational discourse in the fin de siècle Vienna of Wittgenstein, Hugo von Hofmannsthal, and Fritz Mauthner. Gustav Klimt and Arnold Schoenberg, in their respective aesthetic media of painting and music, also pursue the expressiveness of silence. Finally, among myriad postmodern writers and thinkers, from Jacques Derrida and Maurice Blanchot to Samuel Beckett, there is a radical reflection on the inevitable failure of all narrowly rationalizing discourse. This reflection harbors a protest that murmurs all along the course of Western thought, but it resounds most intensely and insistently at pivotal epochs such as those highlighted in this historical synopsis.

It is in this alternative history—alternative even to history itself—that I propose to find the equivalents, or at least the analogues, of this perennial anti-philosophy for which Jullien refers us to China, especially to its founding and most classic texts. At the same time, I wish to stress that Jullien is himself a connoisseur of this other non-history of the non-logos in Western philosophy. Especially worthy of note are his subtle discussions, in *Le détour et l'accès,* chapter 12, section 4, of Damascius at the culmination of ancient Greek apophatism.

Nevertheless, I do not want to give the impression that I am going to take up the advocacy of Western tradition in order to move against the intentions of Jullien to find at the source of Chinese wisdom that which seems to be lacking from the resources of Western thought in its most canonical forms. It is not by *refusing* the displacement to China but rather by *complementing* it through reflections bearing on this *other* Occident, that of the unsayable, that I propose to enter into dialogue with Jullien. The unsayable is that which was never said or thought, except indirectly, all through the (Western) history of thinking of the logos. Through comparison with Chinese thought it can be made to emerge finally as what this thought all along was really about, even while for the most part the unsayable went unidentified and unrecognized because of its inaccessibility to direct, methodical treatment by the logos. In this manner, I intend to integrate the indispensable insight that Jullien has gained through displacement to his Chinese heterotope—that is, by his disciplined exercise of taking up distance, voluntarily, from that which is most his own, in order to be able better to appropriate it with more critical objectivity. In effect, the passage by way of the intercultural has shown itself to be equally inescapable for my own work. An apophatic philosophy, and in any case my own, cannot avoid becoming intercultural. In fact, I was already engaged with the intercultural even before I knew that I was, and I follow Jullien with enthusiasm down this path, which he has opened up and made accessible to me as never before. I recognize in him an incomparable guide and leader in bringing to consciousness the intercultural turn of philosophy that has brought about an irrevocable re*orient*ation of thought in our own epoch—turning us, in this case, eastward.

Thus, far be it from me to wish to abide within the West under the fallacious pretext that there is no need to go to the other end of the world in order to discover what we already have here in our midst, if we only wish to open our eyes. My idea is not to economize on the Chinese excursion. On the contrary, the spirit of apophaticism requires adventure abroad, even in the most foreign parts possible, including that which is foreign to the human altogether—by which I mean, for instance, the divine. Divinity is perhaps the most radical self-estrangement that human imagination can undertake to explore because it claims power and precedence over the human, depriving the latter of its sovereignty. In addition, and inseparably, this incitation to a vertical self-transcendence is expressed and realized concretely in the exigency of exposing oneself without exclusions also to all possible foreign encounters that present themselves along the horizontal axis of our encounter with other human cultures.

It is not, however, Jullien's intention, in the end, to play different civilizations, particularly Europe and China, off against each other. His discourse aims rather at the globality that comprehends the two in a face-to-face encounter: this is a globality that *com*-prehends, or grasps the two together, on the basis of the gap between them. I believe that, at bottom, I am working in the same intent as he, or at least not against him, in attempting to individuate a type of wisdom in the West, too, specifically in its apophaticism, which gives the lie to the sovereign and magisterial pretensions of philosophy. Furthermore, we are united in the attempt to discover in the bosom of philosophy itself an alternative wisdom that is dynamically alive in the work of self-critique.

In my view, then, it is not by categorically excluding the West from the genre of wisdom that China has developed so ingeniously that we will be able better to implement critique of the logos and of its domination over virtually all modes of philosophical reflection. The differences between the two cultures show themselves to be comprehended finally in their common and even, in some sense, universal possibilities. I am convinced, especially through reading *De l'universel, de l'uniforme, du commun et du dialogue entre les cultures*, that it should be possible to reach a certain understanding with Jullien on this head. I suspect that the major difference, the veritable and tenacious bone of contention, between us in this "dialogue" concerns rather our evaluation and, even more fundamentally, our underlying conception of theology.

EPILOGUE

Theology, in the discourse of Jullien, has a tendency to assume the role of that insidious form of thinking which must be surpassed in order to liberate thought from the confining bonds that have too often held it captive in its most canonical expressions in the Occident. It is by means of a contrast with all theologizing thought that Jullien is able to give a more precise (though admittedly only a negative) sense to "the other possible" ("l'autre possible") of thinking that is dear to him—this other possibility of thinking, which he assiduously works to bring to light and to valorize. Theology is deemed in his discourse, in common agreement with a good part of contemporary philosophical discourse in France and in the modern, secular West generally, to restrain and to vitiate the "possibles" of thought, to restrict their full range. According to this widely shared prejudice, the weight of theology and the imprint of the theological on Western thought have been capable of arresting the progress of the authentic wisdom along its natural path, which, in contrast, the sages of China knew how to follow all the way to the end. Theology finds itself accused effectively of leading Western thought into a cul-de-sac.

Starting from this realization, Jullien seems to suggest, we ought to be able better to discern the true possibles of thought in Europe and in China alike, and indeed universally. Thought, finally emancipated from theology would, according to this scenario, be free from extraneous, dogmatic trammels and in a position to deploy itself infinitely. Thought would have failed to do so in the West up to the present because of the sway of the theological incumbent upon the ways and means followed by our thinking, for the most part unconsciously, ever since its Greek and Hebrew origins.

Is it really necessary, however, to inculpate and ostracize theology in this way, as a scapegoat, in order to produce sense and, particularly, in order to bring our thought to its most vital and fecund possibilities? The objective of the thinking that Jullien develops through his reception of classical Chinese wisdom is to break with the practice that consists in making sense always a function of exclusion, thus relying on a binary logic of oppositions. It is rather through an orientation to globality that we seek sense, or rather the *senses,* that necessarily succeed one another and undo each other and—in any event—escape from every supposedly definitive formulation of sense. Jullien performs just such an openly inclusive and endlessly elusive movement of thought, by taking cues from his Chinese models, and I do the same, basing myself on Occidental apophaticism.

A question that presses forward, then, at this point, is that of whether the "possibles of thinking" individuated by Jullien in Chinese wisdom are not available also to the West, specifically in its apophatic thinking. Or even better, should we not perhaps recognize the *im*possibles of thought—those seen and focused especially by what I call apophatic thought—as remaining at the bottom of the two traditions and as establishing the *universal* basis of thought? The possibles of thought exist always already ("immer schon") as specifically determined by the languages and cultures within which they are thought—and thus as separated from one another by cultural and linguistic divides. It is rather in colliding against that which it is *im*possible to think that all forms and varieties of thought meet together in a common impotence, an impotence, however, which can subsequently become infinitely productive. This impasse works productively in differentiated ways across innumerable cultures and their typological variations throughout geographical space and historical time.

Theology, thought negatively, has no thinkable or sayable content. It is not identified with any concept or with any thing at all but consists rather in the denial of the sufficiency of every concept and of every possible enunciation in the appeal and challenge to think them still further and still more deeply. Saint Anselm's celebrated definition of God as "that than which nothing greater can be thought" is already perfectly apophatic. This formula prescribes only the imperative to press always further in pursuing the infinite potential to think always more.[5] This extension of the infinite, just as it excludes no possible from the being of God, likewise excludes none of the inexhaustible connections between all things, which also belong to the creation and thus make up part of the infinite glory of the Creator. In effect, it is only through them and their immanent being that this glory of the transcendent being (*esse*) or God can be known by us, be it ever so little and inadequately. Thomas Aquinas makes this argument explicitly in *Summa Theologica* Ia, question 12 on how God is known by us ("Quomodo Deus a nobis conoscitur"), and it subtends his entire theological outlook.

A note of caution, however, is in order here. The "always more" or "always greater" than we can conceive that is in question signifies for us always more abnegation and always more radical critique of all that which seems to be established or attained. Thus it is not to be confounded with the ideology of heroism or of undertaking to do what is always more, or even most, difficult. Such idealisms are effectively critiqued by Jullien, following his Chinese sources. For example, in his *Traité de l'efficacité*, in pages

---

5. It is so read, notably, by Karl Barth, *Fides quaerens intellectum: Anselms Beweis der Existenz Gottes im Zusammenhang seines theologischen Programms* (Zurich: Theologischer Verlag, 1981 [1931]), trans. Ian W. Robertson as *Fides quaerens intellectum: Anselm's Proof of the Existence of God in the Context of his Theological Scheme* (Pittsburgh, PA: Pickwick Press, 1975).

on "Doing nothing" ("Ne rien faire"), Jullien shows, in an apophatic spirit, that very often less *effort* produces more *effect*: remaining in retreat, holding back, not acting, can often prove more efficacious than charging ahead with all the force and impetuousness of overt, determined, swashbuckling action.[6] The focused nature of deliberate, willful action might after all be detrimental to moving in step with and remaining receptive to the overall process of reality in which all things are accomplished. As is observed in chapter 37 of the *Daodejing*: "Dao does nothing, yet nothing is left undone." We have to be able to look beyond our own projects so as to be able to see what is really done or left undone in the order of things that matters more than we can know or understand. What apophatic thought recommends, finally, is going always further only in the *dissolution* of all of the positive structures that shackle thought. This precisely is what the kenotic spirit of Christianity also does, and this *self-critical* practice is what apophatic theology raises to a level of conscious philosophical reflection.

In translating itself onto an existential and ethical terrain, theology valorizes itself as the most radical critical negation of self because it implies a renunciation and abandon of the very faculty of self-judgment. My own critical power subjects me to a judge who is other than and more just than I. The radicality of unlimited self-critique and the radicality of the recognition of the other meet a certain limit in theology. For God is other with respect to all my thoughts and with respect to my very world itself, other to the point of being able to dispose of my being and of having a certain authority to command even my freedom, which can no longer take itself for absolutely sovereign. Theology aims toward a sphere beyond every concept, even beyond every supposedly theological concept. One can and certainly must mistrust any instance that claims, in the guise of a superior subject, to authoritatively command one's own freedom. But one must remember that every *representation* of such an authority finds itself also immediately undermined by the uncompromising critique that is carried out by negative theology. What is aimed at in this recognition is reality itself beyond every particular representation, reality as manifest rather in the course of things met with in the world as a whole. God is the God of all and is therefore revealed in all and everywhere instead of being confined to any one place or culture or language. This "All" may even include how things ought to be, beyond how they simply are already, since such a comprehensive reality cannot be opposed to idealities or to anything else.

---

6. *Traité de l'efficacité* (Paris: Grasset, 1996), chapter 6.

The first absolute exigency of a negative theology is thus to take into account the globality of all. Of God, as ultimate reality beyond our capacity to know and even simply to conceive, nothing can be predicated, but nothing can be denied of or excluded from such a God either, as Pseudo-Dionysius clearly recognizes in *De caelesti hierarchia,* chapter 2, 141b. Everything is theophany and all things together constitute God's self-revelation, as Ibn al-'Arabi likewise affirms in *The Bezels of Wisdom.* At least at the level of the effective verdict, the course of things in the world is somehow the final judge (even if the world is never completely final either, not *this* world anyway). Classical Chinese thought, according to Jullien, tends to refer to this ongoing process as the unique effective regulation of the world and as without appeal. It is not that this "natural course of things" can be seized in a realized form or as a fixed concatenation of causes, nor that it can be made immediately evident. It is certainly not to be identified with empirical reality. On the contrary, it, too, is invisible and even, I would add, inconceivable as such and yet, at the same time, omni-conceivable: all possible conceptions grasp and reveal an aspect—or aspects—of it. The unlimited potential to remain in contact with all these possibles is what distinguishes the better part of wisdom.

One will surely object: but what need of the word "God" to say this? In effect, there is no logical necessity. Still, the fact is that the conceptions of God, as well as of the divine and the sacred, belong to the landscape, so to speak, or to the historical record of the nature-and-culture of humanity, which does not exclude certainly the dimension of *being a person* from the whole of things. It is not by eliminating the personal from our conception of either the divine or the sacred, or even simply of nature, that we discover the truth in its nakedness. It is rather by inclusion of all that which belongs to history as well as to nature (the two being inconceivable, at least for us, except in their mutual reciprocity) that we are able to attune ourselves to the natural course of things, and this includes our own evolution as well. Not to presume to guide this process but rather to give or surrender oneself to it by realizing one's own potentials without limit, considering that in any case one cannot escape from this larger, all-encompassing context, is the theological gesture par excellence when it is stripped down to its epitome. That this whole be personalized or not is not the essential thing, given the fact that the concept of the person, like every concept, serves only to open thought up to that which surpasses every concept—in this case, specifically, every concept of the person.

In trusting oneself to the whole to which one belongs, the theologically believing "person" recognizes that which is "God" or "transcendence" or "the unconditioned" or "the absolute" or. . . . In fact, all these terms are employed only in order to be subsequently emptied of sense, in order to be broken open to the inconceivability of the infinite relations that traverse us and that constitute us, even as they constitute the world. Neither is the essential thing the manner in which one conceives of the theological or figures it at the outset, considering that every conception, like every figuration, is irremediably inadequate and serves only for being surpassed. It is in accepting the "apophatic" conditioning of our historically evolved being that we are best able, starting from our own different situation as Occidentals, to reach the wisdom promulgated by Chinese classics in their most authentic and potentially valuable possibilities for us. If I persist in qualifying this procedure as "theological," I do so out of respect for the history of this discourse and its preeminence as a matrix of some of the most radical, searching, and sophisticated reflection on the limits of language and its necessary failure vis-à-vis the real. In theological tradition, discourse is rendered particularly *fertile* in its relation to the reality of ultimate, extreme possibles, but also in relation to those possibles that are the most banal and omnipresent.

The theological, conceived thus, is not a theme or a content or a concept. It is of the order of the imaginary and of the practical as well—of the practice of infinite critique for the purpose of opening oneself to the inconceivable totality of the world that can only be imagined (or be thought metaphorically). This does not amount to representing the world definitively as any representable thing or as circumscribed by any notion or by no matter what concept. The world intended here as apprehended by theology is nothing delimited but is rather in the process of transcending *itself* by means of becoming always other. I submit that allowing this self-transcending to take place and to be realized by means of dismantling all our restrictive conceptualities is the effective operation of the theological such as it is carried out by apophatic critique throughout Occidental history—but equally, even if in other words and terms, by Chinese wisdom such as we are led to discover it in its remarkable apophatic subtlety by the studies of Jullien.

Theology has generally seemed, to Jullien and to secular-minded philosophers of comparable cultural background, to be on the side of the foundational, the assured, the ideal. However, thought negatively, it is in fact just the opposite: theology opens thought to its own abyss. Moreover, apophatic theology thinks not only on the basis of abstractions, but more essentially on the basis of the incarnate, of the flesh and the sensory, which are always inexhaustible and thus ungraspable in their concreteness.

In France, protagonists of the famous "theological turn" of phenomenology have been particularly insightful in demonstrating and in underscoring this indefinable, infinitely interpretable and fertile valence of names such as "God." This is verified by the metaphors deriving from the superlatively rich archives of theology concerning the phenomenologically "given" in the works of Michel Henry, Jean-Luc Marion, Jean-Louis Chrétien, and others. Thomas-Olivier Venard and Jean-Ives Lacoste also deserve mention as authors who, in our time, are leading the way in renewing theological language in its apophatic registers.

Of course, there is a certain dogmatic theology that is stagnant in its refusal to think anything new, a kind of theology that could and perhaps should be delivered up for ritual banishment and sacrifice, if only that gesture were able to preserve or restore to health the community of thinkers. But should that "theology" alone be allowed to represent what is understood under this name by contemporary thought striving to become genuinely open to all possible senses and challenges? This sclerotic theology, which repeats its fixed formulas without (re)thinking them, exists, but it is not what "theology" at its best represents. It does not give us a right (and much less a good reason) to ignore the incomparably rich resources for the most original thinking that are also treasured and transmitted by theology in its astonishing range and creativity in virtually every epoch of culture. Neither should we neglect theology's unlimited potential as a form of thinking that reaches beyond the limits of the logos and is capable, consequently, of defying and unsettling, and thereby renewing, thought still today. In effect, we stumble here upon exactly the same objectives as those expressly advanced by Jullien.

One can treat *negative* theology as a variant or deviant form of theology, an attempt to recuperate it and so to save it from succumbing to otherwise devastating critiques; or else, inversely, one can understand negative theology as the first matrix of theological thought and, more broadly, of critical thinking per se. Negative theology provides the key for recognizing the fundamentally negative predicament of thought as such. Jullien is acquainted with negative theology and even expounds some of its source texts, particularly ones in Plotinus and Damascius, but he considers it essentially as derivative rather than as standing at the origin of theology and of the logos as such. One ought to consider, however, as he well knows, things in their first arising and full potential (*essor*) rather than only in the limited actualizations that derive from them. It is not the pious repetitions of the platitudinous *discourse* of theology that one must view primarily but rather the seminal insights and creative inspiration from which it springs.

Every meaningful discourse is preceded, or is at least potentially exceeded, by an event of thought, of illumination in darkness. This is emphatically underscored by apophatic thought, which in this respect corresponds to Chinese wisdom as it is revealed to us by Jullien.

This leads us to confront the delicate question: is there not, after all, something that is quasi-theological in China, something held in common between Chinese wisdom and theological wisdom, specifically in its apophatic form—which is to say in its being *un*formed or without form, according to the slogan "the great image has no form" that is taken by Jullien from the *Book of Dao* and pressed into service as a guiding motto? Something of this order is what I am attempting to place into evidence. And yet negative theology is nothing definable. It escapes from every attempt at characterization. It intimates truth only in giving the lie to every effort to lend substance and an assured status to the real in its foundations (figured as divine). Therefore, a philosophical approach can proceed only by indirect and incisively critical routes. Indeed, negative theology finally does not even "exist," as Jacques Derrida already suspected in his efforts to take on this "impossible" subject.[7]

In an analogous manner, "the evidence of things" evoked by Jullien insistently and confidently cannot be grasped directly but rather only via the negation that it implies. Therefore, given that negative theology does not have any consistency that would permit it to be grasped as such, and that it is perceived only by its effects, exactly like Chinese wisdom in Jullien's exegesis of it, and that it does not perhaps even exist, it cannot be made manifest except negatively, through demonstration of the vanity of the attempts to refuse it, or even to undermine and deny it.

I will just note in passing that it is possible to glimpse here the great question of a truly fundamental difference between a thinking axised on reflexivity, such as that of the West all through its philosophical tradition, including negative theology, and an approach that ignores reflexivity, one of thought that simply opens itself to the other naturally, as if by instinct. And yet, to denote the spontaneous, automatic quality of such opening of thought, we could also say that it thinks "by its reflexes." The word is significant! Thought can and perhaps must be understood as reflection from

---

7. See especially his essay "How to Avoid Speaking: Denials," in *Derrida and Negative Theology*, eds. H. Coward and T. Foshay (Albany: State University of New York Press, 1992), 73–142, originally "Comment ne pas parler: Dénégations," in *Psyché: Inventions de l'autre* (Paris: Galilée, 1987), 435–95.

its earliest beginnings. In the end, Jullien does not maintain that Chinese culture is not just as reflective as Western culture. And, conversely, neither does the *via negativa* exclude the movement "upstream" ("en amont"), to a stage preceding reflection, in order to find a completely "instinctive" response that no longer retains anything negative. The *negatio negationis*, too, might eventually take away all negativity—ἄφελε πάντα, "take all away," as Plotinus urges—and teach us to reflect no longer. This has indeed been the approach typical of numerous mystics in their quest for utter simplicity. As thought negatively, reflection endeavors to reflect itself out of the circle of reflection altogether.

Apart from these possibilities, which exceed the limits of philosophy, the justification for evoking negative theology consists in the insufficiency of any philosophy based on a description of the world that excludes such possibles. Hence the insufficiency of pure "immanence" understood as the exclusion of transcendence. We know well that the theological question can play itself out also in terms of transcendence versus immanence. Employing one of the most common modes of rejecting the theological, Jullien often insists on immanence as the key to Chinese thought. He emphasizes how Greek thought, in contrast, from Plato onwards took the way of transcendence, with his theory of ideas, which are also ideals. Jullien emphasizes, furthermore, how even before Plato, notably in his teacher Pythagoras, the bias towards transcendence was already inscribed in the penchant for mathematical formalization that exits the world of the sensible and concrete in favor of abstractions. The same goes for the laws and even for law as *eros*, whether as object or as engenderer of desire: all of these foundations of Western civilization display a sharp tendency to turn elsewhere and to look beyond the evidence of lived reality as it is given to the senses for the principles that found, justify, and motivate the course of the world. They postulate a base separate from this apparent reality in its concrete and immediate manifestation.[8]

However, Jullien knows that it is not enough to make himself the advocate of immanence without taking account also of the transcendence that it only nominally seems to exclude. His choice, like that of opting for China, cannot be simply a choice for immanence to the exclusion of transcendence—if, indeed, it were even a matter of a choice, since human choices, in this view, are always only secondary to the propensities of things

---

8. This is Jullien's theme especially in *L'invention de l'idéal et le destin de l'Europe* (Paris: Seuil, 2009).

themselves. This genre of discourse always runs the risk of falling into binary dichotomies from which, in reality, Jullien in theory wishes to liberate us. Accordingly, it is necessary to recognize the weight and operativity of a certain species of transcendence even in classical Chinese culture.

Jullien affirms, for example, in the concluding chapter of *Dialogue sur la morale* that Chinese wisdom, in the form of moral consciousness, gives access to the unconditioned, but he denies that the unconditioned can be represented in a stable or adequate manner. In other words, "heaven" is an expression for that which constantly escapes from every finite representation but which, nevertheless, must be pursued infinitely by a chain of metaphorical indications and incitations that is never terminated nor even terminable.

My approach begins from the observation that we cannot think of immanence as a separate thing or as an objective fact. At the most, we can speak of *representations* of immanence and equally of *representations* of transcendence, and at this level of representation it is perfectly clear that the one, immanence, is the negation or the opposite of the other, transcendence, and for that reason is implicated in it—of course, as denied, but nevertheless as at least *implicitly* thought, conceived, said. Therefore, it is not a question of choosing one rather than or without the other. Transcendence *is* immanence, and vice versa, whenever one withdraws from and despairs of the very possibility of its representation. The whole is there in immanence, in the *between* (Jullien's *entre*): the beginning and the end are only representations projected from this between. Yet the "between" itself remains unsoundable and inexhaustible. The mystery and the unconditionedness of transcendence are always already there, fully present and potent in the "between." All that is real and lived in transcendence is effective prior to its representation: the representation can and must be dispensed with. It is the same procedure as in negative theology, which likewise dispenses with representations of God, the transcendent par excellence. Presumably, liberation in the name of immanence would mean that one has no need of transcendence, but it is only by negating the *representations* of transcendence that one conceived of immanence in the first place. It is finally only the outside and the beyond of representation that is cogently aimed at in this term "transcendence," and the same holds for "immanence." Thought radically, either term means and reminds us that any given world of representations is not sufficient unto itself but is compelled instead to explode into an infinite series of representations suspended over what defies and withdraws from every form of representation.

Apophatic consciousness constrains us always to pay attention to this difference that the fact of representing or of saying something makes. Jullien finely analyzes this predicament in his book *Si parler va sans dire: Du logos et d'autres ressources* on whether "speaking" goes without "saying" and on the resources of the logos. Things and reality in their globality are not accessible for us, except as so many negations of our sayings. Things as such are always that which cannot be said. They are in this sense *impossibles* of thought—and *impossibles* of saying. Thought and its possibles thus meet a certain unsurpassable limit simply in real things, a limit that is impossible for thought to think past. But it is starting precisely from here that we must think—thus without being able first to establish a foundation that is justified and capable of accounting for itself and susceptible of systematic elaboration. I believe that, despite their hailing from two culturally and historically different worlds, Chinese wisdom and Western apophatic discourse are comparable in the face of the radical failure of saying to be able to grasp the real in the way envisaged by the logical proposition. The two cultures have no common measure, but they share one and the same problem, to which they respond in their respective styles, and these are as different as can be.

I would wager to say, finally, that the predisposition of Chinese wisdom to rely on the natural inclination of the heart (心 *xīn*), and thus to follow the incessant natural course of change inherent in things themselves, rather than to impose formal models of thought on the basis of theoretical considerations, amounts to a manner of incarnating the *dis-position* that is infinitely open and which I call "theological"—in a negative sense, of course. It is only in distrusting the artifice of thought that is not guided by the natural evolution of things, and consequently in negating our own constructions superimposed on reality, that we let things be what they are and permit them to manifest their *thus* (*ainsi*, in Jullien's vocabulary) in the spirit of *Gelassenheit* or "letting be" as described, for example, by Meister Eckhart.

The authentic theological mode of thinking does not consist essentially in positing a concept of the Supreme Being or of anything else, whatever it may be, but in the fact of giving over every concept to a higher understanding and a more all-encompassing consciousness than one's own. God is for us the inconceivable par excellence. To recognize God or the divine is nothing else but trusting oneself in practice and in life to the order of things as they might be "upstream" from every intervention concocted by human thought and institutions, with their models and ideals, their differentiations and definitions. I say "God" in the first place because things are infinitely variable and in this sense ungraspable and therefore susceptible to being expressed in the richest and most fertile vocabulary we possess for indicating the infinite, the interminable, and the unfathomable. I have no illusions that it will be easy for us to be in agreement about this. Only our lives themselves can persuade us of one or another vocabulary as being more adherent to or more revealing of the depth of our experience—and of its fecundity. Philosophically speaking, it is only critique that forces us to change our points of view, permitting us to no longer keep to our own particular perspectives but, instead, to allow them to evolve without fetters. Such critique requires that we hold our "convictions" in suspense, at least rhetorically, however indispensable they may prove to be in practice.

Of course, such a reflective posture of suspicion, even vis-à-vis oneself, is an attitude characteristic of the Occident: it is Cartesian par excellence in its prizing philosophical doubt as a self-evident value. Jullien denies that such a predisposition to doubt is prevalent in classical Chinese thought. Nevertheless, I propose self-suspension as a particular approach to a common, or even a universal possibility—one which would be neither an affirmation of a position, nor a position at all, but rather the abandon of all fixed determinations, and this *is* quintessentially characteristic of classic Chinese thought as Jullien construes it. For this purpose, it is necessary to look beyond language and its fixed forms and categorical norms. It is only the dynamism of language, or poetic language in its creative emergence, which can indicate this "beyond" of language itself, where the word strives toward its destination through a constant suspension or transcendence of itself. François Jullien himself observes how in China "this commonality which is the condition of possibility of discussion never arises in the discussed" ("ce commun qui est la condition de possibilité de la discussion n'affleurant jamais dans le discuté"), and thus "the veritable stake of the word finds itself always outside the word and the true conversation is tacit" ("l'enjeu véritable de la parole se trouve toujours hors parole et le véritable entretien est tacite," *Si parler va sans dire*, 106). I think that this is valid not only for China, but universally.

The common for the Daoist is found not in that which is articulated in a discourse, or more exactly in a dia-logue, but rather in the retraction of words, or in the retreat from linguistic formulations in the face of the unconstrued course of things. This is necessary in order to remove the partial, biased, and exclusive viewpoints inherent in words, as Jullien says in specifying that the common intelligence aimed at by the Daoist thinker realizes itself "by reabsorption of words accompanying the dissolution of points of view" ("par résorption des paroles accompagnant la dissolution des points de vue," *Si parler va sans dire,* 109). That means reabsorption into the total receptivity that reigned at the stage before all enunciations and before the inevitably exclusive choices made by any discourse. All this converges completely with the modalities of apophatic discourse. Accordingly, I find that Jullien develops, in exemplary fashion from his Chinese sources, exactly what I understand to be apophatic philosophy.

If I might, nevertheless, be allowed to avow what I find, all the same, to be a limit to the opening in principle without limits discovered in the works of my partner in this "dialogue," I would observe that there are some factors in contemporary lay French culture which militate powerfully against a com-prehension of theology and that commonly conspire in devaluing, delegitimizing, and deriding it or even, much worse, in rendering it obscure. Among these factors are anticlericalism and certain triumphalistic versions of the philosophy of the Enlightenment. Jullien, like his public, is sensitive to these factors, and to such an extent that they are practically preconditions of the very intelligibility of discourse, or at least of its persuasiveness, in the highly laicized French intelligentsia of today. This is, after all, the intellectual milieu or community of interpretation that François Jullien most directly addresses through his ideas and writings.

As much as political correctness in France hardly allows laicism to be questioned, nevertheless history furnishes much evidence that wherever religion and civil society are cut off and isolated from each other, both turn out, as a result, to be denatured and become, in certain respects, incomprehensible to one another. The authentic religiosity of the human being is not something other than its social tie, not therefore something to exclude from social transactions, and neither does society hold together without taking into account this dimension, among all the others, including the infinity of the relations with others that constitute us as human. The true or the best comprehension of human affairs is found "upstream" ("en amont") from divisions and separations such as those constituted by the dictates of laicism—this holds even for the purpose of understanding the advantages and perhaps the practical necessity of a compromise arrangement such as that of laicism itself. Laicism, I submit, needs to rediscover its own religious roots, in a negatively theological sense, of an unavowable, unconfessable, but nonetheless indispensable, community.[9]

I believe that the thought of Jullien, in its continuing evolution, is on the way to placing into question these prejudices typical of his intellectual world. His work itself may begin to suggest how these fixed positions, these biases, as well as their opposites, are at risk of becoming cultural blindnesses or atavisms. Most recently, Jullien's *De l'intime* develops a reflection giving

---

9. Cf. Maurice Blanchot, *La communauté inavouable* (Paris: Minuit, 1983) and Jean-Luc Nancy, *La communauté désavouée* (Paris: Galilée, 2014). This has, after all, been the view of that most outstanding representative in our time of the philosophy of the Enlightenment, Jürgen Habermas, especially in *Glauben und Wissen: Friedenspreis des deutschen Buchhandels 2001* (Frankfurt a. M.: Suhrkamp, 2001). See also Giorgio Agamben, *La comunità che viene* (Turin: Einaudi, 1990).

to transcendence its full phenomenological value within the experience in question. Here he taps sources such as the fathers of the church (Gregory of Nyssa and Augustine in particular) for their valuable illuminations.[10]

Nevertheless, reflex and sometimes scornful and contemptuous rejections of all imagination of an other world or of a life after death still appear in the texts of Jullien. These rejections serve as fixed points and ready references for an assured common sense, a reliable basis of consensus for the philosophy that Jullien is in the process of elaborating. Yet the definitive exclusion of the sense that such imaginations of the otherworldly might have for the cultures and communities that invented them, that made them evolve, that believed in them, and that lived in and through them, does not seem to me to accord with the exigency of hospitable reception for all possibles of thought. This reception, of course, must be highly differentiated and must take account of our own context and positioning. However, it is necessary to find the means of recognizing their part of possibility in each of these beliefs or ideologies or visions of the world, whatever they may be, without any exclusions in principle, on the sole condition that they be authentically held and lived out by human beings.

I do not expect that my own *parti pris* for theology will be shared, but I can nonetheless advance a critique and protest against the exclusion of a form of thought that participates essentially in human culture and its evolution. Some, taking up one side alone of Hegel, would maintain that the historical role of theology is obsolete. Yet such teleologies always have in them something paradoxically ideological and practically theological in a very positive sense. That this purported historical advance is illusory is difficult for us "postmoderns" to ignore, for we have become hyper-conscious of the insidious traps of belief in ideologies of progress.

The possibility that there is something beyond the process of the world—namely, transcendence, or God—is for thought a question of how to represent the world—as either with or without gaps—that is, as opening up to its own exterior, or else not doing so. The two positions are possible and perhaps even necessary—as in Kant's antinomy of the world as finite and as infinite, both being necessary and yet mutually exclusive hypotheses. It is not a question of choosing between the two but of inhabiting the divine milieu from which the two possibles—and all com-possibles—emerge. God, or transcendence, cannot be represented except as the condition and at the same time the *negation* of all possible representations—that is, as the unrepresentable, as the unconditioned, which is nevertheless indirectly or virtually

---

10. *De l'intime: Loin du bruyant amour* (Paris: Grasset, 2013).

manifest in all representations. Such is the theology that I draw from the sources of apophatic wisdom. I believe that Jullien envisages something not terribly different, at bottom, when he interprets the *Dao* as follows:

> By the virtuality that it owes to its constant arising, upstream from the concrete, it refuses to let itself be confined within any particular actualization making it manifest within the visible. But it is also from this inexhaustible effectiveness at work and too subtle and diffuse not to remain invisible, that every manifestation of existence proceeds.
>
> (Par la virtualité qu'il doit à son constant essor, en amont du concret, il ne se laissera cantonner dans aucune actualisation particulière le manifestant au sein du visible. Mais c'est aussi de cette effectivité inépuisablement à l'œuvre, et trop subtile et diffuse pour ne pas demeurer invisible, que procède toute manifestation d'existence. (*Si parler va sans dire*, 86)

This conception of the origin of the phenomenon as without bottom excludes only a simplistic and realistic conception of God as a thing, the greatest and most powerful thing of all. And such a reifying conception is likewise resolutely to be excluded, or rather relativized, by negative theology. I would specify, however, that an agreement on this may be valid for us in our habitual context among modern, self-reflective intellectuals, but not necessarily in all other contexts. In any case, it is not valid in the same way and according to the same mechanisms. Historically, the least reflective beliefs in God might be expressive of the most authentic experience on the part of a certain people in its course of evolution. The exclusion of crudely idolatrous belief sanctioned by this argument is only an exclusion relative to our situation and its exigencies and priorities. And philosophy itself certainly belongs among these culturally relative modes of life and relation.

In the end, philosophy itself, as articulate, categorizing, divisive discourse, is perhaps a species of vanity. Philosophical discourse such as it is revealed in the light of Chinese wisdom according to Jullien might be destined to annihilate itself, to draw back before a wisdom that exists only in order to withdraw from its own word. In this, Jullien would join, *malgré lui*,[11] not only the sages of ancient China but also the apophatic thinkers of

---

11. Jullien dissociates himself from the figure of the sage, explicitly in part 2 of *Un sage est sans idée*.

Europe and of all times and places: the universal would reveal itself, before all, as that which cannot be said.

CODA

This "dia-logue" has unfolded by necessity in and through words. The question I am left with is this: does it pass through (*dia*) words (*logoi*) in order to go beyond them? Otherwise expressed, is there something else here to savor besides the words? One could ask in an analogous fashion, is there something else to be lived besides life itself? Death, for example? These are questions that remain open and that intrigue me, the more so since I sense that the (disavowed) wisdom of Jullien would likely tend in a completely different direction, one opposed to my own *parti pris*. I conclude, therefore, that there is still much more that I can learn from him.

Appendix

ANALYTIC TABLE OF CONTENTS

List of Illustrations	xi
Preface and Argument	xiii
Historical-Autobiographical Introduction	xv
Introduction to an Intercultural Philosophy of Universalism	xvii
Acknowledgments	xxi
Chapter 1 All or Nothing? Nature in Chinese Thought and the Apophatic Occident	1
The Nature of *Dao*, or the *Dao* of Nature	7
In Praise of Blandness: Litotes of the Neuter	12
Transcendence and Immanence of the *Dao*	22
Mencius, or the Naturalness of Morality: Is the All without Transcendence?	27
Chapter 2 Nothing and the Poetic "Making" of Sense	37
The Art of Effectiveness: Doing or Saying Nothing	37
Poetic Approaches to the Limit of Expression	42
Neo-Daoism and Neoplatonism: An Uncanny Historical Parallel	53
Western Apophatic Poetics	59
One and Other, All or Nothing, East and West	65
The Absolutely Other and the Movement of Transcendence	74
(Negative) Metaphysics (or Pre-Physics) as Poetry	79
Coda on Chinese Expression of Negativity	83

Chapter 3	Immanence: The Last Word?	85
	From Figures of Immanence to Formless Transcendence: The *Yijing* and Negative Theology	85
	Immanence and the Ineffable	94
	The Matter of Method in Intercultural Philosophy	99
	China and the Sense of Transcendence	107
	Secular Self-Critique and Theological Transcendence	119
	New Debates on the Relevance of Transcendence to Classical Chinese Thinking	126
	Reality That Representation Fails to Represent	135
Chapter 4	Universalism, or the Nothing That Is All	141
	From the Globalism of Nature to the Universality of Thought	141
	Historical Permutations of the Non-natural Universality Forged by Thought	148
	Beyond Cultural Relativity and the Construction of Universality	154
	Transcendent Universality and the Negative Way: Reclaiming the Enlightenment for Religion	161
	Universality in the (Apophatic) Gap between China and the West	166
	The Common Broken(open)ness of Cultures	175
	The Self-Negation of Culture by (Negative) Theology	181
Chapter 5	An Extra Word on Originality	199
Epilogue	Intercultural Dia-logue and Its Apophatic Interstices	213
Appendix	Analytic Table of Contents	235
Index		237

INDEX

Terms: ff means "following pages"

absolute, interdiction against seeking it, 113; opened by the intercultural, 157
abstraction, 145–46
Adorno, Theodor, and immanence, 22; and self-critique, 22; and micrology, 23; and minimalism, 23
afterlife, xvii
aging, 6–7
Agamben, Giorgio, and absolute immanence, 193; archeology of knowledge, 206; *Homo sacer*, 154
Ainsi (thus), 228
Alain de Lille, 3
all, call to think it, 98, 143; as comprehensive ought, 221; in evolution, 55; immanent, 6; as mystery, 143; as Nothing, 10; without exclusions, 40
allegory, in Chinese tradition, 74–75, 161; medieval, 3
allusion, incitative, 209; poetics of, 42–43, 50; versus mimesis, 68; versus symbol, 52
Ames, Roger, 99–127; *Confucian Role Ethics*, 110–11
Analects, 40–41
analogy, natural, 3; for conceiving God, 104; disanalogy more accurate, 112; evades concept, 193

Anselm, Saint, as apophatic, 220
anticlericalism, 20, 80–81, 132, 165, 229
anti-philosophy, 128, 173, 217
anthropology, 149; cultural, 216; negative, 156
Apel, Karl Otto, 176
Apophaticism, 213–14; as critique of concept, 214; between cultures, 134; and bodies, 192, incarnate, 223; in China, 214ff; and the Other, 215; in West, 57, 179
Aquinas, Thomas, *Summa Theologica*, 112, 220; on Creator's transcendence, 125; on language for God, 161
Aristotle, *Metaphysics*, 144
Armstrong, Hilary, 215
art, as spiritual practice, 209
Assmann, Jan, 135, 185

Badiou, Alain, and event, 97; and Paul, 150
Barbier-Kontler, Christine, 207
Barths, Karl, 220
Barthes, Roland, 15; on China, 20–21
Baudelaire, Charles, 5; "Correspondances," 44–46, 52
Beckett, Samuel, 217
being, non-Being more originary, 54, 90

Benjamin, Walter, history in crisis of present, 172; pure language, 186
Berenson, Bernard, 14
between, the, 227; as divine milieu, 231
bible, translation, 158–60
Billeter, Jean-François, 20n, 169ff
binaries, escape from, 219; produced by being defined, 175
Blake, William, 50
Blanchot, Maurice, 1, 217; and community, 230; and the extraordinary, 113; and space of literature, 44, 88; and vision, 52
blandness, 12; as "le fade," *dàn* 淡, 13, 79; as impartiality, 78
Böhme, Jacob, 136, 216
Book of Documents, 110
Boulnois, Olivier, 72
breath (*qì* 氣), 49
Burke, Kenneth, "to beyond," 69
Burik, Steven, 111–112

Cai, Zongqi, 26n, 207
Capra, Fritjov, 12
Caputo, John, 43; his theology of the event, 97
Carlson, Thomas, 156
Celan, Paul, 44, 189
citation, art of, 48
Cheng, Ann, 170
Cheng, François, 208–209
China, *Zhōng Guó* (中国), xvi; as empire, 149, without God, 157; its uniqueness, 170
Chinese character, depicts action, 203; as ideogrammic, 201ff; as natural and pictorial, 201ff
Chrétien, Jean-Louis, 224
Christianity, opposition to, 52; and universalism, 151; as unnatural, 152, 157
Chūnqiū (*Chronicle of Springs and Autumns*), 48

coincidentia oppositorum, 22
Coleridge, Samuel Taylor, 209
common, as brokenness, 175; as empty, 167; as quest, 180; understanding, 35; as universal, 181
communicative competence as exclusionary, 178
communicability as universal, 178, 180
community, unavowable, 230
comparative philosophy, contrastive, 101; method of, 66–67, 103
concept and non-concept, 98; conceptual thinking from Socrates, 144; as lacking, 98
Confucius, and ethics, 25; *Four Books* (*Sì shū* 四書), xvi; as Master Kong (*Kŏng Fūzĭ* 孔夫子), 24, 40; refusal of words, 39–40; and religion, 128–29
connectedness, 28
consciousness without knowing, 194
contingency, unconditional, 27
correlation, as method, 67
Corpus Hermeticum, 10
Creatio ex nihilo, 27, 131
Critical Theory, 178
critique, immanent, 176; self-critique, xviii
culture, of absolute, 157; and alterity, 92; its "between," 174; its "beyond," 91, 157; and comparison, xv; homogenizing, 180; hybridization, 170–71, 199; its intelligibility, 180; intercultural as "revelation," xviii; its paramount importance, xvi; as realm of immanence, 91; its relativity, xi, xvi; and religion, 157; supra-cultural, 188; total, 183ff, 188
Cusa, Nicholas of, 41, 80, 216; *De docta ignorantia*, 23

Dalferth, Ingolf, 137n

INDEX

Damascius, 54, 62, 216
Dante, 15, 35; and Beatrice, 72; *Divine Comedy*, 63–64; and otherworldly vision, 50; *Paradiso*, 76; *Vita nuova*, 47
Dao, as transcendent, 25; translated as "way-making," 99, 112; as without nature, 8
Dào–dé–Jīng, 7–11, 24, 73, 90, 113, 221; *Dào kě dào, fēi cháng Dào*, 186
Daoism and anarchy, 24; Neo-Daoism, 53ff; and pragmatism, 176; and rules, 176–77; and social responsibility, 177
Davie, Donald, 201
de Bary, William Theodore, 25
de Meun, Jean, 3
deference, 119
Deleuze, Gilles, 89; "L'immanence . . . une vie," 187, 194–96; life itself, 194; on pure consciousness, 195; and transcendental field, 195
Derrida, Jacques, 43, 79–80, 217; and negative theology, 92, 93, 225
description, its authority undermined, 136
Desmond, William, 59
Deus sive Natura, 27, 186
Dickinson, Emily, 60–62
difference as gap (*écart*), 175, 182; greatest resource, 180
Dilworth, David, 131
divination, in Greece, 216
dōngxī (東西), thing, 70
dualism, 135, 174–75

Eckhart, Meister, 41, 80, 195n, 216; *Gelassenheit*, 228
effectiveness, 221
Eisenstadt, S. N., 109n
enlightenment, xii; ideology of, 52; as intercultural, 165; as negative-theological, 165; as self-empowerment, 183; as unlimited critique, 165
epic, as lacking in China, 35, 87
equality, ontological, 135; of all with all, 163
Eriugena, John Scott, 80, 145, 216
ethics, non-conventional, 109
etymologies of Is, Be, Not, 203
exceptionalism, European, 151; Chinese, 169
expansion, poetics of, 44

Falque, Emmanuel, 65
Fenollosa, Ernest, 200ff; "The Chinese Written Character as a Medium for Poetry," 201ff; his universal vision of language, 206
figuration beyond figuration, 43; kenotic, 51
Fingarette, Herbert, 25, 193
formalization, mathematical, 226
formlessness, 118, 123, 124
Foucault, Michel, heterotopy, 188; history of present, 172
Framings, immanent, 41

Gabriel, Markus, 15
Gauchet, Marcel, 92
Gernet, Jean, 158
Ghil, René, *Traitee du verbe*, 49
globality, xvi, 219; in Chinese thinking, 103; of reality, 73; of sense, 67; and vision, 53
God, in China, 107ff; as Creator, 27, 90, 130; as image, 32; incarnate, 184; as inconceivable, 103; as not simply Other, 104; as person, 222
gods, in ancient China, 108; for Confucius, 129
Graham, A. C., 99–100
grammar, Chinese lacks morphology, 182; of transitive sentence, 203; of

grammar *(continued)*
  intransitive verbs, 203; as unnatural, 204
Granet, Marcel, 30

Habermas, Jürgen, 91, 165, 176; on community, 230; *Diskursethik*, 178
Hall, David and Roger Ames, 99ff
Hansen, Chad, 68, 127, 210
harmony, of all, 32
Heaven (*Tiān* 天), 74; does not speak, 29; heaven's mandate (*Tiān ming*), 110; as nature, 147; as source of regulation, 32; translation as "sky," 100
Hegel, 34, 231; on China, 20–21; on concrete universal, 152–53; beyond metaphysics, 96
Heidegger, Martin, 102; and age of world picture, 104; and *Ereignis*, 113; and *Gestell*, 144; *Holzwege*, 169; and ontology, 124; *Sein und Zeit*, 97
Henry, Michel, 224
Heraclitus, before metaphysics, 96
Herder, Johann Gottfried, 132
heroism, as ideology, 220
Heubel, Fabian, 23–24, 170ff
Hildegard of Bingen, 43
Hölderlin, Friedrich, 189; *Patmos*, 132, 134
Hofmannsthal, Hugo von, 217
honesty (*chéng* 誠), as perfect and endless, 191
Huang, Yong, 107ff
humanism, as exclusive of God, 30; secular, 184
human rights, 153–54
Humboldt, Wilhelm von, 182
hypostatization 66; avoiding, 71; of language, 94–95; of subject, 94

Ibn 'Arabi, 216; *Bezels of Wisdom*, 222

identity, as differential, 180; and non-identity, 83; self-identity as sterile, 89, 139
image, great, no bottom-line, 73; has no form, 56
imagination, religious, 34
immanence, 11, 85ff; as absolute, 193; and Adorno, 23–24; as apophatic, 85; in Deleuze, 161; as enclosed sphere, 91; as fund, 55–56; immanent framings, 41; its insufficiency, 226; presupposes transcendence, 192; self-negated and self-transcending, 193; as total, 27, 193; as totalization of transcendence, 31; and transcendence, 26; as unsayable, 161
im/possibles of thought, 219–220, 227
indeterminate, the, 87, 117; as potential, 114
India, 54
indirectness, art of, in poetry, 43, 47; in politics, 48; strategies of, 79; in war, 37
ineffable, the, 57, 94ff, 214; Jullien against, 95, 184–85; poetics of, 72
infinity, of divine, 220; of sense, 49
insipidity, 21–22
Inter, 83
Intercultural, 35; difference, xvi; introduction, xvii–xxi; and normativity, 14; philosophy, xi, xiii; as philosophical imperative, 217; as reorienting thought, 218; versus transcultural, 133
Isaiah, 36
Ivanhoe, Philip J., 210

Jabès, Edmond, 44
Jakobson, Roman, 78, 209
Jaspers, Karl, and Axial Age, 107
Jesuits, 169
John of the Cross, *Noche oscura*, 59–60

Jonas, Hans, 177–78
Joyce, James, 35, 43, 62
Jullien, François, xvii; anti-theological polemic, 183, 189, 219; *Chemin faisant*, 179; *De l'intime*, 93, 230–31; *De l'universel, de l'uniforme, du commun et du dialogue entre les cultures*, 142ff, 218; defense, 175; *Dialogue sur la morale*, 28, 36, 147, 192, 227; *Du "Temps," Éléments d'une philosophie du vivre*, 148; *Éloge de la fadeur*, 12ff; *Figures de l'immanence. Pour une lecture philosophique du Yiking*, 85; gap (*écart*), 96, 199; his apparent binarism, 169–70; his originality, 210; intecultural method, 181; *L'écart et l'entre*, 77, 185, 199; *L'invention de l'idéale et le destin de l'Europe*, 58, 77, 226; *La Grande image n'a pas de forme*, 14; *La propension des choses*, 51, 95; *La valeur allusive*, 197; *Le détour et l'accès*, 37, 48, 53ff, 166, 217; partisanship for Chinese, 77; *Pont des singes*, 169, 184; *Procès ou Création*, 173; *Si parler va sans dire*, 152, 227–29, 232; summary of, 67; *Traite de l'efficacité*, 220, 221; *Transformations silencieuses*, 6, 94ff; *Un sage est sans idée*, 216
jūn zǐ (君子) consummate human, 110
Jung, Matthias, 137

Kabbalah, 216
Kant, 29; and aesthetic judgment, 164; binding but not logical, 178; and disinterestedness, 152; and genius, 199; *Kritik der Urteilskraft*, 154
Keck, Frederic, 170
Keightley, David, 161–62
Keller, Catherine, 76

Kennedy, George A., 205
Kenosis, of Christian subject, 150, 221
Kierkegaard, Søren, 102; and paradox, 188
Kipling, Rudyard, 82
Khôra, 88
Kubin, Wolfgang, 128ff

Lacan, Jacques, le réel, 187
Lacoste, Jean-Ives, 224
Laicism, French, 51
landscape, shān–shuǐ (山水), mountain-water, 68
language, its beyond, 117, 228; as culturally embedded, xviii–xix; human per se, 94; its incompleteness, xvii; inescapable rhetoricity, 161; as inherently negative, 3; metaphorical, 161; translation into, 159; as unfixed, 228
Laozi, 7, 16
Leibniz, Gottfried Wilhelm, 158; and negative theology, 159–60
Leopardi, Giacomo, 4
Lessing, Gotthold Ephraim, 132
Levinas, Emmanuel, 101–102, 193
Lǐ (禮), 25, 26, 160
Li, Minghui, 121
Li Bai, 129
Liu, James J. Y., 205
limits of verbal expression, 105
linear perspective, 16
Liu Yuxi, 51
logic, apophatic, 19; Greek, 39; non-exclusive, 16; suppresses subjectivity, 145; Western and medieval, 205
Longobardi, Niccolo, 158
Lucretius, 4

Macao, *Aò Mén* (澳門), xv–xvi
Maimonides, 104
Malbranche, Nicolas, 158

Mallarmé, Stéphane, 45, 49; *Coup de dès*, 50; poetics of suggestion, 50; and second-order Cratylism, 202
Mao Tse Tung, 38n
Marion, Jean-Luc, 224
Martin, Michael, 115
Mauthner, Fritz, 217
Mechthild of Magdeburg, 43
Mencius, 27–35
Mendelssohn, Moses, 132
Merton, Thomas, 23–26
metaphor, expresses relations, 204; as infinite chain, 227; for invisible, 204, 208; language for God, 161; reveals unseen order, 208; for transcendence, 111; versus concept, 204; for whole, xix
metaphysics, as crypto-theology, 189; as poetry, 79; as strategy, 79
Milton, John, and blind vision, 53
mimesis, 68
modernization, xiii; and China, 170; and Judeo-Christian monotheism, 135; as trauma, 170, 174
modulation, Confucian, 39
Møllgaard, Eske, 126–28
morality, as unconditional ideal, 28; as voice of conscience, 29
Moses de León, 216
Mou, Zongsan, 121
multicultural, xiii
mystical, the, 21–22, 127; apophatic, 95; in philosophy of Wang Bi and Plotinus, 54ff; as uniting Sufis, Kabbalists, and Christians, 55
myth, xi; as anthropomorphizing, 90; definition of, 86; demythologizing, 64; and dogma, 93; as exclusionary, 26; of China's externality, 179; versus history, 170

Nagarjuna, 131
Nancy, Jean-Luc, 52, 92, 166; on community, 230
nature, as All, 7; as apophatic, 5; as culturally mediated, 5; as kataphatic, 4, 8; as imperceptible, 5; as Mother, 1, 8–9; natural propensity, 36; as negation, 1, 3–4; as normative, 146–48; as Nothing, 10; as repugnant, 5; as transcendent and emergent, 42; as universal, 207; *zì rán* (自然), 74, 84, 87
negation, as fecund, 149; key to access to cultures, 66; of negation, xviii, 167; as powerful, 209; as process, 56; self-negation, 56, in West, 53
negative theology, xiv, 10; abstract or concrete, 65; as critical resource, 215; does not exist, 225; and *Ereignis*, 111; infinite, 215; as internal critique of metaphysics, 95, 215; as not existing, 92; as operativity, 187; as self-critique, 196–97
neoplatonic negative theology, 10, 53ff, 216
net, versus veil, 71
neuter, 13, 76
Neville, Robert, 112, 120ff, 130ff
Nietzsche, Friedrich, 79, 152; with hammer, 92
Ni Zan, 16, 17, 18
nominalism, 123
non-duality, 52
normativity, 30
nothing, 10; of blandness, 27; as neutral, 12; in poetry, 42–43
Novalis, 21
nuance, as apophatic, 45; nothing but, 81

objectivity, its limits, 119
Odes, Book of (Shi Jing), 42; allegorical program of, 75; and art of citation, 48
one, the, 54ff
oppositional binaries, 74

oracle bones, 161–62
originality, and access to universal, 200; as cardinal virtue, 199; and nature, 200; as nothing specifiable, 199
Other (the), cultural, xvii, 168; interior, 215; other world, xvii; rejected, 231; as unsayable, 67

painting, as absolute, 16; landscape, 14–16
Paranomasia, 136
Parmenides, 91, 102
Paul, Gregor, 115
Paul, Saint, 150; *Galatians*, 151; and law, 177
Peirce, Charles Sanders, 130
perfection, of Heaven, 32
person, as metaphor, 35
perspective, having none, 27, 31, 70
pivot, of the Dao, 69–70
Plato, *Cratylus*, 202; and ideas, 45, 226; and other world, 68; *Parmenides*, 53ff, 144; *Sophist*, 143–44
Plotinus, 193; *Enneads*, 53ff, 216; ἄφελε πάντα ("take all away"), 226
plurality, irreducible, 105
poetics, apophatic, 50
poetry, as aligned with science, 205; American modernist, 202; as language of things, 201; of metaphysics and theology, 32, 78; seventeenth-century metaphysical, 60; as visionary, 51
postmodern crisis, xiv
Pound, Ezra, and Fenollosa, 201
pragmatism, 100–101; American pragmatism, 106, 133
pre-Socratics, as apophatic, 216; as bridge tradition, 105; thinking the All, 142
process, great process of the real, 89; regulated, 20

Proust, Marcel, and time, 97
Pseudo-Dionysius the Areopagite, 216; *De caelesti hierarchia*, 222
Pythagoras, 226

Qu Yuan, *Lisao*, 46–47

Real (the), as absolute, xvi; as globality, 71
rectification of names (*zhèng míng* 正名), 102
reflexivity, context-transcending, 109, 225–26
regulation, 39; as immanent, 63; Way of, 147
relation, of all with all, 136, 144; Chinese relational thinking, 174; as mode of thinking, 67; as unlimited, 163
relativism, lazy, 165
relativity, cultural, of representation, 33
religion, does not exist but informs, 30; the religious, xiii; as unformulatable, 33; as *religere*, 31; as universal, 33; religion without religion, 43; as social tie, 230
rén (仁), as benevolence, 119; as humanity, 30; as human virtue, 25, 40, 147; as indefinable, 83
representation, 15; beyond of, 69, 231–32; Chinese, 138; consciously extravagant, 72; flight from, 41; as infinite series, 227; its inadequacy, 27; its limits, 116; metasemiotic, 137; as open to infinite, 19; on plane of immanence, 16; transcendence of, 104–105, 125, 136, 227
responsibility, as infinite to one another, 197; as prospective, 177–78
revelation, China without, 87; Christian, 71; as negative, 31
reversal (*peritrope*), 62–63
Ricci, Matteo, xxv, xvi, 157, 158, 160

Rilke, Rainer Maria, *Sonette an Orpheus*, 202
Rimbaud, Arthur, 49; "L'éternité," 73–74
rites, 25; "rites controversy," 160
Robinet, Isabelle, 81–82
Roetz, Heiner, 109ff
Roman Empire, 149
Rorty, Richard, 106
Rousseau, Jean-Jacques, 29, 169
Rubens, Peter Paul, 2
Rumi, Jalal al-Din, 60
Russell's paradox, 144

sage, 63; Daoist, 176; without distinctions, 41; as without words, 31
Sartre, Jean-Paul, 194
Saussy, Haun, on allegory, 75; on Fenollosa, 201–205; on grammar, 182; on postmodern, 127; rhetorical recasting of negative theology, 160–61
Schelling, F. W. J., 216
Schleiermacher, Friedrich, *Der christliche Glaube*, 27
Schwartz, Benjamin, 107–108
Scotus, Duns, 133
second-problematic thinking, 105
self-critique, 66, 155; unlimited, 121, 128
self-reflection, in China in Axial Age, 109; human, 188
sense, deployed indefinitely, 72; philosophy of, 52; totality of, 67
Set theory, 144
Shang dynasty, 34
Shàngdì, (上), Lord on high, 34, 90, 158
Shén (神), 123, 158
Shitao, 15, 16
Sikong Tu, 43
silence, in music, 65; poetics of, 44

Sima Qian, 38n
simplicity, as produced by negation, 3
Slingerland, Edward, 172–73
Smid, Robert, 115–116, 120–21, 125
Socrates, 30; and definition, 39; shift to logical thinking, 142
Solomon, Robert, 121
Spinoza, 193
subject, ancient Roman versus Christian, 151; cultural, 180–81; consciousness, 39; against hypostatization of, 94
Sun Bin, 38n
Sunzi, 38n, 166
symbolism, and Western hermeneutics, 42–43; as lacking in Chinese aesthetics, 47; symbolisme, 49

Tao of Physics, 12
taxonomy, as method, 118
technology, as framing, 144–45
Tertullien, *De carne Christi*, 192
Theism, 27, 34
theology, about the Other, xviii–xix; as ball and chain, 155, 219; and China, 225; as a "dimension," xiii; dogmatic, 224; as fertile matrix, 223; as form of culture forcing finite content to its limits, 190; as essentially negative, 224; as generous heritage, 93; as imaginary and practical, 223; as necessary resource, 91–92; as negative dis-position, 227; opens thought to own abyss, 223; as scapegoat, 219; as self-critique, 92, 155; as radical self-negation, 190, 221; thinks beyond limits, 224
Theological turn in phenomenology, 65, 81, 224
Tianzhu shiyi, 158
Tillich, Paul, 30–31, 190
time, subjectified as myth in West, 97; as universal notion, 148

trace, 87
Traherne, Thomas "Eden," 60
transcendence, anti-transcendence, 119; apophatic, 80ff, 124; in China and West, 223, 227–28; in Chinese tradition, 107ff, 184ff; and democracy, 135; as dimension, 126; its exclusion, 101ff; as formless, 118; immanent and active, 19, 22–26; incarnate, 192; as indeterminable, 81; as inward, 110; metaphysical, 111; as natural, 22; as representation, 125; of representation itself, 136; refusal of, 75, 110; and secularity, 118, 119ff; self-transcendence, 55–56, semiotic, 137; separative, 76, 124–25, 138–39; "strict," 110; as taking place of all, 127; theorization of, 121; as total, 27; as totalization of immanence, 28; turn back to, 126ff; as ungraspable, 76, 192; as unrepresentable, 104–105, 227; as wholeness, 103, 116
transcendental ideal, 164
transcendental pretense, 99, 116, 121
translation, 99; infinite, 186; untranslatabilty, 185; unlimited, 185
Trauzettel, Rolf, 197
Trouillard, Jean, 215
truth, as tying together, 31; not objective, 138
Turner, Denis, 59

unconditioned, the, 30, 33, 153–54, 164, 191, 193, 197, 223, 227, 231
understanding, tacit, 179, 229; as cultural unconscious, 181
undifferentiated, the, as ground, 58; as Nothing, 65
universal communicability, 155
universality, xiv; apophatic, 156; through abstraction, 145; Christian, 151; as the common, 181; communicability, 178; as concrete, 153; in history, 153; and identity politics, 163; implicit, 215; as incarnate, 151; as negative, 164; of Nothing, 55; as open, 187; as open wound, 132, 189; its operativity, 156; as radical equality, 163; as self-transcendence, 156; as transcendental ideal, 164; *Universalpragmatik*, 176; unsayable, 59; unthinkable, 153; vertical, 218; as void, 156; of what is not, 175, 215
unity, in Chinese tradition, 105–106; as ineffable, 54; ungraspable, 137
unknown, the, 111, unknowing, 129
unrepresentable, 15; as common ground, 32
unsayable, 214; as inaccessible to method, 217
unthinkable, 187, 194

vague, signs and hypotheses, 130–31
Valéry, Paul, 209
variation, infinite, 71
Venard, Thomas-Olivier, 224
Verlaine, Paul, "Ars poétique," 45; on death bed, 81
Vico, Giambattista, 137
Virgil, 149
Voltaire, 4, 157

war, art of, 38
Ward, Keith, 131
Watson, Walter, 131
Watts, Alan, 84
Way, 30; as inconceivable, 32; as translation of Dao, 99ff; "way-making," 99, 112
Wang Bi, 47
Weber, Max, 109
Weil, Simone, 92
Wenning, Mario, 178, 179

Wenzel, Christian, 182
Whole, as coming first, 124; thinking *kata holon* (κατά ὅλον), wholeness as a form of thought, 142–43
Wisdom, extra–philosophical, 173, 216; alternative to philosophy, 218, 232–33
Wittgenstein, Ludwig, 217; (ladder), 114
Wolff, Christian, 157
Wong, Kwok Kui, 20n
Words, as fluctuating, 74; as incitative, 40; as seeds, 40
Wordsworth, 4
World, this and other, 51, 68, 80, 96, 231; two-worlds model, 73
World picture, 104
Writing, origins in divination, 207
Wu Wei (無爲), not doing, 84
Xavier, Saint Francis, 157

Xu Shen, *Shuōwen jiě zi* (*Explanations of Simple and Compound Characters*), 207

Yeats, William Butler, 47
Yijing (Book of Changes), 85ff, 162; as manifesto of immanence, 187
Yin and Yang, as irreducible duality, 103
Zhang, Gang, 122ff
Zhang, Longxi 26; on allegory, 74; 206
zhì rén 至人 (consummate person), 199
Zhongyong (*The Doctrine of the Mean*), 136, 191
Zhou dynasty, 34
Zhuangzi, 69; dependence on unfixed, 190–91; and excess, 71; on happiness of fish, 162; on *Kun* fish–bird, 70; no static formulas, 138; *Wuwu* (無 無), 167–68
Ziolkowski, Eric, 109n
Zuozhuan, 48

www.ingramcontent.com/pod-product-compliance
Lightning Source LLC
Chambersburg PA
CBHW060947230426
43665CB00015B/2090